Coal,
and Rugby

A
Monmouthshire
Memoir

by
Alan Chivers

THE OAKWOOD PRESS

© Oakwood Press & A. Chivers 2005

British Library Cataloguing in Publication Data
A Record for this book is available from the British Library
ISBN 0 85361 643 4

Typeset by Oakwood Graphics.
Repro by PKmediaworks, Cranborne, Dorset.
Printed by Cambrian Printers, Aberystwyth, Ceredigion.

To Ann

About the Author

Like his father, Alan Chivers attended Pontywaun Grammar School. He then read modern history at Cardiff University, after which he was ensnared by the National Service Act in 1954. Thirty years in uniform were to follow when he served in the instructor branches of both the Army and Royal Air Force and together with his family, enjoyed four overseas tours. However, two years in the Ministry of Defence's Air Historical Branch, where he could indulge his taste for modern history were particularly enjoyable. There he wrote official narrative histories of the RAF's post-World War II campaigns. He also lectured at a number of universities in the United States, and after retiring from the RAF, lectured for five years at Sandhurst. After his final retirement he dabbled with genealogy and perceived that a valuable cohesive narrative could be fashioned around his father's career. Alan enjoyed school and club rugby in Risca, played for a number of service teams and retains an enthusiastic interest in the modern game.

Published by The Oakwood Press (Usk), P.O. Box 13, Usk, Mon., NP15 1YS.
E-mail: sales@oakwoodpress.co.uk
Website: www.oakwoodpress.co.uk

Contents

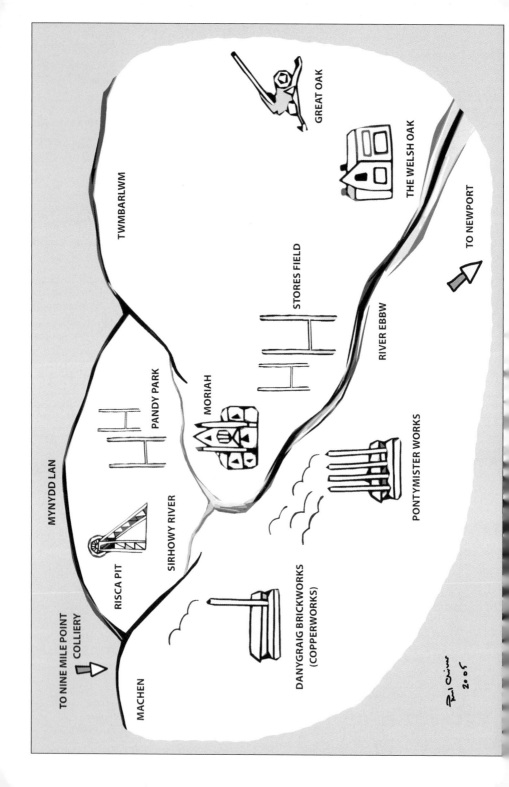

Foreword

On a Sunday morning, together with three other impressionable teenagers, I was taken down Risca pit by Mr E.P. Chivers, a friend of my father. Under his supervision we walked and crawled along the underground workfaces. The experience reinforced our belief that study was a more attractive alternative to working as a collier, which I suspect was one of the objectives of the exercise. We had no idea that within 20 years the mines would have closed, soon to be covered over and grassed.

The beginning of the 20th century saw the coal and iron industries in the Welsh valleys reach a peak of production, then enter a slow but accelerating decline and finally close down in the 1960s. During this period valley towns, of which Risca is typical, experienced a radical change in their way of life. As in the rest of Britain, the changes were initiated and sustained by the inexorable advances in science, technology, education and communications. They were compounded in the valleys, however, by the contraction in the two basic industries that gave employment to the great majority of the men.

In the first decade of the last century the accepted way of life of the people, although only just over 100 years old, was firmly established with its own patterns and mores. Each village was a tightly-knit community containing large extended families. Living in terraces in relatively small communities brought the people into close contact with each other. Local chapels, shops and pubs provided further opportunities to share news and common problems. As Mr A. Chivers writes, a symbiotic relationship existed between the workplace, the chapel, local politics and sport. This can be illustrated by the spontaneous services, led by laymen, entered into by miners during the stay-in strikes at Risca and Nine Mile Point collieries; and even in the spontaneity of the singing of hymns at international rugby matches. Mutual help societies gave financial assistance in times of unemployment as well as for medical care and funeral expenses. All these institutions and activities reflected the inter-dependence of the men in the mines as far as mutual safety, help and support were concerned.

The majority of boys left school at 14 and immediately went to work in the local mine or steelworks to augment the family income. Until they married the girls went into service or the retail trade. It was accepted that married women did not go out to work; they had their hands full raising large families, maintaining the home and making ends meet. People rarely left the valley except for occasional shopping trips to the nearest big town. Even more rare were trips to the seaside. The young men often spent Saturday afternoons, after working a morning shift, playing rugby or watching their local team. On Sundays the majority of people attended chapel and the children went to the large Sunday schools. Choirs, bands and local dance halls also claimed their allegiance. All these activities were voluntary and self supporting.

World War I took many men away, and their experiences in the conflict greatly affected their viewpoints and attitudes when they returned to civilian life. Coal was in great demand during and immediately after the war, and the mines offered good wages. Foreign markets lost during the war, however, were never fully regained. Some countries imported cheaper coal from Germany and Poland, while others turned to oil and hydro-electric sources of power. Ships throughout the world abandoned coal for the more convenient oil. In order to compete, the coal owners called for the cheaper production of coal, and one of the measures they took was to make a substantial reduction in the pay of the miners. This provoked strikes and lockouts and led to a further depression of the industry. Unemployment increased dramatically; there were few opportunities for alternative employment. During these years there was a large scale emigration of young people and families to England and abroad seeking work.

The decline was arrested temporarily just before and during World War II. Labour was now needed and young men, the Bevin Boys, were drafted to the mines as an alternative to the armed forces. After the war the drift from coal continued. The use of oil and gas was augmented by the discoveries under the North Sea. Large electricity generators were built and fuelled by oil or nuclear power. The railways converted from steam to diesel driven trains. Even the homes of the valleys turned from coal to gas or electrical fires, central heating and cooking appliances. This all led to most of the mines closing in the mid-1960s.

During these years the birth rate dropped and the population aged. Families split up as the young left the area, and there was a marked decline in the community spirit. Attendance at chapel gradually fell away, out of town supermarkets replaced the local shops and interest in local rugby declined. The people had fewer communal activities, many of which were being replaced by the all-pervasive television. As a relic of former times there was a flowering of Senior Citizen Organisations. As the members of these clubs frequently commented, 'We are living in a new and very different world'.

Unexpectedly, though, the closure of the mines did not lead to more depression but the valleys entered a period of prosperity and an increased standard of living as the majority commuted to work in nearby towns and cities.

This book offers snapshots from the life of a person who lived through these momentous years, as recounted through the eyes of his son. It provides glimpses of a way of life which, together, contribute to a fuller picture of a period so unlike our own. It reveals the accommodation of Mr Chivers' father to the harshness of the conditions under which the miners were forced to live and work. At the same time, it shows that, through the harshness, there was a will to survive and a capacity to serve, manifested in a community spirit and a sense of belonging. As well as offering details of the history of the mines, Mr Chivers provides vignettes of social life, including his father's time he served in the Home Guard. I am sure that all this will remind older readers of a time past, and provide a few surprises for younger readers. Mr Chivers' view very much comes from the front row centre.

J.H.A. Roberts

Preface

This memoir tells the story of my father's life.

I have set out Ernest Percival Chivers's career under eight separate headings. His sporting prowess with the Risca and Cross Keys* rugby clubs had always intrigued me, partially because of his anecdotes about the games in which he had played and his colourful descriptions of his fellow players. However, his rugby was a pastime. The real business of earning a living took him 'down the pit' at three collieries, Cwmcarn, Risca and Nine Mile Point. This meant that I had to give more than a nod in the direction of some of the Western Valleys' mining history in the 20th century and present a brief overview of Risca and Nine Mile Point collieries during the years that my father worked in them. It was also essential to examine his links with Moriah Chapel in Risca and his membership of the Home Guard during World War II. Those endlessly interesting friends who came to our house in Brookland Road during my childhood were certainly worth scrutiny, while those friends whom I never met but who cropped up in conversations also needed acknowledgement. The eight essays are chronologically linked in a slightly haphazard manner, but fall short of a meticulous biography.

My father's parents, Thomas Herbert Chivers and Amelia Martha Chivers (née Tucker), settled in Risca either in 1892 or 1893. They migrated from Cwmbran in the wake of the 1892 purchase, by Southwood Jones and Company, of the old Copperworks site in Risca. Here the company was to manufacture refractory firebricks, a process at which Amelia Martha's brother, William Tucker, was expert. He was to play a vital part in the company's Danygraig operations, having, in all probability, gained his experience and skill at Southwood Jones's Graig Ddu brickworks in the Eastern Valley. Thomas Herbert and Amelia Martha were accompanied by their three children who had been born in Cwmbran: Harriet Mary Chivers (aged five); Thomas Henry Milton Chivers (aged three) and David George Harold Chivers, a babe in arms. The family group included Amelia Martha's mother, Grandma Tucker (née James), the widow of a miner, John Tucker. They settled in one of the tiny cottages adjacent to the Old Copperworks buildings and Thomas Herbert Chivers was taken on as a moulder in the brickworks, employment which may have been arranged by William Tucker and which probably encouraged the family to move from Cwmbran. Between 1894 and 1905 four more children were born: Ernest John Chivers, in 1894; William John Chivers, in 1897; Ernest Percival Chivers, my father, in 1903, and Miriam Doreen Chivers in 1905. Ernest John died in infancy.

Another of Amelia Martha's brothers, Edgar Tucker, also migrated to Risca from the Eastern Valley at about this time and provided some colourful background to my father's childhood. Family lore maintained that Edgar had been a boyhood friend to Lionel (Nello) Southwood Jones who became the 'hands on' proprietor at the Danygraig Brickworks, and that the two boys had been sent to the same boarding school, with Edgar's bills paid by the Southwood Jones family. My father's recollections of Edgar centred on his uncle's considerable thirst. He would urge my father to gaze into his mouth. 'See anything?', he would ask. The answer was always the same: 'No, Uncle Edgar'. 'Well you should - there's a whole row of houses gone down there!'

* Although Crosskeys is now shown on maps as a single word the rugby club is always shown as Cross Keys.

BROOKLAND PLACE, RISCA

My parents lived at No. 10 Brookland Road from 1932 to 1968. They had previously lived at Kymin (No. 26), which is the third visible house on the left-hand side of the photograph. In this 1920 photograph a car is parked outside No. 10.

Collins & Powell

My father's parents *circa* 1898. The children are, *left to right*, Thomas Henry Milton Chivers, William John Chivers (born 25th January, 1897), Harold George Chivers, Harriet Mary Chivers.   *Author's Collection*

My father with his sister, Doreen, at their home in Bridge Street, *circa* 1909. *Author's Collection*

Edgar's enthusiasm for poaching led to clashes with Lord Tredegar's gamekeepers. During one of these encounters his backside was peppered with shot. There was, too, a brief, peacetime enlistment in a cavalry regiment from which Amelia Martha 'bought him out' with a barely-affordable £25, a formidable sum in the early 20th century. He was unsuited to a career in a mounted regiment where the training featured a harsh reproof from the Roughriding Corporal whenever Edgar fell off his horse: 'Who told you to dismount, Trooper?' Edgar also contracted an unpleasant social disease and was attended by a local doctor who used the kitchen table as an operating surface. My father recalled that, 'Edgar's screams could be heard all over Danygraig!'

The Chivers family could provide role models for my father that were slightly more worthy and reputable than that offered by Uncle Edgar Tucker, although there was an almost Dickensian whiff to the family's tale. In some cases, there had been prosperity, but in another, this was decidedly limited and had been followed by degradation and alcoholism. The first Chivers to arrive in South Wales from the family's 19th century 'base' in Ruardean, Gloucestershire, had been Thomas Chivers whose 1827 marriage certificate described him as an 'engineer'. His bride, Hester Phillips of Pembrokeshire, signed the document with a cross. Thomas and Hester settled in Aberdare but then moved to Ireland where Thomas was an engineer in an iron ore mine. Thomas's brother, Jacob Chivers, also born in Ruardean, prospered greatly, becoming the owner of the Kidwelli Ironworks, some lead mines in Spain and a vessel described as a 'yacht'. He was also a Kidwelli magistrate and one of the founders, if not *the* founder, of a Methodist chapel in that town. However, Jacob's prosperity did not rub-off on Thomas, who returned to Aberdare, sometime in the 1840s, with a small family, including a son, Caleb Elijah Chivers, born in Cork in 1838. Thomas became involved in the iron business in Aberdare and documents of the 1840s refer to 'Chivers & Co' in that town, where Thomas probably used a foundry in Mill Street. When Caleb, Thomas's son, married Mary Hughes, of Aberdare, on 5th August, 1861 in the Merthyr Tydfil Register Office, the marriage certificate showed his occupation as 'Fitter' and that of his father as 'Iron Founder'. Mary's father, Hugh Hughes, is described as a 'Flueman', an occupation that may have irritated the groom's father. In the following year, Mary gave birth to a daughter, Miriam.

Caleb and his wife, presumably accompanied by their daughter, migrated to the United States in 1865, where, at Scranton, Pennsylvania, on 15th December, Mary gave birth to a second child, Thomas Herbert Chivers, destined to become my father's father. The effort and discomfort involved in sailing to America in those days underlines the gritty resolution of the voyagers. What induced the family to leave Aberdare? The Welsh iron trade was not at its best and the newspapers of the period advertised passages to America. That elusive witness, family lore, holds that Caleb had been attracted to the United States by the prospect of work on a new bridge that was to be built across the Susquehanna River in Scranton, a town which, nevertheless, proved to have limited appeal. The aftermath of the American Civil War that had ended in April 1865 brought a certain ruggedness to Scranton's inhabitants' lives and more dangerously, a

My father with his sister Doreen, *circa* 1911. The family's prosperity extended to a photographer's studio and fashionable sailor suits, garments which reflected the Royal Navy's popularity. There was a national obsession at the time with the need to match Germany's ship-building programme.   *Author's Collection*

sinister outbreak of cholera. Perhaps this was the clincher in the Chivers family's domestic discussions about returning to Aberdare, which they did when Thomas Herbert, my future grandfather, was six weeks old.

Some 12 years later, Mary, Thomas Herbert's mother, was killed in an accident on a railway siding and Caleb remarried. His stepmother failed to charm Thomas Herbert and he left home, though apart from tales of his time as a boatman on the Monmouthshire canals, few details of his life have survived. It was said that he walked from Cwmbran to Stoke in search of work, but I have not found any reliable confirmation of this adventure, other than the perennially uncertain family lore. His grandfather, Thomas, described in the 1871 Census as an 'Iron and Brass Founder, employing 15 men and a boy', was now established at Aberdare's Gadlys Foundry, though the halcyon days of the Welsh iron trade were over. His wife, Hester, died on 30th September, 1870 and Thomas married Mary Jane Bird, a 47-year-old widow. This union ended in May 1876, when Thomas died of 'paralysis', leaving Mary Jane a widow for the second time and effects of 'less than £100'. His brother, Jacob, a virtual princeling of Kidwelli, left £9,923 1s. 9d. when he died in 1883.

So much for contrasting fortunes in the iron and tinplate businesses. Thomas's son, Caleb, appears to have left no mark on these years and family lore, which as always, provides insubstantial evidence, relates that after the marriage of his daughter, Miriam, to a clergyman and despite his second family, he became a nuisance caller at her home. As the years passed, Caleb took to the bottle, eventually dying of 'Chronic renal disease' in the County Asylum at Bridgend in March 1904. The death certificate showed his age as 64. My father was generally aware of the Caleb saga and during my childhood was fond of quoting the slogan about there being 'sack cloth and ashes' after two generations. It is unlikely that he knew about Jacob's prosperity, otherwise I would have been told. Only when researching this project did I discover Jacob and his affluence.

Dad's upbringing, first on the Old Copperworks at Danygraig and then in nearby Bridge Street, seems to have featured all the characteristics of a close-knit Edwardian family with strong roots in the Victorian era. Both parents were strict and strove for respectability. Chapel going, Sunday School attendance and, eventually, success in the 'Scholarship' examination for Pontywaun* Intermediate School in Pontymister, were significant features of Ernest Percival Chivers's up-bringing. There were also family bible readings in collective acts of domestic worship. Their 'standard issue' family Bible, so frequently seen in the antique shops and marts of the 21st century, has survived, and contains valuable information about births, deaths, marriages and other 'Family Events'.

My first essay begins when my father was impatient with his studies at Pontywaun School and restlessly sought to leave to become a wage-earning miner. The Pontywaun School documents in the Monmouthshire Archives at Cwmbran show that he was admitted to school on 13th September, 1915, aged 12 years and six months, and that he was a 'School Scholarship Holder'. This meant that no fees were payable because he had earned his place by virtue of academic skills and intelligence. He left school on 23rd December, 1916, a departure that he soon regretted and which always influenced the advice which

---

* Pontywaun School is variously alluded to as the 'County', 'Intermediate' and the 'Grammar School'.

he passed to me and indeed, to anyone else perceived to stand in need of encouragement. It is interesting to speculate about his parents' failure to compel him to complete his studies. His three brothers had either ceased to contribute to the family's income or their contributions had been severely reduced. Harold was married in 1914 while Tom (in January 1915) and Bill (in October 1915) had respectively joined the Army and the Royal Navy, organisations with notoriously poor pay. The family's comfortable standard of living would certainly have been affected by these changes. During his declining years, my grandfather reminisced to me that the period before World War I was the most prosperous time he had known. Although he did not say so, enough money had been available to finance his trips around the country in support of the successful Welsh rugby teams of that era. The pay-packets which Harold, Tom, and Bill had 'put on the table' supported this lifestyle and so the prospect of young Percy's pay packet may have modified parental opposition to him leaving school.

The organisations and personalities that have helped with this project are acknowledged on another page. However, I must offer a special word of thanks to Hugh Roberts who very kindly agreed to write a Foreword. The links between the Roberts and Chivers families can be traced to the early part of the 20th century. They were neighbours in Bridge Street when the patriarch Jonah Roberts was a figure of consequence in 'The Fed', the South Wales Miners' Federation. He also enjoyed a high profile in local government as a Risca Councillor and as a Monmouthshire County Alderman. When my father's brother, Bill was severely wounded at Beaumont Hamel on 13th November, 1916, the Royal Navy evacuated him to a hospital in Chatham. It was forever a source of our family's gratitude and admiration when Jonah paid Bill a bedside visit and left a half-sovereign on his locker. My father was a close friend of one of Jonah's sons, Ivor, and they played rugby together in the 1920s. Hugh is Ivor's son and has enjoyed a distinguished academic career in addition to serving as the Mayor of Islwyn and as a City of London Freeman. His book, *A View From the Hill* (the Cwmbran Community Press 1986), blends the history of Risca with that of Moriah Chapel. I have found this work to be exceptionally helpful and I am grateful to Hugh for his kind permission to quote from its pages.

Chapter One

The Search for Black Gold

My father left the Pontywaun Intermediate School, Pontymister, on 23rd December, 1916 and probably began work at the Cwmcarn colliery soon after. He always reminisced that leaving school was certainly a bad move but stressed that the allure of a pay packet was hard to resist. This was especially so when his friends who were miners could display some affluence as workers in an industry that offered good rates of pay. After the war, the mine owners perceived an urgent need for retrenchment, thereby initiating a lengthy period of industrial turbulence. My grandparents were unable, or perhaps unwilling, to force Ernest Percival Chivers to stay at school. Unlike his brother, Harold George Chivers, he suffered no physical disability that might have inhibited manual labour. Harold's apparent poor health, that produced growths on his hands, made it obvious that a rugged mining career was not for him. The doctor operated on his hands at the house in Bridge Street and he was found a lowly office job at the Southwood Jones brickworks, where his father was a moulder and where his mother's brother, William Tucker, was the foreman and acknowledged fireclay expert. William's son, Willy Herbert Tucker, also worked in the office and had some expertise in accountancy. Harold was to rise to become Company Secretary in an environment that suited him to a 'T', but my father would have been unhappy in a factory where he might have been expected to tip his hat to 'Nello' Southwood Jones. Also, he would have been overseen by his father and bossed by his uncle. His other brother, Tom, addressed 'Nello' as 'Sir', a form of speech which would not have been to my father's fancy.

So my father was taken on as a collier's boy at Cwmcarn colliery This colliery, nowadays grassed over and a part of the locality's Scenic Drive, had been in existence since 1876, when it was the ventilation pit for the neighbouring Abercarn colliery. Lack of space in that spur of the Western Valley meant that all the spoil extracted in the mining process had to be stored underground, and so there was no unsightly tip on the surface.[1] By 1912, the colliery, owned by the Ebbw Vale Steel, Iron & Coal Company, employed 292 men, a group that would have grown by 1916 and which my father eagerly joined, probably early in the following year. The only evidence of Dad's working days at Cwmcarn was his account of how Risca people made their way to the pit. Today's generation, accustomed to the motor car, or at the very least to a bus service, would be appalled by the long walk from the nearest railway station at Cross Keys* to the Cwmcarn pit-head. My father's routine involved a brisk walk from Bridge Street to the Risca railway station, probably through the Victorian development known, after its builder, as Sponford's and up a flight of steps close to the Bridgend pub in order to reach the station. The workmen's train, with its special wooden seats, carried him to Cross Keys, from where he had a tedious walk, through Pontywain and then along the railway line, around the Medart mountain, to the colliery. The return journey, after a strenuous shift, must have been an even greater chore.

* The Great Western Railway station was always shown as Cross Keys (two words).

Some, or perhaps all of the workforce at Danygraig Brickworks (the old Copperworks) just before World War I. My family is strongly represented. Third from the left in the back row is my father's brother Harold who became Commercial Manager; fourth from the left, wearing a turned-down hat, is my grandmother's brother, Will Tucker, the foreman and an expert on brick manufacture. Third from the right, with a dark moustache is my grandfather, Thomas Herbert Chivers. Second from the right is Will Tucker's son, Willy Herbert Tucker, said to have been an accounts expert or perhaps a book-keeper. In the middle row, fourth from the left, is my father's brother Thomas Henry Milton Chivers, who later became a successful haulier and coal merchant. The heavily-built man at the extreme right of the middle row is Ted Lloyd, who married my grandmother's sister, Lucy and was destined to become the grandfather of the operatic bass, Robert Lloyd. The strong family representation certainly discouraged my father from seeking employment at the brickworks when he left school.

An excellent photograph of my father aged 13, wearing the Pontywaun School uniform. In his lapel is the badge of the Royal Navy Division, presented, no doubt, by his brother Bill who served in that unit from October 1915 to August 1917. *Author's Collection*

Cwmcarn Colliery.

Cwmcarn colliery, looking back down the valley towards the village of Cwmcarn. Sinking had commenced in 1910 and the colliery was in production by 1913, when this photograph was probably taken, judging by the newness of the brickwork.   *Neil Parkhouse Collection*

A shaft had been in existence at Cwmcarn since 1876 and was used as a ventilation pit for Abercarn colliery. The owners, the Ebbw Vale Steel, Iron & Coal Company sank a second shaft to the Black Vein (Nine-Feet) seam in 1912. The shafts were 843 ft deep.   *David Williams Collection*

Perhaps tiring of this routine, my father transferred to Risca colliery which was somewhat nearer home and where he was soon working alongside his brother, William John Chivers, my Uncle Bill. Grievously wounded at Beaumont Hamel on 13th November, 1916, Bill was discharged from the Royal Naval Division in August 1917. Records of some of his time at Risca colliery are logged in one of the colliery's many surviving ledgers, where he is shown working as a 'stower' from October 1917 through to April 1918.[2] The two brothers were to work side-by-side at Risca and were soon involved in the business of actually extracting the coal. Risca colliery, despite its name, was in Crosskeys. The pit dated from 1878, was owned by the United National Collieries and employed approximately 2,200 personnel in 1921. Two underground explosions, the first in 1880 (which killed 120 men and boys) and the other in 1882 (which killed four), left a permanent scar on the community's memory.[3] In all probability, the Chivers brothers, as they walked along Pandy Lane (more correctly, Gladstone Street), from the station to the colliery in the early 1920s would not have been greatly worried by this background of local disaster, although the dreadful trauma of the Senghenydd colliery explosion of 1913 would have been an ever-present memory for the entire workforce. Together with approximately 271,000 of his fellow workers in the South Wales coalfield, my father was now set on a career in which he was dragged through the awful economic and industrial turbulence of the 1920s and 1930s. It was an experience which left him with a cynical and slightly apprehensive attitude to the industry and which was to damage his health in the period leading to World War II.

He told me how Bill insisted that they walk side by side when going to or from work. Bill's war wound (he had been left with one leg shorter than the other), slowed him up and could only be emphasised if his younger brother forged ahead and so the dignity of seniority - Bill was six years older than my father - was maintained. My Uncle Bill left a small memento of his time at Risca colliery, although I feel confident that it was a legacy known only to its immediate beneficiaries, all of whom, sadly, are now dead. This relic of a humorous but determined man is crystallized in one of my father's many anecdotes. It seems that during a shift underground at the colliery, an argument arose amongst a group that included Bill and my father about who was entitled to fill some coal 'trams', or tubs, that had been shunted into the work area; whoever had access to these trams could fill coal and earn money. Out of the argument, one voice rose above all others: one miner, a prominent Methodist layman and part-time preacher, said, 'Let us revert to the Scriptures. Let us cast lots for who is to have the trams'. Bill dealt speedily with this quasi-theological intrusion. 'Bugger the Scriptures!' he said. 'I'm having those trams!' Bill was to display a prescience that did him credit and exchanged mining for the Civil Service, a career which gave him the time and the opportunity to become the Secretary of Maesteg Rugby Club in the 1930s, when the Ministry of Labour transferred him to its outpost in the Llynfi valley. A later deployment saw Bill and his family on the Isle of Wight, where he was to manage the Labour Exchanges at Cowes and Ventnor.

In a sense, a petty dispute about who was to have the chance to fill a couple of coal tubs mirrored the difficulties of the entire Welsh coalfield at that time.

My father's family in a Newport studio *circa* 1915 or 1916. *Front row, left to right:* Amelia Martha Chivers, Miriam Doreen Chivers, Thomas Henry Milton Chivers, Thomas Herbert Chivers. *At rear, left to right:* Harriet Mary Jenkins (née Chivers), William John Chivers, my father, Harold George Chivers.

Author's Collection

The young Percy Chivers, whose 18th birthday fell on 5th March, 1921, just before the miners' strike of that year, must inevitably have been buffeted by the pressures and changes which the entire region endured in the years following the Great War. Although ineligible to vote, he would have noted the results of the so-called 'Khaki' General Election of December 1918, when Charles Edwards, a 'Fed' stalwart, was first elected as the Labour member for the Bedwellty constituency, one of 10 seats captured by the Labour party in Wales at the election which returned a total of 57 Labour men to the new House of Commons.[4] If this was a pointer to a rosier future for the Left, then the old social hierarchy of 1914, characterised by the ascendancy of the Established Church and the landed gentry, had totally collapsed. The Welsh Church was disestablished in 1918 - not that my father, a Sunday School pupil from an early age in Moriah Baptist chapel, would have cared very much about that. Nor would the fragmentation of some of Lord Tredegar's estates have caused him much anguish. His Lordship disposed of much of his urban property in Monmouthshire during the war, a realisation of assets copied by other landowners in the county and which may have disappointed my grandmother, Amelia Martha Chivers. She caused my father some irritation with the maxim, 'God bless the squire and his relations and keep us in our proper stations'. The impact of this antique slogan must have diminished in Risca as the years rolled by. Not only had the Church been disestablished and the landed estates fragmented but a major power throughout the immediate post-war years was, of course, The South Wales Miners' Federation, handily referred to as the 'Fed'. By February 1921, with a membership of over 200,000, this trade union had never been larger or stronger and was poised to assert its members' interests in the distinctly unfavourable circumstances of the post-war era.[5]

During the war the Government had nationalised the South Wales collieries in an effort to obviate the labour disputes which bedevilled the region and hindered production. This was followed by the nationalisation of the entire British coal industry, so, when the war ended, a decision was needed about its future. Were the coalowners to resume control or would nationalisation continue, as the unions wished? A Royal Commission, chaired by Mr Justice Sankey, came down in favour of nationalisation. After first appearing to accept the Sankey Report, the Government eventually changed its mind and in 1921 the coal industry was handed back to its original owners. The unions' disappointment at this decision was to fester throughout the next 25 years until nationalisation was achieved. In 1921, however, the immediate result of the decision to return the mines to their original owners was a strike. In South Wales, the coalowners argued that wage rates had been excessively increased during the war and that it was time for retrenchment, especially in the face of lost overseas markets and foreign competition. They required the unions to accept lower rates of pay or men would be laid off. The strike that followed was not confined to South Wales and on 1st April, 1921, one million miners in Britain were locked out.

The strike's impact in Risca was far from trivial and although my father recalled the purity of the River Ebbw at the weir, near the feeder to the steelworks, where that summer he swam with his fellow strikers, greater matters were afoot. An athletic 18-year-old, absorbed with the 1920-21 rugby

Police at Cwmcarn colliery during the '21 strike. They have set up a field kitchen to sustain their Newport colleagues tasked with guarding the colliery. The mine owners required access for maintenance teams so that the pit would be ready for work after the strike.   *Collins & Powell*

Risca colliery depicted on a picture postcard. Notice the mineral wagon bearing the legend 'United National Collieries'.   *John Ryan Collection*

Risca Colliery.   Cross Keys.

season which was then drawing to a close, he could hardly have failed to notice the Government's Emergency Powers Act and, on 14th April, the appointment of Sir William Mitchell-Thomson as the Civil Commissioner for South Wales and Monmouthshire. This man, with his headquarters at the Cardiff law courts, was, according to the *South Wales News* in its edition of 15th April, required to maintain food supplies and other public services. But it was the bustling nature of the deployments of police and military units in Monmouthshire and elsewhere that would have caught the attention of any nascent and politically aware adult. The arrival of three charabanc loads of Newport policemen in Abercarn on 11th April showed the authorities' determination to maintain law and order, and in this case to ensure that the pumpmen at Abercarn colliery should work without interference or intimidation from the strikers.

Royal Navy personnel, rousingly headlined in the *Argus* as 'Bluejackets', descended upon Abertillery on 12th April. This deployment could not have been given a more benign connotation by the newspaper. The sailors played football in the grounds of the local Drill Hall and they were 'Already popular with the girls', said a headline . However, smaller print said,

> During the afternoon the detatchments detailed for duty at the Arrael Griffin, Vivian and Gray Collieries, marched to their posts with full kit and wearing the familiar wartime tin-helmets…

That same evening the *Argus* reported the arrival at the Newport Barracks of 'about 200' reservists from Chester, and the paper seemed pleased to add that there they joined more 'Bluejackets'. The *South Wales News* reported, also on 12th April, that the battle cruiser *Malaya* and the light cruiser *Excellent* had put into Newport docks, while 'several hundreds' of Newport's locally-enlisted reservists had been sent, by train, to Edinburgh. The Government's resolve to deploy military personnel who were unfamiliar with the localities to which they were sent, ostensibly to maintain the peace, was a tried and tested pattern. While my father would have read the papers and probably observed the occasional charabanc laden with unfamiliar police or military, his historical awareness would have included the Chartist riots of 1839, when Newport's Westgate Hotel served as a bastion for soldiers of an English regiment who fired on the rioters. Although Risca colliery was relatively peaceful for most of the strike, a demonstration there on Friday 8th April added to the authorities' worries about the imminence of serious strife. A group of about 700 miners marched down the Sirhowy valley from Nine Mile Point colliery to Risca colliery in order to persuade the management not to allow the use of maintenance men to keep the collieries' pumps going. This kind of work was essential if the pits were to be re-started successfully if and when the stoppages ended. The *Argus* of 9th April reported that, 'There were no incidents and the demonstration was orderly'. The demonstrators sent a deputation to interview the company's agent and acting colliery manager, E.W. Jones, who agreed, after 'considerable discussion', to withdraw all the maintenance men and the colliery's horses by 10 am on Saturday morning. The press carried a slightly different story, however, during the following week. Under the headline 'Pumping at Pits - Monmouthshire Mines Protected', the *Western Mail* reported on Thursday 10th April that the whole of the industrial portion of Monmouthshire was again in a perfectly peaceful state by Wednesday and 'safety work was being carried out everywhere by the officials of the various companies without any interference'. The newspaper was pleased to be able to report that the constabulary was contributing to the overall tranquillity of the Monmouthshire valleys, with Police Superintendent Porter of Risca and his colleagues from other police stations, all of whom 'have a perfect knowledge of mining districts', carrying out their duties 'in a tactful way'. My father was probably present at a meeting of Risca colliery miners on Tuesday 19th April and he would have paid respectful attention to the meeting's Chairman, Jonah Roberts, a figure of considerable significance in 'Fed' and local government matters.[6] The question of the continued use of maintenance men was prominently on the agenda and a delegate was dispatched to a regional conference on the Wednesday. The *Argus* report of the meeting at Risca colliery included a highly sensitive allusion: 'The men were strongly advised not to apply for parochial relief except in cases of absolute necessity'. This was an important matter, given the distress occasioned not only by the strike but by the curse of unemployment which afflicted the entire coalfield. Harold Finch, soon to become the Secretary of the Tredegar Valley District of the 'Fed' and Charles Edwards's eventual successor as MP for Bedwellty, claimed in his memoirs that throughout the United Kingdom, in March 1921, there were over 2 million unemployed.[7] In South Wales in the winter of 1920-21, that is, before the strike, there had been a growing number of miners out of work. By the end of February 1921 it was estimated that about 80,000 Welsh colliery workmen were unemployed 'through trade depression'. In the accounts of the South Wales Miners' Federation the payments to unemployed workmen (which totalled £29,202 in 1920) amounted to £216,000 in 1921.[8] The state unemployment benefit for a single man was 15s. per week and 12s. per week for a woman. A married couple received 20s. per week, with a 'a few shillings for the children'.

In the Spring and early Summer of 1921, therefore, there were two categories of people who were out of work, the unemployed and the strikers. Now, family lore has made no reference to the Chivers family of Bridge Street being 'on relief'. Unemployment as a result of depression in the mining industry would affect my father later in his working life, but he fully understood, as did the rest of the family, that if unemployment benefit, 'the dole', was insufficient, then recourse was to be had to outdoor relief, administered, for Risca, by the Newport Board of Guardians. The receipt of this type of hand-out became a carefully recorded debt which the recipients were expected to discharge when they were in funds and about which Jonah Roberts and his 'Fed' colleagues had warned the Risca strikers at their meeting on 19th April.

The records of the administration of outdoor relief for Risca in 1921 are available in the county archives at Cwmbran. By July of that year the Newport Guardians were many thousands of pounds short of their requirements to meet their liabilities. Payment in kind seems to have been the norm and there are letters about the difficulties which the local tradesmen encountered. On 23rd June, 1921, the Abercarn Risca and District Grocers' Association complained to the Newport Guardians,

...that owing to the abnormal conditions the Members' financial resources and trade credit are almost exhausted and unless there is a decided improvement the members will not be able to carry on. In the circumstances it was hoped that the Board would pay all accounts within 7 days in future...

Another letter from The Abercarn, Crumlin, Risca and District Master Bakers' and Millers' Association dated 22nd June expressed the membership's dissatisfaction with the way the Board of Guardians were paying accounts,

...due to us from the supplying of goods on the relief notes and owing through [sic] the abnormal conditions we find through the limit of our financial resources we are unable to carry on . We therefore respectfully ask you to pay our accounts sent in to you within seven days and thus render us some assistance.[9]

Despite the pressing nature of these problems, my father would have shown little or no concern for the predicament of the local tradesmen. However, his brother Tom's business venture probably made a greater impression. Tom, who had married Gwendoline Pearce of Newport on 6th October, 1917, quite clearly had set his sights on some kind of business career when the war ended. Aided by a gift of £30 for the purpose from his father, Tom bought a horse and cart and embarked upon a career as a haulier. This business was to prosper and eventually supported a number of lorries and inevitably, their drivers. My father was also offered £30 by my grandfather for the same purpose but he turned it down. Not for him the hum-drum life of delivering domestic coal or carrying a family's furniture from one part of the county to another, although my grandmother, Amelia Martha, made sure that whenever it was feasible my father would put his shoulder to the wheel of his brother's enterprise. Never was there a better illustration of the proverb about a volunteer always being better than a pressed man. The haulage business offered no delights for my father and whenever he spoke of the occasional jobs which he executed for Tom, there was never any enthusiasm in his voice.

This was not the case with his stories of life on the farm. The Harris family, Lord Tredegar's tenants at Pontymister Farm, could seemingly provide an abundance of casual work, as was the way with small hill farms in those days. Of particular attraction was the farmer's horse trading, which, in the nature of things, provided Dad with free riding lessons and ample opportunity to travel. The farmer, Alf Harris, a figure of some consequence amongst the Tredegar tenantry and in the Risca community, would buy ponies and horses of different heights for the coal mines, mostly from the Llandinam-Llanidloes area of mid-Wales. This involved collecting consignments of animals from the Church Road and Risca railway stations but also a certain amount of foot-slogging (when the animals were sold on), from Pontymister to and from Llwynypia in the Rhondda, Llanbradach and Penrhiwceiber. Alf's son, Reg Harris, was my father's exact contemporary, having been born in 1903, and the pair filled vital roles as the deliverers of horses, on the hoof, to those collieries, mostly in the 1920s. Reg's daughter, Mary Prosser, has very kindly provided me with details of this business in which her father was involved from the age of 10 onwards:

L & N W R CEMENT BRIDGE, NEAR NINE MILE POINT.

The bridge in the foreground carries the London & North Western Railway over the Sirhowy River. Nine Mile Point colliery forms the backdrop.

John Ryan Collection

After purchasing maybe 12 horses/ponies they would have spent time training the animals to work in shafts. This was done by my father [Reg Harris] and his brother Harry. The Colliery Manager and a vet and the underground manager who was responsible for the horses whilst underground, would come to Pontymister Farm and decide which they would want to purchase, maybe the 12 or sometimes less! It was really quite a thriving business!

Dad's time at Pontymister Farm provided a pleasant, cheerful background to his work at Risca colliery or enabled him to occupy his time, at some small profit, when the pit was idle. The '21 Strike' must have offered ample opportunities for this bucolic spree on the hillside above the steelworks and although most of the Welsh miners returned to work on 4th July, 1921, it is highly likely that he made it his business to be available for that year's harvest, if only for the opportunity which it offered to enjoy one of Mrs Harris's harvest suppers. These feasts were mentioned briefly during my childhood and once again, I am indebted to Mary Prosser for some solid detail. She recalls how 'mounds of cold beef' were minced and supplemented by home-made chutney or mustard. There were, too, 'loaves of sandwiches' together with her grandmother's 'superb Victoria sponges and yeastcake (everyone's favourite)'. All the harvest workers would sit in the 'bailey', or yard, outside the farm kitchen. This was a stone-walled area with a stone seat built into the wall and as Mrs Prosser writes, 'It was a wonderful, very happy gathering of lovely men and boys'.[10]

My father's opportunities to keep up his membership of this happy band, at harvest-time or at any other time, diminished, obviously, when Risca colliery resumed work, after the strike, at the beginning of July 1921. The coalowners had achieved their eagerly sought reduction of wages.The new pay-scales for adults working 'on the coal' comprised 10 shillings per shift for a six-shift week, a reduction of 7s. 10.2d. per shift, or 44 per cent. Labourers were to receive 7s. 3.28d. per shift, which was a reduction of 7s. 6.22d. per shift, or 50.82 per cent.[11] Whichever scale applied to my father would have seen him earn slightly less because he was only 18 years old. Twenty-one-year-olds received the full scale. The 'Fed' had accepted defeat after the promised support from the Transport Workers and Railwaymen had not materialised and a Coalfield Conference narrowly voted to return to work under the terms offered by the owners. This decision would have been hard to bear, particularly in what seems to have been a widely admired 'Fed' lodge at my father's workplace. Harold Finch records in his memoirs how, as a young man, he had admired the ability, courage and devotion of the Risca committeemen. The three 'Fed' officials, John Woodward, John Powell and Jonah Roberts, were Monmouthshire County Council aldermen and members of Risca Urban District Council. With their Nonconformist background, they were men of great integrity who held the confidence of the miners and the general public for many years. 'Their wise leadership', writes Finch, 'gave the Risca Miners' Lodge considerable influence in mining circles in South Wales. The men had complete confidence in their Committee'.

If only the distillation of this committee's wisdom had been appreciated at Nine Mile Point in the following year. Nine Mile Point, so called because of its distance from Newport, was sunk in 1904 and was to become a cockpit for inter-

This brother and sister photograph of my father (the elder by two years) with Doreen, was probably taken in the garden at Bridge Street *circa* 1920.   *Author's Collection*

union rivalries later in the century. The events at 'The Point' in 1922, of which I am about to present an abbreviated account, had nothing to do with my father, but anyone with historical awareness, and my father was certainly in that category, would have grasped their significance. It can be argued that when eventually he became the colliery's Training and Welfare Officer, just after World War II, an appreciation of the slightly sinister happenings of February 1922 must have been very helpful. At that date, a rumour swept through 'The Point' that the owners, the United National Colliery Company, had decided to close down the pit indefinitely. One Monday morning, when the men gathered for work at the pit-head, they discovered that the lamps of about 65 of their number had been 'stopped', which meant that they could not descend. The 800 miners who were present went looking for the manager, Mr Huxham, with the idea of having the decision altered and the withdrawal of about 80 notices that were pending. They also sought the settlement of a number of cases where a money question was at issue. Once again, I have relied upon Harold Finch's memoirs for a description of the scene:

The men's feelings were running high. They smashed two holes in the office windows and surged along the passage leading to the Manager's office. They made a dash for Mr Huxham and in the disturbance, broke a large table. Mr Huxham was dragged onto the main road and hustled along. Ex-police Sergeant Powell tried to protect the Manager, but was hurt in the mêlée. Soon after reaching the main road, Mr Huxham made a bid for liberty along the bank but some men dashed after him and again dragged him back to the road and onwards to the Workmen's Hall in Cwmfelinfach. There were threats to throw him into the colliery reservoir, but more sensible counsels prevailed. Despite his slight build, Mr Huxham withstood the rough treatment stoically, though he received a number of bruises. Mr Huxham was rushed into the hall. Superintendent Richards and other police officers arrived, but there was then no need for their services. At the hall Mr Huxham was subjected to a long debate and ultimately was forced to sign a document.

Years later, during one of those pleasantly soporific Sunday evenings with the immediate family, that really were rather boring for a small boy, I heard my uncle, David Jones, who witnessed Mr Huxham's persecution, say to my father, 'You see, Perce, some of them wanted to hang him!' Mr Finch points out that, eventually, 16 men appeared before Blackwood magistrates before being remanded to the county assizes, where three of them were given six months' imprisonment; four were each sentenced to three months' imprisonment; two were bound over for 12 months and six were found not guilty. One man was acquitted. Nine Mile Point was the scene of more incidents in 1923, 1929 and, famously, there was a stay-down strike in 1935, a catalogue of activity which my father would have recalled when he was assigned to the post of Training and Welfare officer at the colliery in 1945. His emergence as a 'staff' man, however, seemed an unlikely career move during the turbulence of the 1920s. In April 1924, about 600 men employed on the Five Foot seam at Risca colliery were given a fortnight's notice by the management and their employment ended on Thursday 1st May. The *Argus* correspondent, probably Fred Porter, was told that this was because the work on which they had been engaged was 'unremunerative'. Firmer details than this are just not available, and I have no idea if my father was one of those who were cast aside in this way. However,

The Risca Division of the Monmouthshire Constabulary in 1925. There are no smiles and clearly, life is very serious. The group contains a sprinkling of be-medalled ex-soldiers while the two seated figures with peaked hats are obviously the seniors.

Collins & Powell

the causes of the trouble were inevitably linked to the mining companies' need for retrenchment and the cataclysmic developments of 1926 soon enveloped the coalfield. The General Strike of that year began with a national miners' strike, the refusal of the government to continue a subsidy to the coal industry and the implementation of further wage reductions. The solidity of the labour movement, which saw the country paralysed for nine days from 3rd May, lasted only for that period and the miners were left alone to endure the hardships of a long strike. Community and inter-community collaboration was remarkable during the strike and Harold Finch's memoirs recall how, for example, soup kitchens were organised in Risca for the unemployed, and how the public and the local tradespeople helped to organise such a system. Finch tells how,

> ...a club for unemployed folk was formed by public-spirited men and women. A meeting was held in an old building and Mr Evan Rowlands (later Chairman of Risca Urban District Council) presided...Subsequent developments included the formation of a carpenters' shop for the unemployed and a boot repairing shop...Later it was decided to start educational classes...A Professor Price was invited to a public meeting and he helped to establish the classes...A good deal of interest was evinced in economics.

Much later, in the mid-1930s, my father was to study economics at evening classes taught by his close friend, Noel Evans, but it is likely that in 1926, aged 23, he would have been preoccupied with his rugby career. After all, the Welsh Rugby Union, at its meeting on 16th April, suspended him for fighting in a game against Talywain at the Stores Field on 13th March, 1926 and so perhaps the onset of the General Strike was of slightly diminished significance for him. Of course, much has been written and spoken about the strike and of how the police are supposed to have played football with the strikers, a characteristic which baffled some of this country's European neighbours whose constabularies would undoubtedly have maintained a more robust approach to a similar situation. Indeed, Risca's Superintendent Richards accepted some bread and cheese from marching miners at Bassaleg, while at the same time, he forbade them to continue their march on Newport where they wished to make representations to the Guardians about the payment of relief. The cheese incident provoked laughter at Newport magistrates' court on Saturday 29th May, 1926, when William Lewis, a checkweigher from Wattsville, and Robert Gilchrist, a miner from Ynysddu, were charged with unlawfully impeding Superintendent Richards in his application of the Emergency Powers Act. Approximately 600 miners had been involved in the march and the police witness pointed out that it was more practical to bring charges against the two accused than against the entire body of marchers, a combined group from Risca, Nine Mile Point and Bedwas. Despite the Superintendent's frustration at being unable to hold up the march, it had nevertheless passed off peacefully and the cases against Gilchrist and Lewis were dismissed.[12]

However, this incident had occurred at an early stage in the strike and before attitudes had hardened. By August, there was a barely perceptible tendency for small numbers of miners throughout the British coalfields to return to work. Such groups angered their fellow unionists, and during my childhood Dad was quite free with his use of the terms 'scabs' and 'blacklegs', to categorise those whose behaviour had diminished the solidity of the 'Fed'. The events at Quarry Level near Pontypool on 30th August, 1926 blended two components which shaped my father's approach to such matters. Firstly, there was a small group of workers who sought to work and not to strike and secondly there was police action under the direction of a man shortly to be posted to Risca, Superintendent Lawrence Hubert Spendlove, whose activity on this day was ever after to cause my father concern as to how such an officer might discharge his duties in Risca.

'Riot at Colliery' said the *Argus* headline on Monday 30th August. It gave a lurid precis of events:

> A riot occurred at a small colliery near Pontypool on Monday, when police, who were escorting 15 men from the colliery where they had been working, were attacked by an angry crowd of between 600 and 700 men. Volleys of stones and pieces of rock were thrown by members of the crowd, and the police retaliated with their truncheons, laid out four or five of their assailants, and scattered the others up the mountain-side. Panic reigned for some time, and women and young girls rushed about screaming hysterically, and the men tried to reform themselves into groups in order to have another 'go' at the police.

This piece of high-profile industrial drama played well in the magistrates' court and subsequently, in November, at the Monmouthshire Assizes. On the rioters' side, some of the leading actors prosecuted for rioting turned out to be men of local eminence, such as County Alderman Arthur Jenkins, the Miners' Agent (later a Member of Parliament for the Pontypool constituency and at the time of the riot, father of the six-year-old Roy Jenkins, later Lord Jenkins of Hillhead). Another figure of consequence to be prosecuted was William Coldrick, also a member of Monmouthshire County Council and the Deputy Miners' Agent for the Eastern Valley. All told, six of the rioters were sent to the Assizes, one, Bryn Thomas, being discharged by the judge because the evidence against him was said to be thin. Of the remainder, there was the exotic figure of a Japanese steelworker, Ichitara Nishizawa, aged 27, said to have lived in the district since boyhood, when he had abandoned a circus career; the two remaining defendants at the Assizes were Messrs Edwards and Keenan. So much for the union's *dramatis personae*. On the side of the law was Superintendent Spendlove and various constables who had formed part of his force. Spendlove was always a figure of interest to me, during my Risca childhood. For a start, his police uniform carried chainmail on the shoulders and my father assured me that this was a legacy of the great man's days 'in the cavalry'. Research for this project has revealed that Dad was on the right track: Spendlove came from Army stock, as the *Argus* put it, and reported that he had seen service in 'the Dragoons' in India, Egypt and South Africa, ideal training grounds for containing industrial riots in Monmouthshire. Undoubtedly, the paper had sent an excellent reporter to cover the Pontypool disturbances and the journalist's report carries the full flavour of the unpleasantness at the Quarry Level on that day.

As the perceived strikebreakers (whose profiles, for obvious reasons received no press attention), left the colliery, walking between a line of policemen, the crowd's anger erupted:

There was considerable booing and cries of 'You dirty rotters', 'You rotten scabs' and 'You*******. Someone shouted, 'Let them have it ... Let the police have it as well. Down with the ********. About 300 men then rushed the police and the workmen. Clods of turf began to fall among them, and eventually about 100 climbed higher up the hill and started to bombard the police with stones and pieces of rock. Fortunately, no-one was struck, for the police were protected by a row of trucks which lay between them and those higher up the hill but the crowd closed in upon the police. Suddenly, Superintendent Spendlove shouted 'Charge!' Truncheons were drawn, the crowd scattered in all directions and a moment later, three figures lay prostrate on the railway line leading to the colliery. Superintendent Spendlove cried, 'Up the hill at them', and the crowd scattered in all directions. Two men, Harry Merchant, of Pontnewynydd and a man named Pike, of Garndiffaith had their heads split open by truncheon blows, and three or four others received minor injuries. One man who stood on the brink of a steep part of the hill, received a blow on the head and rolled down a considerable distance. Mr Arthur Jenkins rushed up to Superintendent Spendlove and started to expostulate angily, but the Superintendent retorted: 'Who started it? Who started throwing the stones from the top?'

After this first-hand piece of reporting, the case progressed through magistrates' courts and to the Monmouthshire Assizes in late November. At each stage, the *Argus* relayed the evidence to its readership. One prosecution witness, a constable in Spendlove Force, who was seen to have clubbed a rioter, admitted under cross-examination that, yes, he certainly had experienced crowd control problems of that nature earlier in his career. When would that have been, the defence asked. The answer was that he had encountered that kind of trouble during army service in Ireland. My father would have followed all this closely, especially when it was announced that three of the accused, Arthur Jenkins and Messrs Edwards and Coldrick were sentenced to terms of imprisonment, with Jenkins being kept the longest - until February 1927, in Cardiff Gaol. Today, a considerable body of responsible journalism might criticise the police for their violence and the learned judge, Mr Justice Swift, for his summing-up. In his address to the jury, Swift said,

If in the course of the case up to now or in the course of my remarks, it occurs to one or other of you that I take a particular view about a particular fact, you must not allow that to influence you, unless of course, you think it a right and commonsense view.

It was not disputed, said the judge, that at a particular moment, when there were shouts, booing, hustling and throwing of stones - there was a riot on that particular day. Spendlove's bobbies came in for a particular tribute from the bench. The learned judge said that,

They were very brave, very courageous and what they did was in perfect fulfillment of their duty...To my mind it was wonderful how these little bodies of policemen in twos and threes drifted over the mountainside as they got the telephone messages...There were 15 or 17 policemen to a crowd which they estimated at 800 to 1000 and which the defence admitted was 400 to 600.

In their book, *The Fed,* Francis and Smith deliver a devastating indictment of Mr Justice Swift's sentencing and point out that as he had relied entirely on police evidence he seemed by implication to question the suitability and role of the overwhelming Labour dominance in the public affairs of the valleys.

> Your position is deplorable [he said to the mild-mannered Jenkins]. You were a man of high position not only in the Miners' Federation but in the county and it was above all things your duty as a public man, as member of the County Council and as one of the Standing Joint Committee to have assisted the police and maintained order.

This kind of language would have caused my father immense irritation, setting the learned judge in the coalowners' camp and certainly as a member of the establishment that his mother, Amelia Martha, had always urged him to accept, with her 'God bless the squire' slogan. My father was not alone: throughout the valleys the police had lost the confidence of the communities and their credibility was correspondingly diminished.[13] The standing of the constabulary was however, an irrelevance in a setting which saw the resumption of work under a General Agreement signed in November 1926. Most collieries 'opened their gates' for work on 1st and 2nd December, as the *Colliery Guardian* (on 28th January, 1927) put it, but in our corner of the Western Valleys things turned out not to be that straightforward. The ownership of Risca colliery had changed with the United National Colliery Company being replaced by the Ocean Company. The new owners were reluctant to implement the November agreement and bitter wrangling dragged on until February 1927. A side-issue of considerable importance was whether the Risca miners, who had refused to work because the Ocean Company would not implement the General Agreement, were therefore entitled to benefit - a dispute which an official Umpire resolved in the men's favour.[14] One can almost sense the atmosphere in the Primitive Methodist Hall, Crosskeys, on Saturday 12th February, 1927 when union representatives and the striking miners gathered to debate the resumption of work. The *South Wales Argus* of 14th February reported an event, which if not quite historic, is certainly noteworthy as having finally ended a dispute which had begun in May 1926 and which had imposed much hardship:

> A mass meeting of Risca Colliery workmen,was held at the Primitive Methodist Hall Crosskeys on Saturday afternoon. Alderman J. Powell, JP, presided. He was supported by Alderman J. Woodward, JP, Secretary, Mr F. Pettiford (Vice Chairman) and the Works Committee. Alderman Powell, in a report on the position, stated that the representatives of the Ocean Company (Mr E. Edwards, Managing Director and Mr W.P. Thomas, General Manager), had agreed to a resumption of work on the terms existing prior to the national stoppage. The Company were very wishful to have the hearty co-operation of Risca workmen to make the concern a paying and prosperous undertaking. Alderman Powell, on his own behalf and on behalf of his colleagues on the Committee, made a strong appeal to the workmen to give the new Company all the assurance possible to make the concern a success. The meeting unanimously decided to accept the recommendations of their officials and to commence work on Monday morning…

I have no idea whether my father attended this meeting. A Saturday in February would have been a day for a game of rugby with Risca but I have not uncovered any evidence of this. Had he been in 'The Prims' hall, he would, in company with the other veteran strikers, have surely opined that the Ocean

Company's wish to make the concern 'a paying and prosperous undertaking' was all very well. If, however, as the authors of *The Fed* point out, the 'dictated terms in South Wales included an eight-hour day and such a loose agreement which allowed for the erosion of earnings per man shift from ten shillings and three farthings to nine shillings and twopence halfpenny', the arrangement was to the company's advantage and hardly benefited the miners. Their defeat seems to have turned many of them towards conventional Labour Party politics and away from what Francis and Smith call the 'quasi-syndicalism' of industrial action. The Labour party, with my father assuredly voting for it, strengthened its support in the valleys so that in the 1931 General Election, when Labour was decimated everywhere else, South Wales was the only big coalfield to hold all its mining seats, with four candidates returned unopposed.[15] Charles Edwards, the member for the Bedwellty constituency of which Risca and Pontymister formed a part, would most certainly have received Dad's support.

After the strike,the 'Fed' was shattered for nearly a decade, lodge officials and activists were victimised, blacklists abounded, a rival 'scab' union appeared and Ablett, one of the coalfield's most respected militants, was suspended by the 'Fed' for having signed a premature settlement. I am indebted, once again, to Francis and Smith for their crisp analysis of the post-strike situation.

All the assets painstakingly built up by the mining communities, colliery customs, medical schemes, chapels, football teams, the Institutes and their libraries, dramatically declined. Enormous family debts needed to be repaid to the local shopkeepers and the Poor Law Unions, amounting, according to one estimate, to at least £2,500,000 for South Wales alone.

Of greater immediacy in Risca was a report that council house tenants owed £7,000 in arrears of rent, a figure which increased by £400 each month.[16] The Newport Board of Guardians, whose remit for relief included Risca, anticipated a total demand of £126,800. This was the highest sum ever required by the Board, being six times the amount that had been needed in 1911-12 and nearly four times the amount required in 1919-20.[17] Probably the most significant socio-economic result of the 1926 stoppage was the impetus which it gave to the migration of workers from the coalfield. My father's attempt to leave hearth and home was not entirely an impetuous reaction to the depressing events of the year but was linked to a phenomenon of valley life, the obsession of so many workers with their favourite sport, rugby union football.

The Welsh sporting press of those years was replete with reports that so-and-so, a famous or perhaps a not so famous player, had 'gone north' to play professional rugby for one of the Northern Union rugby league clubs. Clearly, my father was not quite of that calibre but when he discovered that London's Metropolitan Police Commissioner was keen to recruit Welshmen for a rugby team, he appears to have been off to London with all dispatch. His seven-year-old nephew, Elwyn Chivers, Harold's son, wrote a neat letter to his cousin, Marian Chivers, on 14th July, 1928: 'Uncle Perc is gone to London he caught the 12 o clock train last night and he might catch the 12 o clock train tonight or the 1 o'clock...'

An unidentified group at 'The Risca Unemployed Club' in the 1920s. The photograph lends credence to Charles Edwards' House of Commons speech on 28th February, 1928 in which he said that in the mining villages men who 'used to take pride in their dress … had lost heart and dressed anyhow'. *Collins & Powell*

This shows some of the principals and the workforce at Danygraig Brickworks in 1937. The owner Lionel 'Nello' Southwood-Jones wears a trilby, and third from the left is my father's brother, Harold, by this time a senior management figure. Yet another member of our extended family, John Rhys Tucker, my father's cousin and Brickworks foreman is on the extreme right. *Collins & Powell*

This could only have been my father's vain (as it turned out) attempt to become a policeman, and many years later he told me that he had been one eighth of an inch too short at five feet eight and something, or perhaps it was five feet nine, I forget now. The syntax and punctuation of an article in the *Argus*, some 10 days later, was not much better than that of Elwyn's letter, but shed a little more light on my father's motivation.

> Many athletic men from South Wales [it said] with experience in the rugby game , have recruited for the Metropolitan Police...The Metropolitan Police are encouraging rugby and it is desired that all members of the force with acquaintance of the game, and others who may be joining the ranks from South Wales should get into touch with Inspector F.H. Hutchins, Cannon Road police station, Secretary of the Metropolitan Police Rugby Football Club and representative on the London Welsh. Men of prominence in addition to the very favourable prospect of a place in the Metropolitan Police team will also have a trial for the London Welsh. As it is impossible for the sports officials to know personally of every man who has played rugby before his enlistment into the force, the latter should not wait for an invitation but communicate at once with Inspector Hutchins.

This episode is surely one of the family's great what-might-have-beens. Dad's distaste for Superintendent Spendlove's forthright methods of riot control notwithstanding, the blend of the coal industry's difficulties with the possibilities of profiting by proven skills at rugby football could have led my father down an entirely different path. We can only speculate about Hitler's blitz on London and whether we would have coped.

Economically there had been every incentive to leave South Wales. Despite the encouraging tones in the *Argus* after the restart at Risca colliery in 1927, the subsequent year did not hold out encouraging prospects. On 31st January, 1928, the newspaper reported that 1,500 men had been idle for a week at Risca and the paper's edition of 25th February, 1928 said that the colliery was working irregularly 'and had been idle at times for two or three weeks at a stretch on account of depression in trade'. The entire picture was given a depressing but realistic gloss by Charles Edwards, the Bedwellty MP, in a speech in the House of Commons on 28th February and reported in the *Argus* on the following day:

> It was terrible to walk around the mining villages now. They met men who used to take pride in their dress, in themselves and in their children. Now they had lost heart and dressed anyhow...The conditions, added Mr Edwards, constituted a perfect scandal. Vagrancy was on the increase to an alarming extent throughout this area. The state of things there was something of which the House should be ashamed.

While it is hard to envisage any member of the Chivers family in Bridge Street as being dressed carelessly or engaging in any form of vagrancy, another of my father's anecdotes sheds light on their lifestyle. My Uncle Harold, undoubtedly comfortably and responsibly established as a valued member of Nello Southwood Jones' office staff at the Danygraig Brickworks, was appalled to see the condition of my father's work-clothes when these were dropped on the tiled kitchen floor. According to my father, a small puddle of perspiration from the garments spread over the tiles. Harold was disgusted. 'I'd sing in the streets first', he said. Whether these clothes had been used for work in the brickworks or at the neighbouring quarry is unclear, although in default of underground work, my father would probably have overcome his prejudices against his relatives' powerful positions at those establishments. Underground work would not have been easy to come by. At the end of May 1928, 300 men were idle at Nine Mile Point and 500 idle at Risca,[18] although from the scant documentary evidence which is available, it is hard to be definite about the exact circumstances of Dad's working life at the time. He appears in Risca colliery's National Health and Unemployment Insurance Register for the half-year ending 3rd July, 1927 where his National Insurance contribution of 4s. 1d. is duly logged. He also appears in an identical document for the quarter ending 1st January, 1928 when no contribution was recorded, an omission which probably points to there having been no work available. These entries are my first pieces of documentary evidence about his working life.[19] From the coalfield's glory days of 1913, however, when 233,139 miners had worked in South Wales, by April 1928 only 169,000 were in employment, while of these, 72,981 were 'Fed' members.[20] Set against these statistics, and given the circumstances at Risca colliery, my father's attempt to join the Metropolitan Police probably made sense.

For those disposed to be hypochondriacs, and again, the Chivers family was not in that category, the County Medical Officer of Health's report for the previous year made depressing reading. On 5th June, 1928, the *Argus* stated that Dr Rocyn Jones had been trying to cope with an epidemic of smallpox that had been 'raging' in the county since February 1927. The figures dealing with maternity and child welfare were poor. The county's birth rate 'again' showed a decline. The rate of 17.5 per thousand of the population for 1927 was 2.8 below that of the previous year. The *Argus* reported that the 'infantile mortality rate' per thousand births was 87.3, as compared with 66.1 for 1926. This was, seemingly, the highest since 1921 and was higher than the rate for England and Wales as a whole, which was 69.

We can be as sure as it is as possible to be, after such a lapse of time, that my father did not travel to Hereford, via the Wye Valley when, in August 1928, Risca colliery's 'afternoon shift' enjoyed the 'first of their annual outings' to such a pleasantly scenic area. Young men of that period, even if they were in employment, would not, in all probability, have wanted to be working 'afternoons' and so the cheery group, of which the 'chairman' was Mr W. Hawkins (Overman), is more likely to have been on the comfortable side of 30 and in all probability comprised a majority of married men. The *South Wales Argus* on 24th August reported that Hawkins 'took control' of the party and was presented with a silver-mounted umbrella. At Tintern, they held a concert in which the *artistes* were the brothers Duffield, Albert Hawkins, and Eli Marsh, while Mr John Moon gave a conjuring exhibition. In the midst of such depressing economic circumstances (by 11th September, 2,000 men at Risca colliery were reported to be working half time),[21] such a cheerful news item could only have been a benison to the soul of the newspaper's editor. After all, in such difficult times, money had been found for the excursion and for the purchase of the silver-mounted umbrella, to say nothing of the necessary refreshments.

It was probably at about this time that my father took steps that were to lead to matrimony. Zion Baptist Chapel in Cwmcarn had initiated the type of social events at which, in those days, a young man might meet a young lady under conditions of perfect respectability. According to the account which my mother gave me, many years later, she met Dad at a 'social evening' at Zion, and it seems that this is where their courtship began. My mother, Eva Evelyn Waite, was the eldest surviving child and the eldest daughter of John James Waite and Rebecca Waite of 47 Newport Road, Cwmcarn. There were six surviving children of that marriage and John Waite was a miner at the Celynen colliery, Newbridge. My mother described herself on the marriage certificate as a 'tobacconist's assistant' and worked at a shop in Newport Road, Cwmcarn, owned by Mr Tom Miles. She had been determined never to marry a miner, a resolve which had obviously faded by 8th September, 1929, when they were married at Duckpool Road Baptist Chapel, Newport. My father was described on the marriage certificate as a 'coal hewer', a phrase which although not carrying any particular social distinction at the time, certainly held implications of strength and virility. Why Duckpool Road Chapel was chosen is something of a mystery, given the links which the bride and groom had, respectively, to Zion, Cwmcarn and to Moriah, Risca. My mother was within a month of her 28th birthday but is shown on the marriage certificate as 27 and my father as 26. Although there seems not to have been much money about for a reception, the happy couple honeymooned in Sidmouth, a resort which may have been chosen after recommendations by my uncles Tom and Harold who knew of it from Risca RFC's trips to the West Country.

It can only be a cliché to describe my father's wedding as a major new step in his life. Thus far, he had worked at two collieries, Cwmcarn and Risca. He had experienced the drastic post-war downturn in the fortunes of the coal industry, and had endured the major stoppages of 1921 and 1926. Subsequent lay-offs at Risca colliery, caused mostly by unremunerative production, had probably driven him, in 1928, to try to join the Metropolitan Police. He faced the new decade with a partner and helpmeet. In common with thousands of others, the difficulties they faced were colossal.

My father's elder brother Harold, *circa* 1914.   *Author's Collection*

Chapter Two

That Old Football...

My mother's description of the noble game of rugby football will always stay with me. It was a part of my upbringing, really. Of course, her's was not a lone voice. She would have heard the pejorative phrase used by women of her generation whose menfolk were obsessed with the sport. In those days, before the Welfare State and before professionalism, families could suffer severe financial penalties if the breadwinner was injured while playing rugby, for no reward, on a Saturday afternoon. However, the enthusiasm for rugby football that permeated the valleys in those days would brook no denial from the women of the family. My father's birth, on 5th March, 1903, coincided with a golden era for Welsh rugby and those of a romantic disposition could say, with some legitimacy, that he acquired his enthusiasm for the game from his mother's milk. Indeed, his mother, Amelia Martha Chivers, appears to have made a mysterious allusion in her diary to a local sporting hero, one J.E.C. Partridge, son of Jason Partridge of Risca. She wrote, in 1908, 'J.E.C. Partridge born on 13th June, 1879 he is now 29 years-of-age. Wore colours of team 1905-6'.[1] Partridge, sometimes known as 'The Bird', was a sporting gent who played rugby for both Newport and Cardiff and became a referee of some repute.[2] Why Amelia Martha logged him in her diary - if indeed, the entry was hers - must remain a mystery. Her husband, Thomas Herbert Chivers, was certainly a rugby fanatic whose principal hobby in those prosperous days before World War I was quartering these islands in pursuit of the glitteringly successful Welsh XVs of the time. He visited Dublin, Inverleith and Gloucester and had witnessed the All Blacks' defeat, at Cardiff, in 1905. Two of my father's elder brothers, Tom and Harold, were also enthusiasts. Tom played for Risca in the immediate pre-war years and was selected for the representative Monmouthshire League XV. In August 1919, the *Football Argus* reported that Harold had been appointed as the secretary of Risca Rugby Football Club and extolled him as, 'The best secretary in the valleys'. Therefore, the family setting in which the young Percy Chivers grew up and the close-knit community where the work-place, the chapel and the rugby club all exerted their influences was to provide him with a rugby career that was interesting without being outstanding.

Indeed, he was to start off with the Risca club, claimed to have been a power in the land since 1876. The hard physical labour that began in Cwmcarn Colliery after he left school in 1916 strengthened his physique to the point where the undoubted 'rough house' style of the game suited him down to the ground.

Setting aside, for a moment, those early days with Risca, it will serve the purpose of this narrative to leap forward for a few years and to review a game which my father played for Cross Keys against Llanelli, at Stradey Park. On 4th February, 1924, he was a month short of his 21st birthday, hardened by seven years of pit work and by a few seasons with Risca in the abrasive Monmouthshire League. To play at Llanelli, then as now, was a tall order. They were a first class side with a sprinkling of international players, including the brilliant Albert Jenkins who had already been capped for Wales at centre-threequarter and his tally of caps would eventually reach 14. It is not difficult to imagine the chilliness of west Wales on a February afternoon but the new experiences that were to assail the young Percy Chivers are perhaps harder to appreciate. Travelling to the ground in a horse-drawn brake, from the pub where they had changed into their black and white club colours, was a touch unusual for the Cross Keys players and being pelted with missiles, *en route*, by the local urchins, even more so. This bombardment emphasised that they were truly up against it on that cold Monday afternoon. The game, which produced a victory for the home side by eight points to nil, was a dour encounter and bewilderingly, the Llanelli players spoke to each other in Welsh, a tongue with which most of the Cross Keys players were not over-familiar. In effect, they did not understand a word of what their opponents said. One Cross Keys forward, whose name has not survived, kept repeating his only Welsh phrase throughout the game, 'Chwarah teg, Llanelli, chwarah teg!' ('Play fair Llanelli, play fair!'). Whenever the ball reached the great Albert Jenkins, the crowd would keen, 'Albert bach!' rather in the style of an opera chorus. In those days, before television and when radio broadcasts were in their infancy, such men were idolised through the medium of the printed word. Jenkins was not the only 'star' on view that day. The Llanelli half-backs, David and Arthur John, were a formidable combination, the former, already with three 'caps' to his credit, was to be awarded two more.[3] The Cross Keys scrum-half, Freddie Reeves, had three Welsh 'caps' and one of my father's colleagues in the pack that day, Ron Herrera, later won eight, while the Cross Keys outside half, Harry Rowe, would soon migrate to the West Country where he would win a county 'cap' for Devon. 'Play throughout was very keen', said the now defunct *South Wales News* 'although Llanelli, who had the better of matters territorially, contributed some pretty passing movements'. The *Western Mail* reported that 'The visiting forwards were a hefty and vigorous lot', while the *South Wales News* said that Cross Keys were 'well served by a robust pack', descriptions that would surely have caused my father to have swelled with pride.

Dad's visit to Llanelli, even allowing for some of his other games for Cross Keys at Bath and Bridgwater for example, was undoubtedly the high-light of his rugby career. It represented an almost magical transformation from his apprenticeships with junior teams in Risca and with the Risca team itself. The Risca first XV with whom he played prior to his migration to Cross Keys, enjoyed a formidable reputation at the time, especially in the Monmouthshire valleys. After 80 years or so, tracing a player's progress through junior teams to a senior XV is far from being a straightforward process. Despite the Risca club's reputation and position in those days, devices such as match programmes which may have survived, are an unlikely luxury for the researcher. On the other hand, the good old *Football Argus*, carefully filed and bound between hard covers, or on microfilm, at the Colindale Newspaper Library, provides valuable information. De-coding a reporter's phraseology and allowing for printing errors that could have stemmed from an indifferent telephone line between Risca and the *Football Argus* office in Newport, six miles away, must form part of the researcher's technique. Take, for example,the report of a game in which a Risca team, probably the 'Firsts', played against the 'Spillers and Bakers' on 6th September, 1919. The *Football Argus* printed its report of this game in two halves and on two different pages of the paper, reflecting, probably, the opportunity which the half-time break gave the reporter to file his copy. The first half of the report mentioned a player called 'Chiver'. Naturally, I was pleased to have found this, perhaps my father's first mention in print. It went on to say that this 'Chiver' had headed a forward rush. Sadly, however, the second part of the report, on a different page, said that this feat had been accomplished by a player called Shiner. I had better luck with the newspaper's edition of 2nd October, 1920 which reported the Risca first XV game at Machen and listed a W. Chivers amongst the Risca forwards. Again, I had to be cautious in assuming that this was my father, P. Chivers. It was certainly not his brother, William Chivers, whose war service had left him with a badly damaged leg. If it can be assumed that this W. Chivers was a misprint and that it was really P. Chivers who had played, then this may have been the first recorded mention of his career in the Risca colours. He would only have been 17. Irritatingly, apart from telling the reader that there was no score at half-time in this game, no final result was recorded in the paper.

On 21st January, 1921, the name Chivers again appeared in print when Risca Harlequins defeated St Julians, from Newport, at Risca, by 28 points to 6. The *Football Argus*, much to my satisfaction, reported that 'A rush by the home side saw Allsop score a try which he converted. Directly afterwards, Chivers got another try for the Harlequins'. Even Jack Strickland's famous book, *Risca Rugby - Days of Glory* is vague about the status of the Harlequins. Perhaps they were the team, which, according to my father, once waited patiently in Risca, one mid-winter afternoon, for a coach that was inordinately late turning up for their fixture in Tredegar. When eventually, they reached their destination, darkness had fallen but there was a bright and clear moon. Nothing daunted, the teams changed and the game proceeded by moonlight!

That kind of enthusiasm was by no means undiluted. Although the Risca RFC mascot, a live goose, made its first appearance when the club defeated Abercarn, at Abercarn in the last fixture of 1919, public support seems to have been patchy in the post-war period. The region's industrial turmoil, dealt with elsewhere in this work, may have had some impact on crowd attendances. On 29th October, 1921, the *Football Argus* carried the following, rather bitter commentary, under the heading, 'A Complaint from Risca - Adequate Support not Forthcoming':

> The Risca Rugby Club do not get the support they deserve. Some two years ago certain people protested against clubs accommodated on licensed premises. If this state of things were altered, so it was stated, the people would support 'The Cuckoos'.[4] Consequently, the pavilion was erected, but the promised support is not yet forthcoming. Then people said, 'What language we hear on the football field'. Again, the Committee made a strong effort to cleanse the grand old game. Notices were posted up and the committeemen constituted themselves as vigilance officers and much good was done. And yet the promised support is not forthcoming.

This was probably written by Mr Fred Porter, occasionally known as 'Captain' Porter but who used the *nom de plume*, 'Bwana', both handles derived, allegedly, from his war service in East Africa. Fred Porter's complaints continued into the new year and on 4th February, 1922 he wrote, in the *Football Argus*, '…that the Risca club is not getting the support it deserves, in spite of the fact that it has produced one of the greatest forwards in the Principality. Local patriotism is dead at Risca'. Porter was undoubtedly referring to one of my father's heroes, the mighty Tom Roberts, who was capped from Risca against Scotland, Ireland and France in 1921. He later transferred to the much more prestigious Newport club.

Evidence about Dad's career at Risca in 1921 is scant. The *Football Argus* reported on 3rd September, 1921 that in the previous week's trial match my father had played for 'The Whites' against 'The Stripes' and that 'The Whites' had prevailed by 18 points to nil. A week later, the same paper pointed out, in a commentary on the trial that, 'There were plenty of good forwards - strong, lusty young fellows in the pink of condition, but badly in need of coaching'. My father probably read that with mixed feelings.There was further confusion of the names Chivers and Shiner in the *Football Argus* report of Risca's home game against Newbridge on 7th January, 1922. The team listing mentioned W.E. Chivers, but Porter's account alluded to Shiner. Risca won, by three points to nil, and Percy Bunce, in his pre-Cardiff career, scored the game's only try. In a retrospective article in the paper published on the following Saturday, Mr Porter said that the Newbridge game had been 'a grim struggle'. My father, it seems, had to wait until the 1922-3 season for another game with the first XV. On 13th January, 1923, the *Football Argus* reported that in Risca's home game at the Stores Field, against the Newport-based side, Pill Harriers, 'a round of passing resulted in Chivers scoring easily'. This did not save him from being dropped, however, and on the following Saturday, 20th January, 1923, he was chosen for 'Risca Seconds' for their home fixture with Roath Park and on the week after that he was listed for the same team for their game at Tredegar against 'Tredegar Reserves'. At the beginning of the 1923-4 season, the *Football Argus* reported my father's game for the Risca first XV against Treherbert at the Stores Field, which Risca won by 19 points to 10. On 16th October he played his last game for Risca for the time being, when they entertained Ynysddu, at Risca. Then, within the short space of four days, the young Percy Chivers, at the age of 20 years and seven months, took the major step of transferring to Cross Keys.

The rules about transfers between clubs in those far-off days of almost undiluted amateurism were probably sufficiently elastic to accommodate a move at such short notice. Clearly, Cross Keys needed his services in fairly short order for their imminent game against Bath, at Bath, on 20th October, 1923 and perhaps his brother, Harold, the Risca secretary, oiled whatever wheels needed to have been put in motion. The Bath game, my father's baptism in first-class rugby, ended in a draw, with each side scoring an unconverted try. Although, many years later, this game cropped up frequently in our conversations, I ought to have interrogated my father more thoroughly, I suppose. After all, for such a young player, a coal-miner who was hardened to muscular fitness by hard work, a debut on the neatly-mown surface of the Bath Recreation Ground was something to shout about, especially when elitism and class-consciousness dominated all aspects of rugby union football.

If rugby in South Wales was the game of the people, there was altogether a more middle-class aspect to the game in England, and Bath was certainly in England. The flourish of initials before many of his opponents' names on the team-sheet and the honorifics of 'Doctor' and 'Lieutenant' that appeared amongst the Bath listings that day, could have irritated my father, who was only too anxious to leave the shadow of his mother's acutely class-conscious invocation on behalf of the squire and his relations. In their definitive work, *Fields of Praise*, David Smith and Gareth Williams point out that during the 1920s, Cross Keys, 'one of the leading clubs of the decade', frequently fielded sides in which only four players were in employment of any sort, the remainder being victims of the appalling economic conditions.[5] Eighty years on, it is hardly possible to detect which of the Cross Keys players, at the Bath 'Rec', on 20th October, 1923, was in or out of work. Of infinitely greater interest, today, must be the fact that Bath were in the habit of fielding eight backs and seven forwards, and of course, this five-eighth game as it was called, needed to be matched by their opponents. Bath's five-eighth game predicated a fast and powerful pack and offered the luxury of two outside halves, who, positioned at both sides of the scrum, could mount an attack from either flank.[6] On Monday 22nd October, 1923, the *South Wales News* assessed the game, my father's baptism in first-class rugby football:

Bath's rise to eminence amongst English clubs has been almost meteoric. A couple of seasons ago they were regarded as being little better than second class; now Cross Keys' experience in the Somerset town on Saturday might well serve as a warning to future visitors there. This achievement The Cidermen have attained by dint of perseverance and the exploitation of a style of play in which forwards, like a pack of greyhounds have an important part. Three or four of the Bath seven would make speedier wings than the bulk of those playing for Welsh clubs and this, coupled with a 'pull' they had in the lines out by reason of their greater stature made itself felt time and time again in the game with the Keys. With the result of it neither side has reason for complaint, for each in turn held the upper hand but lacked the ability to drive home their attacks. Cross Keys would have done better if only their tackling was less of an embrace and if they are to retain their strength of last season they will have to remedy this forthwith. The only scores were a try by Trevor Benson, Hicks failing to convert and Chaddock's try for Bath in the second period which Woodward failed to majorise.

The *Football Argus* reported that for Cross Keys, 'Millard and Chivers were prominent for a fine piece of cross dribbling' and surely my father would have been pleased about that. In the pack, he played alongside his hero, the mighty Steve Morris, already the holder of eight caps, while the half-back/five-eighth trio comprised the thrice-capped Freddy Reeves at inside half, while Rowe and Howell were the five-eighths. Bath included a medical man on the wing, Dr Meine, and a Royal Navy officer, Lieutenant Rose, in the pack while Harry Vowles, at inside-half, had been capped for the England schoolboys side.

My father's place in the Cross Keys team was by no means assured, although he played against Pontypool on 17th November, 1923, when Cross Keys won at home, 3-0, and a week later he was in the team that defeated Penarth, at Penarth, 6-0. By the end of the year he had lost his place and on 20th December he played for Cross Keys Seconds against Risca Seconds and scored a try. The *Football Argus* reported that, 'a forward rush by the Cross Keys side resulted in Percy Chivers scoring an

CROSS KEYS SECONDS R.F.C. 1923-1924.

BUSBY'S, Photographers,
122 Chepstow Road,
Newport.

W. RICHARDS (Manager)   T. CHEDDY   A. CREWE   W. MILLARD   H. JEFFRIES (Trainer)

W. STRANGE   R. HERRERA   D. DAVIES   T. EVANS   L. HICKS   J. HEMMINGS   DONALD SINCLAIR (Hon. Secretary)

P. ROBERTS   I. GARDNER   H. PRICE   C. HOWELLS (Capt.)   P. CHIVERS   GEO. JAMES   IDRIS DAVIES

A. MARTIN   G. MILTON

Having played a number of games for the Cross Keys first XV, my father was relegated to the 'Seconds' and lined up (*seated, third from the right*), for this photograph. A player of considerable potential was Ron Herrara (*second row from the back, second from the left*), who was capped for Wales eight times between 1925 and 1927.

Author's Collection

unconverted try'. Father and son never discussed how it felt to play against his old club after leaving them, eight weeks earlier, but at the very least, the scoring of a try must have deflected any criticism. Within a month however, my father had bounced back into the Cross Keys first XV when on 10th January he was picked to play against Bridgwater, at Bridgwater. They changed in a pub, The Duke of Monmouth, named after the rebellious bastard son of Charles II, and although it was unlikely that they derived inspiration from this facility, went on to defeat their hosts 9-3. The *Western Daily Press* reported the game on 21st January, 1924:

Bridgwater lost again on their own ground, Cross Keys deservedly winning by 9 points to 3. Cross Keys gave a capital display under the circumstances. Bridgwater got the lead early in the game through Arthur Spriggs kicking a fine penalty goal, but the visitors then became the stronger side. Their forwards were much better than the home pack, both in the scrums and in the loose and the backs convincing movements. It was a considerable time however, before they overcame the defence. The first score to Cross Keys came from clever play in the loose, James getting an ungoaled try and another was added by Williams after clever work by the backs. They would have got a third try from the best movement of the match had not Hicks given a forward pass to Benson when the latter had only to run in to score. Bridgwater had lost Clement through injury and he did not again take the field after the interval when play developed into a great struggle between the forwards. The home pack were dangerous at times but there were some fine rushes by the Cross Keys forwards, Winmill, the old international, leading them well. The only other score was a try by Rowe, who ran over very cleverly after receiving a pass from Reeves.

This generous account, in a West Country newspaper, although non-partisan, omitted to mention that Reeves, as well as Winmill, had been capped by Wales. The great man, Steve Morris, my father's hero, had other duties that day. He was helping Wales to defeat England, at Swansea by 11 points to 3. Thirty years after the Bridgwater game, I visited the town with Risca RFC when we were returning from a brief Easter tour of the West Country after defeating Honiton and Tiverton. I think that my father was quite pleased when I reported that I had seen both The Duke of Monmouth and the Bridgwater rugby ground, where a game had been in progress.

After the Llanelli game on 4th February, 1924, which I have already described, it seemed that his career with the Cross Keys first team had come to an end. He took his place , possibly with no good grace, in the line-up for the Cross Keys Seconds team photograph at the end of the 1923-1924 season and that, it must have seemed, was that. Looking forward to the next season, he paid heed to wise advice from that shrewd and highly experienced administrator and Risca RFC's Secretary, my Uncle Harold. My father told me that, 'Our Harold said that I would probably get a regular first-team place with Risca', and therefore, on the say-so of his elder brother, he returned to Risca for the 1924-1925 season. The Risca first team had an impressive record to which 'Bwana' composed a fulsome tribute, published in the *Football Argus* on Saturday 30th August, 1924. Under the heading, 'A Popular Captain - P. Bunce to lead Risca, Winners of the League Medals', Fred Porter wrote,

Risca did exceedingly well last season and won the Monmouthshire League medals but they hope even to eclipse that record in the 1924-1925 period. The club have a band of energetic and enthusiastic workers who have not spared themselves to ensure success and as a result of their efforts, the Eisteddfod organised in aid of the funds was a huge success. The Pavilion was a big proposition to tackle but this has been improved and is considered one of the best in the valleys while the playing field has also received attention. The officials, Mr George Lewis (Chairman), Mr Harold Chivers (Secretary) and Mr Dan Jones (Treasurer) are the right men in the right place. Mr Chivers has compiled a good fixture list, including Newport, Weston, Bridgwater, Wellington and Exeter. The captain is P. Bunce, a very fine forward...

Fred Porter's eulogy of Percy Bunce needs acceptance against a boldly coloured background. Destined to appear later in this narrative, Bunce was a very solid figure both as a player and later, an administrator. Porter's comment about Bunce being a very fine forward is rather low-key, compared with Jack Strickland's remarks in *Risca Rugby - Days of Glory*. The latter maintained that the very mention of Bunce's name, even after his retirement from playing, was 'enough to bring on a nose-bleed' for any of his former opponents.[7] Undoubtedly a rough handful who inspired his 'troops' and led from the front, Bunce, like all outstanding Risca players, was to move down the valley to play for Newport and Cardiff and played in a number of Welsh trials before returning to Risca, where he saw out the remainder of his playing career in the 1930s. My father was always pleased to tell of how, in a local 'derby' when Risca played Newbridge, one of Bunce's own side, Ivor Roberts, swung a 'haymaker' of a punch at a Newbridge player. The intended recipient ducked and the blow struck Bunce, who went down, 'as if pole-axed' as my father put it.

Clearly, for the family historian, Bwana 's mention of my Uncle Harold and his excellent fixture list for the 1924-1925 season is quite stimulating. Fred Porter's occasional tributes to Harold deserve elaboration. Harold George Chivers was born in Cwmbran in 1892 and came to Risca with his parents soon after. A serious medical problem, said to have been 'tubercular growths on his hands' had prevented him from following a career involving any form of harsh, menial labour. An operation, allegedly performed by the doctor, 'on the kitchen table', had alleviated the problem and an office job was found for him at the Southwood Jones brickworks at Danygraig, Risca. To use a cliché, he seems to have risen rapidly to a position of responsibility, which some family members referred to as Company Secretary, although as a child, I remember visiting his office, some time in the 1940s, and carefully noting the legend on the door, which read, 'Commercial Manager'. Harold was probably the brightest star in the Chivers firmament, achieving a mention, and having his photograph published in the memoirs of Harold Finch MP, where he is described as having been a student at the London Labour College and as a member of a left-wing study group which met at Blackwood in the 1920s.[8] Family lore made no mention of these important facets to Harold's career but concentrated on his unhappy marriage to Edith May Smith in 1914. The marriage broke up in the 1920s and Harold formed an association with a Mrs Campbell, the widow of an army NCO who had been killed during the war. My father was convinced that Harold's career as a rugby administrator would have taken him beyond the mere secretaryship of Risca RFC and on to the Welsh Rugby Union, had it not been for his marital troubles. Someone, perhaps Harold himself, took care to secure his entry in *Who's Who in Wales* for 1920, where he is listed as, 'Secretary local Sailors' and Soldiers' Reception Fund; Sec. Discharged Sailors and Soldiers' Hostel Fund; Sec. Risca Sports Comm. and Rugby F.C.' Jack Strickland's book, *Risca Rugby - Days of Glory*, records that Harold was the club secretary from 1918 to 1933, a period encompassing, of course, my father's chequered playing career.

Tracing my father's career in the 1924-1925 season was difficult. Diligent research of the *Football Argus* and the *South Wales Argus* failed to produce any evidence that he was playing any games, anywhere. My childhood recollection of when he told of a rib injury, sustained at one stage in his career, might possibly match up with these non-appearances and it was not until I researched the following season that I was able to trace, once again, his career with the Risca club. During this new season, 1925-1926, Bwana continued to write straightforwardly about the club's fixtures and in the process managed to cause offence to my father on a seemingly minor issue that rankled through the years and which Dad resurrected during my time with Risca RFC. The urbane journalist was never confronted with the matter, but now that I have discovered the offending item, I can begin to understand how the reporter's phraseology caused offence. The new season was not very old when Risca entertained Llanilleth on the Stores Field on 31st October, and sadly, lost the game. One week later, in a customary retrospective commentary, Bwana filed an analysis of the game, from which the following lines are an extract:

> Bunce played a useful game in the open while a great deal of credit is due to P. Chivers for the valiant way he attempted to break through the opposition … This young forward is improving very rapidly…

The young forward who was improving very rapidly was not best pleased with this. Although he was 22 years and 8 months old and quite obviously merited the adjective 'young', my father felt that his experience with the Cross Keys first XV should have been acknowledged in a more positive way. The slightly patronising flavour of the report was quite unacceptable to a player who was proud of his achievements which, however modest they appear in retrospect, nevertheless counted for a lot in the valleys in those days.

Risca's subsequent victory over Cross Keys, at the Stores Field on 21st November, 1925 would have offered consolation. Risca scored 13 points to their opponents 3 points, but winning this local 'derby' and the attendance of newspaper photographers was highly gratifying to the home team and their supporters. My father's photograph appeared in the *Western Mail* on the following Monday, 23rd November, and the reporter said that,

> Risca were superior to Cross Keys in all departments and thoroughly deserved their victory in a hard game. The home forwards outplayed the opposing eight, heeling and packing admirably and giving a dashing display in the open.

This was an important game that cropped up from time to time in my father's reminiscences, some of which dealt with a flying tackle that he had attempted on the Cross Keys player, Bert Tovey, later to be our newsagent when we lived in Brookland Road. Sadly, the photograph which my father asserted had caught

My father is the player with the ball in Risca's home game with Cross Keys on 21st November, 1925. Risca won 13 - 3.

the moment precisely, has not been traced. Approximately one month later, on 19th December, 1925, Risca narrowly lost, at home, to Pontypool, by 6 points to 5 and my father scored the solitary Risca try. The *Football Argus* reported that:

> George Milton got possession and attempted a dropped goal. The ball fell short and the home forwards by a strong combined movement broke through the opposition and Percy Chivers got a brilliant try which Bunce converted with a fine kick.

Scoring a try was enough to make people sit up and take notice, but to have been the scorer of a 'brilliant' try was some kind of compensation for Bwana 's earlier comments.

The Spring of 1926 brought a dramatic event. On 13th March my father was sent off the field, for fighting, in a home game against Talywain which ended in a scoreless draw. The *Football Argus* carried a headline that evening which said, 'Two Players Ordered Off', but the report which followed cagily avoided identifying the miscreants.[9] More accurately, three players were sent off, two from Talywain and one from Risca, the latter being my father. It seems to have been the accepted practice not to have identified players who were dealt with in this way and so, what today would be described as 'naming and shaming' had to wait until the disciplinary process had been implemented. A month later, on 17th April, 1926, the *Football Argus* carried the salacious headline, 'Rugby Players Suspended - Welsh Union take Disciplinary Action - International Forward Included'. Sadly, the international player was the great Steve Morris, who was dealt with by the same tribunal that punished my father, for an offence committed while playing for Cross Keys, a coincidence from which my father may have derived some cheer. The report that followed said:

> The Welsh Rugby Union, at a meeting held in Cardiff on Thursday took disciplinary action against several well-known players. Suspensions passed were: Risca versus Talywain: Mr W. Leahy, Newport, reported Percy Chivers (Risca), Stanley Smith and L. Hodder (Talywain). The first two for striking each other and Hodder for charging a Risca player. Chivers and Smith were suspended until September 13th and the case against Hodder deferred until the next meeting.

The tribunal suspended Steve Morris 'up to and including 1st May, 1926' and it might be argued that my father's penalty was slightly more severe, taking him, as it did, to the beginning of the next season.[10]

If my father's idol, Morris, was seen to have had feet that were perhaps, only partially made of clay, there was one game in that great man's earlier career that had a profound influence on my father, so profound in fact that it moved him to write a story. The event was a game at Rugby School, when on Thursday 1st November, 1923, a team from England and Wales played a team from Scotland and Ireland to commemorate the anniversary of that seminal event when a Rugby schoolboy, William Webb Ellis, was supposed to have been the first player ever to have picked up the ball and run with it. The England and Wales XV won by 21 points to 16, but my father's principal interest in the game, together with that of many other rugby enthusiasts in the Western Valleys, was the fact that two outstanding international forwards from Monmouthshire, Steve Morris of Cross

Keys and Tom Roberts of Risca and Newport, played on the winning side. My father's short story, 'The Dress Suit', was clearly inspired by the game at Rugby School and most certainly, by the perceived need for those players attending the post-match function to be immaculately clad in dinner jacket and black tie. The plot centred on the plight of the two heroes, notionally Morris and Roberts, but portrayed with different names, who worried desperately about how, in those harsh days of strikes and unemployment, they were to procure the correct garb. More subtly, it was essential that they should not let down their host, 'The Squire', a man unknown in Welsh Rugby Union circles, but a handy figure nonetheless in my father's demonology and derived from my grandmother's slogan about 'our proper stations'. The heroes scrimped and saved and tricked themselves out in their newly-purchased dinner jackets only to find that, on the night, the Squire wore a lounge suit. The point of the yarn was that the Squire had expected his guests only to have managed lounge suits and so he wished to avoid causing them embarrassment. This story was never published and clearly failed to find favour with the editors to whom my father submitted it in the 1940s. However, as the creation of a coalminer, promoted to Costs and Wages Clerk and then to Colliery Training Officer by the time he tried to have it published, it is an interesting construct.

From Dad's point of view, the Centenary Match at Rugby School had quite obviously been very stimulating. His perusal of the details of the game and the post-match celebrations, published in the *South Wales News* on Friday 2nd November, might well have fired him up. Spectators did not comprise 'an ordinary crowd' wrote Old Stager, 'especially from the viewpoint of a democratic Welshman, for it was composed almost exclusively of professional and leisured classes who are the backbone of the game in England, Scotland and Ireland'. In his after-dinner speech, the President of the Welsh Rugby Union, Mr Horace Lyne, identified a number of handicaps endured by rugby football in the Principality. He pointed out that there were practically no public schools in Wales from which players might be drawn and,

> Wales had the disadvantage of having so many working men players (who) played as fine a game and were as good sportsmen as any, but working men who succeeded at football had big temptations placed in front of them, especially if they were colliers and others on low wages.

The tone of this speech could have irritated my father and sown the seeds for the short story.

However, Lyne's words touched a sensitive issue, the recent depredations of the Northern Union and its financial inducements. In their book, *Fields of Praise*, Smith and Williams tell how,

> Wales's international success up to 1922 flattered to deceive, for the inducements of the professional game were already sapping the energies of Welsh rugby. By the end of 1921, nine post-war capped players had joined the Northern Union. Pontypool began the 1921-2 season with only seven players available because virtually the whole pack had gone North during the summer; by 1922-3 there were 40-50 Welshmen appearing regularly in northern sides.

Although *Fields of Praise* provides ample details of these depredations, it omits Cross Keys' Joe Thompson, who after being awarded one Welsh 'cap' against England in 1923, promptly 'went North', to Leeds, to begin a distinguished Rugby League career.[11]

Smith and Williams censure the Welsh selectors of the 1920s and as a point of attack, seize upon the England victory, by 17-9, over Wales at Swansea in January 1924. The writers complain at the 'sterility' of Wales' back play throughout the 1920s:

> Its limitations were cruelly exposed at St Helen's in 1924. England's 17-9 victory was her first win of the century at Swansea; it was based on a skilful and intelligent pack and threequarters whose strong running and swift passing revealed the Welshmen's imperfect grasp of what was once 'the Welsh game'...England scored five tries against a threequarter line which...resorted to shoulder tackles...Six of the (Welsh) side's nine new caps were in the pack, but while the steamroller theory had been abandoned for dash and youth, it was enthusiasm at the expense of experience, and it was too much to expect the genial Cross Keys collier, Steve Morris, to knit them together...Welsh packs of the twenties were strong but not skilled in their strength for they were unable to control the decisive ball-winning areas of the contemporary game, the tightly bound scrum and the loose heel...

This detail exudes the atmosphere, the ethos, and the attitudes which Dad absorbed through every pore. As meat and drink, such subtleties dominated lengthy discussions at the workplace and in the valleys' football dressing rooms.They surfaced too, many years later, at our house in Brookland Road where Steve Morris easily kept his heroic status.

The great man's international career ended in 1925, though he went on playing for Cross Keys into the 1930s. On the other hand, my father's appearances for Risca in the 1926-1927 season were spasmodic. The *Football Argus* listed him as a member of the Risca first XVs that played against Treherbert and Ynysddu in 1926 but I was not able to find his name again until the paper listed him on his 24th birthday, 5th March, 1927, as a member of the team that drew with Blaina, at Risca. One week later he attracted favourable comment by his play at Newbridge, when 'Pask, Sage and Chivers relieved the situation with a dribble', in a game that Risca won, 8-3. On 9th April, 1927, Risca lost at home to their local rivals, Cross Keys, by 10 points to 5 and Bwana reported that 'Chivers had hard lines in not getting over from a cross-kick by Davies'. However, in a retrospective article compiled by the paper's Crosskeys correspondent and published on 16th April 1927, we learn that in that game, 'The play of Chivers, the Risca winging forward, did not tend to enhance attractive football'. The interesting point here, apart from the light thrown on my father's style of play, is that a forward position is identified. Rarely, in the writings of the day, were such positions named and indeed, Dad always reminisced that in his day forwards simply formed a scrum when required to do so by the referee and he maintained that it was a case of 'first there, first down'. The authors of *Fields of Praise* identify the Welsh Union's reluctance to recognise the need for specialist scrum positions as a contributory factor in the national team's lack of success. As late as 1935, Horace Lyne would be telling his members that 'specialist forwards distressed him for they were spoiling football in all the countries...' The extent to which scrum specialisation was influencing tactics would have been increasingly academic for my father at the end of the 1920s. Indeed, his career seemed almost to have ground to a halt in the 1927-1928 season, when his name appeared on the teamsheet of what was very definitely a junior side, Pontywaun County School Old Boys. The first of these listings was for a game at Royal Oak against Newport High School Old Boys on 20th September, 1927, although the papers carried no information about the result. Next, my father was the 17th listed player among the 20 names which appeared in the *South Wales Argus* on Friday 7th October, 1927, from which the Risca first XV to play Blackwood on Saturday would be selected. This was not particularly flattering for such an experienced player. A useful cliché, perhaps, is to say that he may have made himself 'unavailable' for this game and his name was not included in the team listing which accompanied the *Football Argus*'s report. However, the Pontywaun County School Old Boys' selectors seized their opportunity and included him, the following week, in their side to play the Newport 'Thirds' on 15th October. The Old Boys did not secure his services, but allowing his name to go forward in their published team-sheet may have paid off, for on that date he played for Risca when they lost, 18-3, at Abertillery.

Neither the *Argus* nor the *Football Argus* offer much detail about what is clearly the concluding stage of my father's rugby career. It is probable that by 1928, the social evenings organised at Zion Baptist Chapel, in Cwmcarn, where he met my mother, were turning his thoughts towards matrimony. He made it quite clear to me that she had certainly influenced him in his decision to abandon the sport, although his attempt to join the Metropolitan Police in that year, which I have described elsewhere, would have been stimulated by the Police Commissioner's well-known requirement for rugby-playing recruits. His souvenirs of the sport which the *Football Argus*'s Fred Porter called 'The grand old game' were scant. In 1926-1927, Risca won the Monmouthshire League championship and Dad's medal was collected, on his behalf, at the usual small ceremony, by his brother Harold. They were not amongst his possessions for very long. Later, during the Depression, he was forced to pawn them to help to put bread on the table for his wife and child.

Reminiscences by, or about, rugby players frequently concentrate on the careers of those 'stars' who have played for their country.This account of my father's career sheds light on a seemingly run-of-the-mill performer whose potential may not have been completely fulfilled. Yet, it must surely rate as an achievement at that time, for a player barely into his twenties, to win a first-team place with Risca and more especially with Cross Keys, one of the leading clubs of the decade. His rugby days left him with a fund of humorous reminiscence and an undying love of Bwana's noble game. It was not all about harsh physical confrontation and the macho rivalry between mining communities. There were other, broadening aspects. In the 21st century, when teams cover considerable distances by motorway, by rail and by air, it is hard to appreciate that in those days of depression and unemployment, the rugby club may have been the players' sole travel agent. Often, the only opportunity of free travel was to board a charabanc to fulfil an away fixture. One of Dad's fellow players, when asked if he had ever visited Birmingham, is alleged to have answered, 'No, Risca never played there!'

Chapter Three

Gardener, Father, Fireman, Clerk

My parents began their married life in a council house in Ty-Isaf, but by 1930 they were living in Brookland Road. The Register of Electors for the Pontymister Polling District for that year shows that they occupied 'Kymin', which later became No. 26 Brookland Road, a premises owned by Dad's sister, Harriet Mary Jenkins and her husband, Ernest Frederick Jenkins. Ernest Jenkins worked at Pontymister Works, an enterprise which, according to my father's slightly envious analysis, was mostly strike-free.[1] Hard work and thrift accounted for the Jenkinses' prosperity and their ownership, not only of the house, but of a motor cycle and side-car combination, replaced, first by a Morris 8 and then, just before World War II, by an Austin 12 saloon. By the standards which prevailed in Risca during the Depression, the Jenkinses were comfortably off. They were childless but doted on sundry nieces and nephews, and were loyally supportive to my parents when financial difficulties cropped up.

But, of course, my parents were not the only people in difficulty. The poor state of the mining industry was compounded by the Wall Street crash of 1929, and the Labour Government took the harshest of blows when it was perceived that the sums of money paid as 'dole' to Britain's unemployed masses were unsustainable. Ramsay MacDonald's decision to cut unemployment benefit and public servants' salaries cost him the support of Labour's rank and file in the Commons. From this debacle, the Prime Minister emerged at the head of a 'National' Government drawn from all political parties and which abandoned the gold standard in September 1931. A General Election was held in October which delivered another devastating blow to Labour. In all, only 46 Labour and five ILP members were returned, in place of the 289 elected in 1929. They were opposed by 554 supporters of the Government, Conservative, Liberal and 'National Labour'. However, Labour maintained its position in the Welsh valleys amidst a mood of intense class bitterness that perceived a 'bankers' ramp' and MacDonald's 'betrayal' of his former allies in the working-class movement in South Wales. Some of the flavour of the election campaign may be gauged from a speech at Bedwas early in September 1931, by Bedwellty's MP, Charles Edwards, and reported in the *South Wales Argus* of 4th September:

> Mr Edwards said he could not understand Mr MacDonald. He had done great work for the Labour movement but now he had joined forces with men who had no sympathies with his ideals…In spite of Mr MacDonald's denial, he [Mr Edwards] contended that the Premier had given way to the dictation of bankers and other financial interests.

These were sentiments with which my father agreed wholeheartedly. I have been unable to find my parents' names in the electoral roll for 1931, probably because this was the year when they were driven to migrate. London was an inevitable magnet for South Walians seeking work. In the year preceding my parents' move to Twickenham, the *South Wales Argus*, quoting a magazine called *The Welsh Outlook*, said, '…thousands of young people from the

This photograph of my mother was probably taken in 1929.   *Author's Collection*

This may have been my parents' wedding day (8th September, 1929) photograph, although the bride is covering her left hand and the groom has no buttonhole. *Author's Collection*

depressed mining districts have descended upon the metropolis in search of the livelihood which their staple industry has ceased to give', and predicted further migrations.

During my formative years I discovered a snapshot of my father, wearing a gardener's apron and posing in a large, well-tended garden. I was told, 'That was when we were working in Twickenham'. As early as March 1928, Neville Chamberlain had urged mass transfers of unemployed Welsh miners to other parts of Britain, and indeed Dad's attempt to join the Metropolitan Police in that year might have stemmed, in part, from this advocacy. On 17th February, 1930, the *Argus* reported that in Risca, 'no less than 65 families have been transferred to other districts, eight families sent to Canada and 180 single men transferred to other areas'. Five months later, on 5th July, the paper said that, 'The last four years have witnessed the biggest wave of Welsh migration into London within history', and so, if my analysis of their absence from the 1931 Electoral Roll is correct, my parents' move to Twickenham was part of this pattern. Both of them may have been embarrassed by an episode in their lives which involved a kind of servility. They were employed, it seems, as housemaid and gardener, at a large house in Twickenham. The lady of this house had a foreign accent and expressed considerable surprise when she discovered that her employees were reasonably well turned-out and lacked the poverty-stricken appearance that Londoners had come to expect when encountering those from the depressed areas. It was a rare event for my mother to attempt to guy a foreign accent as, for my benefit, she tried hard to replicate her posh employer's sentence: 'But, you are not poor. I thought you would be poor'. What she meant, of course, was they didn't look poor. The job included accommodation but it failed to hold them and, according to the account which my mother gave to me, they were soon looking to get back to Risca. Cash however, was a problem. My father's sister Hattie, came to the rescue and supplied the train fare. The migration to Twickenham had been a brief and not a joyous episode for the young couple.

The London adventure had almost certainly been encouraged by further industrial turbulence. A coalfield-wide strike about hours and wages lasted from 1st January until 18th January, 1931, and my father's record of National Insurance contributions in the Risca colliery register shows that he worked during the weeks ending on 20th January, 31st January and 7th February. However, the colliery company, which, according to the *South Wales Argus*, sought 'a cut in the price list', gave the Risca miners 14 days' notice on 26th January and after its expiry the pit remained closed until Monday 21st September. My father was not listed amongst the mourners at the funeral of Jonah Roberts, a close and respected family friend. This absence from a funeral reported in the *Argus* on 20th March was uncharacteristic and added to my small collection of evidence that pointed to his migration to London.

The *Argus* calculated in its edition of 31st May, 1932, that, in Risca, approximately 2,000 people were unemployed, which the paper said was approximately 50 per cent of the community's total work force, although it admitted that precise computation was difficult. An interesting commentary on the situation has survived from the archives of Risca's Oxford House Settlement and while this may lack total authority, it certainly paints a useful picture. The

Oxford House Warden, writing on 1st November, 1932 to a Mr Cameron, who was destined in all probability to lecture or to engage lecturers at the Settlement, said,

> So far as I can make out, Risca is affected more by rationalisation than by depression merely…in 'Risca Pit', new methods have been put into operation which cut down the number of employees by about half. Six hundred men are now working there. A thousand is probably about the full strength now, with about 2,000 before the Ocean took it over from the United National…The population of the district is 18,000. It is impossible to get unemployment figures because the Urban District, the PAC [Public Assistance Committee] and the Employment Exchange Area are not conterminous. But the number of men on the Risca Labour Exchange Register has increased during the last twelve months, from 2,000 to 2,600 men, women and children, but of course the great majority of them are men.[2]

A number of government initiatives affected the coalfield and inevitably impacted upon Risca and my parents. Firstly, the the Coal Mines Act of 1930, which forced amalgamations and production quotas on the coal owners, and to which the Oxford House Warden was referring when he mentioned 'rationalisation'. The 10 per cent cut in the 'dole' and in the salaries of public servants has already been mentioned. In 1934, the Chancellor of the Exchequer, Neville Chamberlain, introduced an Unemployment Act that was an attempt to establish a sound financial and logical basis for the payment of unemployment benefit. It aroused enormous resentment for its intrusive approach. There were bitter demonstrations against the Act throughout South Wales and in many industrial areas of the United Kingdom. The *South Wales Argus* reported a 'Risca Demonstration' in its edition of Monday 4th February, 1935.

> Nearly 5,000 people [it reported] from Abercarn, Cwmcarn, Pontywaun, Wattsville, Cross Keys, Risca and Pontymister, gathered at the Church House Field, Risca and protested against the new regulations. County Councillor Edgar Matthews presided and was supported by Mr C. Edwards MP, Chief Labour Whip.

So far, so depressing. My parents, by now, according to the Electoral Roll for 1932, were living at No. 4 (later renumbered No. 10) Brookland Road, a premises owned by the Oddfellows, a Friendly Society for whom Dad's brother-in-law, Ernest Jenkins, was a part-time official and rent-collector. They remained there until 1968. My birth, on 7th September, 1933, imposed an additional responsibility and may have influenced later aspects of my father's career path, if indeed, such an avenue could be claimed by an ordinary coal hewer during the depression. Dr Paterson, our general practitioner, was keen for my mother's confinement to take place in hospital, and with unparalleled expansiveness, at least, so far as our family was concerned, he hired a car from Messrs Baulch (no bill was ever presented), and accompanied my mother to the Cardiff Infirmary. When the time came for my father to visit his wife and child, a bicycle had to suffice for the 15-mile journey to Cardiff. Family lore maintained that a number of dutiful visits were made in this way but I have no idea what transport was used to bring me back to Brookland Road. I was certainly a lucky baby. Monmouthshire's Public Health Report for 1933 states that the infant mortality rate for the year was 71.72 per thousand births, an increase of 4.02 over 1932 when the figure was 67.7.

Astrologers delight in identifying propitious omens for a birth. Might they have linked the imminence of my birth to the Hunger March through Risca on 30th August, 1933? The Monmouthshire Marchers Council based in Queen Street, Abertillery printed a rousing account of the march that began in Brynmawr and Tredegar, gaining marchers and momentum as the contingents plodded down the valleys:

> From Crumlin to Cwmcarn fully 50,000 workers were on the streets, shouting encouragement and giving financial support. Nearing Risca where we spend the night [sic]. It is now 9 pm and dusk. The lights of Risca, dusky shadows between, shouting, cheering, singing. That is how we enter Risca. Straight into Moriah Chapel Schoolroom, where a piping hot bowl of soup awaits on the appetite of every marcher. Tea follows and everybody is satisfied. The Marchers are now ready for the night's kip. But excitement is too high, the situation is too stimulating for sleep and very few marchers sleep that night. Meanwhile the Risca workers who mass outside the school-room are being spoken to by comrade Walter Jones. Walter points out why we are marching against poverty in a county where men women and children are starving midst plenty. He urges the Risca workers to give the marchers a glorious send-off in the morning and urges everyone to mass behind the marchers into Newport...3

The object of the exercise was to appeal to Monmouthshire County Councillors (one of whom, on this occasion, was Mr Aneurin Bevan), at their Newport assembly, to modify the Government's public assistance policy.4 A small deputation of the marchers was eventually permitted access to the County Councillors, who, having listened to them, also agreed to provide all the marchers with free transport home. It is highly unlikely that my father would have been a part of such a demonstration, although his links with Moriah, dealt with elsewhere, could perhaps have drawn him to assist with the hospitality offered to the marchers. However, the imminence of my birth could have kept him at home and would certainly have provided food for thought. There was much to think about. The coal trade was in a slough of despond. By May 1934, 2,822 men were unemployed in Risca, 54.4 per cent of the male insured population.5 The owners, particularly the Ocean Group, were manipulating their workforce so as to encourage the so-called 'scab' union and Risca colliery had a number of safety problems that worried miners and officials. The *South Wales Miner* published a letter from a fireman complaining about rusty corrugated sheeting at the pit-head, which, under the influence of a strong wind, might easily fall down the shaft; the same radical paper urged the Risca colliery workforce to 'Elect militants at Risca...What we require in Risca is a lodge leadership that will organise and lead the men in the pit against the bad conditions and petty tyranny now prevailing...' As my father sought advancement and eventually became a fireman, or deputy, this last issue assumed an importance that affected his health and eventually brought about a radical change to his career. When, as an inquiring schoolboy, I asked my father for some explanation of the troubles of the coal industry in the 1930s, he pointed out that a major cause was the post-war loss of overseas markets for the coal that South Wales produced in such abundance. Statistics are rarely exciting, but helpfully deployed they may shed light. If, for example we note that in 1924, 180,000 men were employed at 356 mines producing 37,000,000 tons of coal in South Wales (and at a barely significant handful of pits in the Forest of Dean), the differences apparent by 1936 are remarkable. In that year there were approximately 266 mines at work in the same region, giving an output of some 25,000,000 tons and providing employment for 96,000 persons.[6] As well as the post-war loss of markets, technological advances that saw the Royal Navy, and other fleets around the world, gradually replace steam with oil for propulsion, were another factor, as were the high-profile trade sanctions meant to punish Italy for the invasion of Abyssinnia in 1935, a campaign completed in the following year. The sanctions seriously damaged what had been a valuable market for Welsh coal. Again, the regulation of output, brought about by the 1930 Act and to which reference has been made, further limited the scope for employment.

My father, together with thousands of others in the coalfield, saw that the coalowners' encouragement of a new trade union, The Industrial Union, was deliberately meant to weaken and rival the 'Fed'. His pithy description of the new body as a 'scab' union was typical of the attitudes of the 'Fed' membership who saw what the owners were trying to achieve. In 1927 the new union claimed that it had 50,000 members but other sources maintained that it never had more than one-tenth of that number.[7] After approximately eight years of highly stressful co-existence with a debilitated 'Fed', the Industrial Union's presence was a catalyst for trouble, particularly at those collieries owned by the Cory and Ocean groups. On Monday 30th September, 1935, 14,000 miners withdrew their labour at those companies' collieries, which included Risca and Nine Mile Point. By this method, the 'Fed' sought to achieve a 100 per cent membership within the groups and to eliminate the Industrial Union in the process. The official strike was called off after 10 days but events took an unexpected turn when the miners at Risca and at Nine Mile Point resolved not to come to the surface, thereby achieving extensive press coverage. At Risca, 170 miners eventually came up after three days and at 'The Point' 70 men stayed down for 176 hours, almost seven and a half days, before a satisfactory agreement was reached between the company and the 'Fed': there was to be no victimisation and only the 'Fed' would negotiate over the re-opening of the colliery.[8]

During these events, which attracted considerable attention from the national press, it looks as though my father was very much on the sidelines. While there is documentary evidence of his employment at Risca colliery by the Ocean company in its 'All Insurances' registers for the years 1930 to 1934 (although these years reveal periods when he was not employed), there is no reference to him in the corresponding documents for 1935 and he only re-appears as a National Insurance contributor at the colliery with effect from 17th April, 1937. To use modern jargon, the Ocean company was clearly 'downsizing' between 30th December, 1933, when the colliery listed 815 employees in its summary of the 'insured', and 6th January, 1935, when the books logged 687 contributors. The books for the second half of 1935 show that a number of men were 'conveyor' operators, allusions pointing very definitely to technological advances which meant fewer workers overall. My recollection of snatches of conversation between father and son, long after these events, hint that in all probability he found occasional work at the Southwood Jones quarry and brickworks, although his mother's death in 1929 had diminished any clout which he might otherwise have had with her relatives there. Perhaps, too, family politics damaged his links to his brother Harold in the Southwood Jones office. A souvenir of this period was a recurring nightmare in which he experienced a dreadful sensation of falling from the quarry face. Another probable source of work, judging from his occasional warnings that I should never, ever, become involved in that sort of labour, was digging holes in the road for Risca Council. This, during bad weather, was soul-destroying.

My father would, most certainly, have had strong views about the disputes at Risca and at Nine Mile Point, with the former, naturally, having greater immediacy, if only because he had worked there and knew many of the strikers. Everyone knew Dan Jones, named in the *South Wales Argus* as a striker at Risca colliery, because he was a member of the Welsh Rugby Union's 'Big Five', but much attention was to be focused on the hitherto obscure Searys, father and son, of respectively, Priory Street, Risca and Herbert Avenue, Rogerstone. If the Industrial Union roused the ire of the workforce throughout the Ocean and Cory groups by its very existence and because it was recognised by the employers, the Searys were loathed at Risca colliery because they insisted on working during the Federation's official strike that began on 30th September. Frederick Seary (senior) was a determined man, an ex-soldier, whose puny physique seemingly belied the courage which he displayed by defying his workmates. Once again, the strikers' anger was of the type displayed at Quarry Level, Pontypool, in August 1926 (and of course, at other locations and on other occasions, throughout the coalfields), when union solidarity was perceived to be flawed. Once again, the strike breakers were exposed to physical intimidation and once again, Superintendent Spendlove and his constables were available to uphold law and order. The Superintendent's zealous reputation was known, not only as a result of the Quarry Level episode of 1926, but from events at Nine Mile Point in 1929, when a police baton charge had featured in a bitter dispute about 'scab' labour.[9] One of the players in the drama staged on Gladstone Street, Crosskeys, between 30th September and 3rd October, 1935, was Risca's first-ever Communist councillor, Ernest Coote. My father might have described Mr Coote as a 'toy', one of his favourite words when he wanted to describe an extrovert, while today's argot might hold that he was 'tasty'. Coote's supporting players were Stanley Jones, Cyril Whatley and Henry Albert Godwin and there was of course, a 'chorus' of large police constables, at least two of whom, Power and Salmon, were well-known sportsmen. Hostile crowds inevitably confronted the Searys as they left Risca colliery after the night-shift, to be escorted by policemen to Cross Keys railway station and thence to their homes. The attempts made by Coote and by Jones, Whatley and Godwin to assault the Searys inevitably landed them in the Newport County Police Court a few days later. On Thursday 10th October, 1935, the *South Wales Argus* reported the proceedings as follows:

Evidence was given by Superintendent Spendlove that there was a crowd at Risca Colliery on September 30th. They numbered about 400 and there was a lot of booing and shouting. 'The crowd were extremely hostile to Seary', said the Superintendent, who was at the colliery with five officers. As the escort, with Seary in front, passed the colliery offices,there was a rush from all directions. 'We were hustled a bit, but I'm not going to say the crowd were hostile to the police', said the Superintendent. 'A man rushed down from behind - like a man going down the wing on a rugby field and without stopping he struck Seary, who had his foot on his bicycle, and knocked him over. Some small stones came over and I shouted to the crowd, 'We don't want any trouble'. When I picked up Seary a number of big stones were thrown. They were not thrown at me, but they very nearly hit me'. On the main road the crowd were dense and there was difficulty in making a way through. For Seary's protection, the police took Seary behind the wall of the Pentecostal Chapel...'Coote rushed past me', said the Superintendent, 'and tackled Seary, striking him from above. Seary actually went down; I do not say he was hurt very much. P.C. Power parted Seary and Coote and we got Seary away...Coote was shouting "I have been out of work four...years...swine." His behaviour was that of a lunatic'.

Both Searys gave evidence, with the son's version of events revealing perhaps, that he had not been made of the same stern stuff from which his ex-soldier father had been fashioned. Seary, junior, said that after the events of 30th September he did not return to the colliery on the following day. When asked in court to explain this, he said that some of the crowd were unfriendly, but the friendly ones asked him not to work and for their sake he stayed away. His father created an entirely different impression, with his assertion, in court, that standing up to the intimidation was a manly thing to do, clashing perhaps with an analysis offered by Harold Jones, a friend of my father's and a local Federation activist. Jones told Alun Burge, when interviewed for an article in *Llafur* in 1994 that,

> Fred (Seary) was a man of small stature...now his wife was a bigger woman... and our theory was Fred was going to work because... there would be a bit of a to-do if he didn't go to work. Pressure was coming from his wife more than anything else...Of course, he was remarkably brave, you couldn't help admire his guts, his character...

Having bound over Godwin, Jones and Whatley, his fellow accused, the magistrates sent Ernest Coote to jail for two and a half months for assaulting a policeman, for assaulting the senior Seary, for inciting others to assault Seary and for 'besetting' Risca Colliery. While hardly a criminal mastermind, Mr Coote did have 'form', in that he had previously served a month in prison for 'threats and assault' and had incurred a £1 fine when on a hunger march in Bristol.[10] However, a much more important evaluation of Mr Coote's status must be his political affiliation. On Monday 24th July, 1933 he had been elected as a Risca Councillor, the first Communist to be so elected, with 522 votes garnered in Risca's South Ward. In the elections which followed his conviction in the Seary case and that were held in the Spring of 1936, Coote topped the poll in the South Ward, this time as a 'Workers' Candidate', attracting 865 votes. These local developments reflected the growth of Communist Party activity and electoral success in South Wales overall, and are unsurprising. The depression, together with the Spanish Civil War, gave the party many opportunities to offer its own remedies to contrasting types of very high profile grievances.[11]

Friends and relatives look towards Nine Mile Point colliery during the stay-in strike in October 1935.

There are a number of other aspects of the Seary case that call for comment. Firstly, Superintendent Spendlove's evidence that on 30th September he was on duty at Risca colliery with five officers usefully omitted the fact that at least a coachload of officers from another force were in attendance either on that date or at other times during the stressful few days when Fred Seary sought to work.[10] There is a slightly more pacific tone to the Superintendent's phraseology, compared with his attitude after the Quarry Level episode. The crowd had not been hostile to the police, he said, while the stones that were thrown by the crowd were 'not thrown at me, but they very nearly hit me'. Perhaps, from the higher reaches of the Chief Constable's office or from the Home Office itself, the word had gone out that, wherever possible, the divisions of 1926 and 1929 were not to be exacerbated. The defending solicitor, Mr Gordon Edwards, requested that all the accused should be bound over now that there was 'peace and happiness in Risca', and he succeeded up to a point, in that Coote was the only one proceeded against. The *South Wales Argus* (on 10th October) reported that the Chairman of the Bench on that day, Mr J.H. Vickery, said, 'The magistrates were gratified to hear what had been said that morning and that there was a prospect of peace. "I hope there will be peace in the coalfield", he added'.

The involvement of entire communities in the situation in October 1935 is partly shown in the recollections of my father's colleague during the post-war days at Risca and at Nine Mile Point collieries, Dick Burnett, who writes:

> My father was involved in the Risca stay-in strike. I was attending Pontywaun School at the time and several times I came home from School to find that my Mother had gone to Crosskeys with hundreds of other women and friends to line Gladstone Street (Pandy Lane) to support the other miners who had not been underground when the decision was made to stay down. They all used to wait for Seary at the end of his shift, to walk from the pit along Gladstone St to Cross Keys Railway Station to get the train to Risca …of course the Police were brought in to protect Seary. Busloads of Police came up from Newport, and one great memory for me is that our neighbour in Raglan Street, Edwin J. James (Johnny to me) was one of the stay down men and his brother Percy James was a Newport Policeman sent to Crosskeys protecting Seary, the only man working.

The authorities' deployment of locally-recruited policemen may have been intended to reduce some of the abrasiveness that had characterised the riot at Quarry Level in 1926. The presence of sportsmen like PCs Power and Salmon, the former an eminent amateur boxer, could have been similarly planned. However, one especially interesting aspect of the inter-union rivalries that had generated the trouble in the first place, was an intervention by at least two of Risca's religious denominations. On 13th October, 1935, the minutes of Moriah Baptist Chapel's Sunday School Committee (with my father present and listed as 'Bro. E.P. Chivers'), show that the committee was eager to register its disapproval of the Ocean Company. The minutes read, 'Prop Bro. Wm Roberts, sec Bro. G. Morgan, that a letter of protest be sent to the Ocean Colliery Co. Ltd re the action of importing workmen into the district in spite of the fact that thousands were willing and able to do that said work in the district'. Apart from the succinct, 'Carried', written against the proposal in the minute book, there is no evidence as to whether such a letter was dispatched.[12] However, the

Above: Fred Seary with police protection at Nine Mile Point in October 1935.
Western Mail & South Wales News

Right: James Griffiths (President of the 'Fed'), *left*, and Alderman Arthur Jenkins (Vice-president) awaiting the 'stay-in' strikers' decision. *Western Mail & South Wales News*

Left: Superintendent Laurence Hubert Spendlove MBE, who later became Deputy Chief Constable of the Monmouthshire Constabulary.
Western Mail & South Wales News

intrusion of this topic at a meeting where the business was the implementation of the Sunday School's perceived spiritual requirements must surely reflect the concern aroused by the troubles at Nine Mile Point and the Seary business at Risca. Not all of the Industrial Union's members were local and according to the Federation's President, James Griffiths,[13] 'There were men in the coalfield who visited derelict villages where unemployed men were tempted by offers of money and wages, shillings per day over what was normally earned'. On 16th October, 1935, an article on the front page of the *South Wales Argus* claimed that non-Federation men had been brought to Nine Mile Point 'from Merthyr and other places'.

Moriah's Baptists were not the only congregation to express concern at this sort of thing. Risca's Anglican Vicar, the Reverend John Evans, appears to have made some kind of representation to the Ocean's Chairman, Lord Davies, concerning the importation of workers from outside the district. Only his Lordship's reply is available, amidst the back numbers of the *Colliery Guardian* at the Colindale Newspaper Library. In its edition of 25th October, 1935, the journal was anxious to point out that the Chairman, in his reply to Evans, was 'defining the Company's attitude towards the dispute at Nine Mile Point'. Lord Davies said that, 'the dispute was not between the employees and the company but between the employees themselves'. He and his colleagues had always regarded it as a sacred right that the individual should be allowed absolute freedom of choice as to what association or trade union, if any, he might desire to belong. It was not true that his company had imported workmen into the district, but they felt they had no right to refuse work to men who genuinely desired it, even though they lived at a considerable distance from the colliery… It is all too easy to place a cynical gloss on the Chairman's letter to the Vicar of Risca. Perhaps someone had advised His Lordship that using the word 'sacred' in a letter to a man of the cloth could only have been beneficial, while the sophistry of the argument about workers who lived some distance from the colliery would surely attract the admiration of the so-called 'spin doctors' of the 21st century.

'Stay-in' strikers at the surface after 7½ days underground.
Western Mail & South Wales News

With my parents, *circa* 1938.

Of the two linked disputes, at Nine Mile Point and at Risca, the former generated the most discontent and publicity and Alan Burge's piece in *Llafur*, entitled 'In Search of Harry Blount', cleverly lays bare the raw, enduring wounds suffered by the communities at Ynysddu and Cwmfelinfach. My father's absence from the roll of Risca colliery's insured workers from 29th December, 1934 until 17th April, 1937 must have been one of the bleakest periods of his career, albeit one that allowed him to view the dramas, of which I have only given a brief description, from the touch line, as it were. I have no idea if he drew any reassurance or comfort from the rapprochement reached by the rival unions, when, in January 1938, a merger between the Industrial Union and the Federation was agreed. My viewpoint is necessarily limited to our corner of the Western Valley and those desirous of a more complete analysis should study Francis and Smith's *The Fed*, where the two unions' agonising struggles, at the Bedwas and Taff-Merthyr collieries, for example, are put in perspective. The new Wages Agreement of 1937 chimes neatly with my father's pithy analysis of the country's economic position: 'There was a war coming, wasn't there?' Francis and Smith phrase it a little more elegantly when they say, 'The economic "boomlet", stimulated by rearmament, allowed an ending of the subsistence wage...' The standard wage rates of 1915 were replaced by higher ones, and the lowest wage rate was to be 8s. 5¼d. per shift. Wage increases varied between 2s. 2d. and 10s. per week and the complicated grading of jobs in the coalfield, with pay differentials, was reduced from the the 13 underground and six surfacemen grades, to four main ones that now ensured one rate for the job throughout the coalfield.

All of this was academic for my father until he resumed work at Risca colliery in April 1937. His entries in the colliery's 'All Insurances Register' began on 17th April and by July of that year the word 'repairer' appears against his name, this label being repeated during the period 8th January-2nd July, 1938. It is now that my father's career follows a path that was to affect all three of us in an important, perhaps even in a dramatic way. He became a Fireman. The position was of ancient origin in the industry and derived from the time when it was the practice to send someone in advance of the workmen into the mine workings to burn off any firedamp - a noxious gas - which might have accumulated. Contemporary practice, enshrined in law, required the Fireman to carry out certain duties about the presence of gas in the district of the mine to which he was assigned, to check the ventilation, the state of the roof and sides and general safety. He was also to check and record the number of persons under his charge and the size of the district of the mine for which he was given responsibility was such as to be capable of complete examination within a period of two hours. He was expected to do this 'in a thorough manner', as the report of the Royal Commission on Safety in Coal Mines stated in 1938. For my father to procure the necessary qualification for his advancement seems not to have been a problem. For a man of his intelligence and high competence in written English and arithmetic, passing the required examinations, theoretical and practical, was a straightforward process and his 'Fireman's Certificate' duly arrived, to be treasured amongst the family's small collection of important papers. The 'All Insurances Register' for Risca colliery includes my father's name as a regular 'contributor' under the Act, from 9th July, 1938 until 30th December, 1939 and against his name is the annotation, 'Fireman'.

I embarked on this project with only a vague awareness of the difficulties which colliery officials faced in those days but a repetition of the detail which I have viewed would take up too much space. Mining was undoubtedly a hazardous occupation and South Wales was a dangerous place. The Royal Commission noted that in 1935 there had been 465 accidents in the coalfield and of these, 89 had been fatal. A short-lived radical journal, the *South Wales Miner*, published in the Rhondda and edited by the Communist unionist, Arthur Horner,[14] harped constantly on the safety theme. In one of its final editions in 1935 (it was cash-strapped by this time), the paper again drew attention to Risca Colliery where,

> At the bottom of the Big Pit...haulage ropes have been rubbing the sleepers with the result that the sleepers are cut half-way through. True, ventilation is relatively good at the pit bottom, but if this is the case at the pit bottom, what is it like at the faces? Friction between steel and wood is an easy way to start a fire...

However, my father was not even employed at the colliery at the time and while he would perhaps have read the *South Wales Miner*, it is more likely that the history of Risca's disastrous 19th century explosions would have played on his mind. There were, too, the awesome events at Senghenydd in 1913 and more recently, the disasters at Gresford and at Markham in Nottinghamshire, where, on 10th May, 1938, 79 miners had been killed. This explosion occurred just eight weeks before his listing as a Fireman in Risca's 'All Insurances Register'.

The Fireman's life was by no means a doddle. The Royal Commission's report included a homily on his routine:

> ...it is imperative that airways should be constantly under examination in view of past serious accidents and the greater emission of firedamp in machine-mined faces. Unfortunately, deputies (i.e. Firemen) are not always able to fulfill the legal obligations placed on them by statute because a number of conflicting interests, and interference by persons with no legal responsibility, whose chief concern is to maintain the output of coal or keep the working costs down at times when it is almost a vital question for the deputy whether the lives of the workmen are being endangered or not. Section 67 of the Act (i.e. The Mines Act) places a deputy in a delicate position affecting not only the economic position of his employer but that of the workmen as well, whose earnings are cut off if and when a working place or district is found dangerous, or when danger is apprehended and many deputies have hesitated to take steps they otherwise could have done when dangerous conditions were apparent, while in many instances others have found themselves on the road, dismissed.

My father's new working arrangements would probably have included the supervision of the so-called 'longwall' working in which there would be 20 or 25 'stalls' with 10 or 11 yard centres. In those 20 stalls there would have been 'doublers', that is, 40 men or perhaps a proportion of men and boys. There may have been four hauliers and a master haulier and perhaps some blocklayers, so his district might have had 60 or 65 men, in all, a group over which one man's span of control could have been a challenge, especially against the background of the increased pressures of the period. In his book, *The Coal Scuttle*, published in January 1936, the President of the Miners' Federation of Great Britain, Joseph Jones, pointed out that there had been an immense speeding up of the work underground and that the working day was just one big effort 'to get as much coal as possible'. Jones believed that such an intensification of effort was caused by officials 'who have to carry out the owners' policy of a maximum output at minimum cost'. My father became another casualty in this battle to wrest the coal from the ground. His problem was not caused by the ingestion of coal or silicate particles, 'the dust', nor was he maimed by a tram 'journey' or a roof fall and, unlike many of his contemporaries, he was spared a fatal accident. Only the vaguest fragments of evidence have been passed down in family lore. He once told me that during his work as a fireman, there had been a requirement for him to order workmen to put themselves at risk and that some of this had involved making them crawl through the most difficult of apertures. As an active member of Moriah Chapel's Sunday School Committee, he told other family members, at the time, that he 'could not serve God and Mammon'. I can remember a particularly unpleasant and uncharacteristic scene at 10 Brookland Road when I was shouted at, and told angrily to go away when I went upstairs, as I had done, happily, on many previous occasions when my father was about to leave his bed. I had expected the usual friendly chat. As I heard my mother describe it, years later, this was when 'Perce had that breakdown'. The intensification of effort which Joseph Jones mentioned was in all probability linked to the conditions identified in *The Lancet* on 6th September, 1947, when it published an item entitled 'Coal Miners', dealing with some of the industry's medical problems. A specialist wrote that in the mines, in particular, 'there was, between the wars, a high increase in psychoneurosis and psychosomatic disturbances'.[15] It is likely that my father's symptoms were linked with one or both of these conditions.

The entries in the colliery's 'All Insurances Register' for the period 6th January, 1940 to 29th June, 1940, certainly show my father as a contributor but there is no longer the 'Fireman' annotation set against his name. For the immediately following period, that is, 6th July 1940 to 4th January 1941, a high proportion of the entries in this register are in my father's handwriting. Some kind of miracle had occurred. He was no longer a horny-handed worker but a member of the Ocean Coal Company's office staff! What had happened? As I remember, his mentor and perhaps saviour, had been the colliery's Chief Clerk, Walter Lewis, who plucked this unwell and unhappy miner from the bowels of the earth and gave him an office job. Lewis recognised that a man who could write clearly and neatly and for whom straightforward wages' calculations presented no problem would be an asset. However, initially there was some kind of apprenticeship to be undergone, not in any formal sense, but perhaps in the style prevailing in all organizations, which meant that the new recruit was handed the least attractive tasks. Working nights and dealing with the office switchboard in the 'silent hours' formed the core of this 'apprenticeship'. There is a page in the colliery's 'All Insurances Register' for the period 6th July, 1940 to 4th January, 1941 that is entirely in my father's handwriting and on which he describes himself as 'E. Percy Chivers', and in the 'Occupation' column he

A page from Risca Colliery's National Health and Unemployment Register for September 1940. All the entries are in my father's handwriting. His name is eighteenth from the top.

Glamorgan Record Office

wrote against his name, 'Phones', a humble enough beginning. A complementary piece of evidence, his Home Guard enrolment paper (Army Form W3066) dated 1st June, 1940, was carefully annotated in someone else's handwriting, 'Working nights, free on Saturdays'.

I was, by this time, old enough to be taking notice and to listen to Dad's anecdotes about his new working environment. The names of his new colleagues were frequently mentioned, many of which I was to recall when, recently, I saw them listed in the 'All Insurances' registers at the Glamorgan Records Office in Cardiff: Walter B. Lewis, E. Percy Knight and Miss Mabel Benson, typist and telephonist, being the most easily remembered. The office staff also included Mel Huntley and Ivor Beacham, the latter soon to become a family friend. As to the colliery's senior hierarchy, the manager was Gwilym Jones, whose official residence was a little way off, in the Blackvein area of Risca, while Sid Beacham, a close kinsman of Ivor's, was an undermanager and an expert in dust suppression. What duties fell to the new clerk, E. Percy Chivers, after his apprenticeship operating the colliery's night-time switchboard? Just before I sat the '11-plus', my teacher at Pontymister Boys' School, Rhys James, asked what was my father's occupation. The information was needed as part of my pre-examination documentation, it seemed. So, that evening, I put the question to my father, who replied, 'Tell him, "Costs and Wages Clerk".' This was early in 1944, by which time, the occupation shown against his name in the 'All Insurances' Register, said 'Office', a quantum status leap, perhaps, from 'Phones'.

By 1947 and after his translation to the post of Training Officer at Nine Mile Point colliery, my father felt sufficiently ebullient to write to the *South Wales Argus* in reply to a correspondent who had criticised a system of which Dad clearly felt that he was an important part. The letter sheds light on the clerk's workload:

> I read in the *South Wales Argus* of the Blackwood miner who was so badly treated during his belated effort to solve our coal problem. After taking a mere eighteen months, (during which the country has suffered agonies through shortage of coal) to make up his mind to return to the mines, he offers to return on his own terms. He demands money, tools, clothes, soap, meat, cheese, etc., and because these rare blessings do not arrive in a few days, he withdraws his services. The industry is well rid of him and his like. I wonder if he, or anyone else, ever spares a thought for the colliery clerk, who, in addition to arranging the supply of the aforementioned commodities, has also to deal with bus tickets and permits, boot permits, war savings deductions, towel permits, travel warrants, bread coupons, and in his leisure moments, perform the normal functions of a colliery clerk.
>
> Yours etc., E. Percy Chivers, Brookland Road, Risca

The letter was published on 19th March, 1947, a mere three months after the Labour Government had nationalised the industry and in common with thousands of others in the coalfield, my father may have been basking in the euphoria induced by this eagerly-anticipated measure. Certainly, well before Vesting Day, his lot had improved tremendously. Evidence about the office staff's wages emerges spasmodically, but I have no reliable evidence about the salary attached to his work in the Risca colliery office in the early 1940s. For example, the Glamorgan Record Office holds a document itemised in its catalogue as 'United National Collieries Ltd (Western Valleys of Monmouthshire): Office Pay Book 1940-1946'. On the face of it, the perfect document in which to discover how much my father earned at the time. No such luck. The paybook has no mention of him. However, a certain B. Edgar Griffiths, described as 'Clerk, Risca', earned £4 6s. 2d. for the week-ending 26th April, 1941. It seems that this would have been a princely sum for my father to have earned and perhaps Mr Griffiths was a man of some seniority and at the top of his salary scale? Perhaps the same caveat must be applied to Mr W.H. Humphreys, a clerk at Nine Mile Point, who, in the same document, is listed as having earned £4 6s. 11d. for the same week's work? If my father had continued to work underground earning the lowest rate under the new (i.e. 1937) pay scales he would have earned 8s. 5s. 1¼d. per shift, or £2 10s. 7½d. per week, before deductions. Wherever my father's office salary scale began, his money was 'regular', as my mother put it, and no longer subject to the vicissitudes of the type they had endured since their marriage in 1929.

The household's regular and carefully-apportioned income was to bring me unprecedented fun. In 1938 we took a holiday in Weston-super-Mare, staying at a bed and breakfast establishment in Orchard Street. As I was only five at the time, not many memories remain, except a snapshot of a rather prosperous-looking and immaculately dressed family and my toy sailing boat, especially purchased for Weston's boating pond. Then, one year later, we were off to Weymouth, in that summer before war was declared. In contrast to my vague recollections of Weston, Weymouth stands out, if only because my father photographed the King, there to review the fleet and because we sighted a former Labour minister, J.H. 'Jimmy' Thomas, who was sunning himself on the verandah of Weymouth's Gloucester Hotel. In the eyes of stalwart Labour supporters, much notoriety attached to poor old Jimmy Thomas, particularly his membership of MacDonald's National Government and his injudicious disclosure of budget detail which Dad always maintained was in return for 'a racing certainty'. I discovered this detail, of course, much later, together with the otiose information that Thomas had been one of the few people who could make the late King George V laugh.

So, with an office job and enough cash to take his family for seaside holidays in successive years, my father's career prospects were vastly improved. His name appeared regularly in Risca colliery's 'All Insurances' register as a member of the office staff, until 28th April, 1945. On that date, in the space where the annotation of his contribution should have appeared, was the abbreviation 'NMP', which stood for Nine Mile Point. He was now, aged 42, on the threshold of a much more interesting assignment in the soon-to-be nationalised industry, where, like thousands of other miners, he had suffered grievously.

Chapter Four

God and Mammon

The first piece of evidence to surface in my search for details of Dad's links with Moriah Chapel was a Sunday School prize dated 31st December, 1912. This book, *The Old Red School House*, by Frances H. Wood, is an improving novel about contemporary life in Canada and was suitable for a literate nine-year-old. The label, or book-plate, stuck inside its hard cover, is incontrovertible evidence that Percy Chivers made 45 out of a possible 47 attendances at Moriah Sunday School during the year. The label is headed 'Moriah Baptist Sunday School, Risca, Mon.' As well as the recipient's name, it lists the Pastor, the Revd T. Cynon Jones, together with the names of those holding the Sunday School offices of Superintendent, Assistant Superintendent, Treasurer, Secretary and Register Secretary. My father clearly operated within a culture of care for his books, for 91 years later, *The Old Red School House* still has the brown paper cover which he gave it and its hard, glossy, red cover which the brown paper has protected for the best part of a century. Of course, at the time, no-one could have predicted that by 1936 his own name would be listed on a book plate as one of the Sunday School officials for that year.

Amongst those for whom such a prediction may have seemed particularly unlikely was his mother, Amelia Martha. She was wont to describe her youngest son as, 'A house angel and a street devil', an opinion reinforced by an episode in Dr Richards' orchard. A policeman caught young Percy scrumping apples and immediately administered punishment to his posterior with the flat of the hand. According to my father, this meant similar punishment when he went home, a double-barrelled retribution which would be impossible in the 21st century. Family lore has nothing further to tell about any other conflicts which my father may have had with the law, although much later, as we have seen, Superintendent Spendlove was to occupy a special position in his demonology. The Sunday School seemed happy with his continued attendances and more book prizes accrued, some of which have survived: in 1915 came *Saxby* by Emma Leslie (a brown paper cover still protects the original); in 1916 there was Ballantyne's *Coral island*, a book that clearly made an impression, because, years later, I was an attentive listener when my father read portions aloud. From the 21st century's perspective, a prize awarded to a 16-year-old in 1919 merits a special focus. This book, by Bessie Marchant, was entitled, *In the Toils of the Tribesmen*, and describes life in imperial India. It was presented to a young miner who paraded at Sunday School on 48 occasions during the year (the book-plate makes this clear) but who was also obsessed with rugby football and who had probably played a few games for the Risca first XV. In a sense, the recipient's position gives more than a hint of the symbiotic relationship existing in the valley communities of the time between the workplace, the chapel and the rugby club. His parents' combined efforts had failed to keep Percy Chivers on the roll at the Pontywaun Intermediate School, but he was obviously prepared to accept similar pressures to attend Sunday School.

For the family historian, these fragments of evidence provide valuable and solid proof of a particular pattern of behaviour. The Welsh religious revival of

Moriah Baptist Sunday School,

RISCA.

Hymns and Anthems

TO BE SUNG AT THE

ANNIVERSARY

TO BE HELD

On SUNDAY, JULY 5th, 1914.

ORDER OF SERVICES :—

In the MORNING at 7 o'clock, a Sermon will be delivered by the

REV. T. THOMAS, Bethany.

At 11 o'clock, the Pastor, Rev. T. CYNON JONES will preach.

The Afternoon and Evening Services will consist of

RECITATIONS, DIALOGUES, &c.,

By the Scholars, and

SPECIAL HYMNS and ANTHEMS

Will be rendered by the Choir, under the leadership of
Mr. M. WATKINS.

Mr. T. E. YENDALL. A. Mus. L.C.M., will preside at the Grand Organ

Collection at each Service in aid of Sunday School Funds.

ON MONDAY, THE

ANNUAL TREAT

WILL TAKE PLACE,

when (D.V.) the Teachers and Scholars will walk in procession through
the principal streets, headed by the NEWPORT MILITARY BAND.
TEA provided for Visitors at 4.30, at Sixpence Each.

Yendall & Co., Ltd., Printers, Risca.

The front page of Moriah's Sunday School Anniversary programme for 1914 - a historic
document carefully preserved in my grandparents' family Bible.   *B. Withers/Galata Print Ltd*

1904-5 would have provided its own stimulus and a family's efforts to meet the community's norms offered both spiritual and social gratification. Sending, or taking the well-behaved and perhaps the not-so-well-behaved members of the family, who not infrequently made three visits to a place of worship on a Sunday, provided the righteous parent with a sense of having done the right thing, both in the eyes of the Lord and in the eyes of the community. In 1912 there were 925 'scholars' on Moriah's Sunday School roll, one of whom was, of course, Ernest Percival Chivers.[1] This statistic underlines the wisdom of those elders who had built a new chapel to replace the old building which dated from 1818 and which was, in any case, on the hillside, in a less than convenient location on the banks of the Newport-Crumlin canal. The new chapel was erected on a site virtually at the heart of the Risca community and at the point where the main road to Newport intersected the road from Penrhiw to the Copperworks. It was also handily placed in relation to the railway station. The new premises was completed by the Spring of 1894, by which time, the Chivers family had arrived from the Eastern Valley to live in a company house on the Copperworks. Amelia Martha's brother, William Tucker, was the foreman and an acknowledged expert in the manufacturing process at the Danygraig brickworks, a Southwood Jones enterprise which employed a number of Tuckers and, more importantly, my grandfather, Thomas Herbert Chivers, shown in the 1901 Census as a 'Fireclay Moulder'. It is unclear whether family members ever attended the old chapel on the hill, but certainly, such an attractive building as the new Moriah would have been their place of worship.

The leaves of their massive family bible have protected some documents of the period, the most interesting being the programme for the Sunday School's anniversary services on Sunday 5th July, 1914. For those disposed to brood on history's many facets, this was to be the Sunday School's last peace-time anniversary celebration for five years. On the preceding Sunday 28th June, 1914, the heir to the Austrian throne, the Archduke Franz-Ferdinand, had been murdered, together with his wife, in far-off Sarajevo, an act that precipitated World War I. However, on 5th July, members of the congregation in their very best suits and dresses, smelling faintly of moth-balls, would certainly have had their minds on other things. The programme, printed by 'Yendall & Co., Ltd., Printers, Risca', told of the order of services. On the Sunday morning, at seven o'clock, a sermon was to be delivered by the Reverend T. Thomas, the pastor of the neighbouring Bethany Baptist Chapel, a respected figure in the community, revered by my aunts Harriet and Doreen, who spoke of him as, 'Thomas, Bethany'. A service at 7 am was of course, unusual in nonconformist chapels, but certainly afforded an opportunity for the faithful to demonstrate their loyalty and spiritual intensity on the special occasion. The programme listed a service at 11 o'clock when Moriah's Pastor, the Reverend T. Cynon Jones, was to preach, while 'The Afternoon and Evening Services' were to consist of, 'Recitations, Dialogues etc., by the Scholars' and 'Special Hymns and Anthems' were to be 'rendered by the Choir, under the leadership of Mr M. Watkins'. The bulk of the programme was taken up by the words of the hymns to be sung, beginning with 'All Hail the Power' and concluding with 'By the Rivers of Babylon'. The programme, printed on pink paper, does not list any scholars and so curiosity about my father's likely participation must remain

My father with his brother Bill (right) *circa* 1918. Bill had been wounded at Beaumont Hamel and after his discharge from the Royal Navy, worked with my father at Risca colliery. He was soon to join the Civil Service. *Author's Collection*

unsatisfied. Only serious illness however, would have stopped him from taking part in the celebrations on the following Monday, 6th July, which the programme hailed as 'The Annual Treat'. Indeed, this listing is worth reproducing in full. It said,

ON MONDAY THE ANNUAL TREAT WILL TAKE PLACE

When (D.V.) the Teachers and the Scholars will walk in procession through the principal streets, headed by the NEWPORT MILITARY BAND.
Tea provided for Visitors at 4.30, at Sixpence Each.

One can pick over the subtleties and implications of this announcement, but for my father, as it was for his son, some 25 years later, such a promise meant an enormous intake of sandwiches and slices of cake, washed down by quantities of tea from gleaming urns, the entire process conducted in the Sunday School rooms (buildings, as I recall that were built of corrugated sheets and adjacent to the chapel itself), under the vigilant eyes of the Chapel's matrons, whose dedication and attention to detail had been largely responsible for the spread in the first place. The bracketed 'D.V.', or *Deo Volente* (God Willing), was a pious invocation, used more frequently perhaps in those days than in today's less spiritual climate, but which could be said to cover such unpleasant interventions as bad weather and the truly awful threat of the imminent European war. We can see today how 'D.V.' might have covered the eventualities spawned by the Sarajevo murders and only wonder about the sequence of events: did the assassinations precede the programme's printing? An answer is unlikely.

When my father collected his prize for Sunday School attendance during the year 1919, he would undoubtedly have held opinions about the recent war that were more clearly formed than any that he might have held in 1914. A snapshot from the war years shows him sporting a military badge supplied by his brother, Bill, who was serving in the Royal Naval Division. This man, my Uncle Bill, was grievously wounded at Beaumont Hamel on 13th November, 1916. The inevitable telegram first told the family that he was 'missing', though they were not to know that the Germans had rescued him from a shell-hole in no man's land and succoured him in one of their forward casualty stations. He was in captivity therefore until, in fairly short order, the German position was overrun by the British and Uncle Bill whisked back to Chatham Hospital, his war over. Another elder brother, Tom, served from 1915 and survived, mostly unscathed, as a Bombardier in the Royal Artillery, until the war's end. His links with the Southwood Jones brickworks caused him to be temporarily recalled from France for his specialised knowledge of the brickmaking process to be utilised for an order which contributed to the war effort. After this remission he returned to France. These close family links to the war would have supplemented my father's awareness of similar situations affecting many Risca families, while the major headlines of the day and the casualty lists in the press made an inevitable impact on an impressionable and aware teenager.

I know from his brief allusions to the topic, that the slaughter on the battlefields caused Dad to be wary of all military thinking and behaviour. He was ready to cite horror stories of how some of our troops, advancing upon the enemy across no-man's land, had shot their own unpopular officers who led

My father's brother, Tom, served in the Royal Field Artillery during World War I. At some stage he was permitted to return from France to work at Southwood-Jones' brickworks on an important Government contract. This may have been in October 1916 when perhaps this photograph was taken. Afterwards he returned to his unit. Muddy boots were highly unofficial fashion accessories meant to show that the wearer had recent front-line experience.

Author's Collection

them. These unsubstantiated and fanciful yarns were picked up, no doubt, from returning veterans in the collieries. His links to Moriah continued, and a small but significant piece of evidence of my father's religious inclinations has survived in the shape of a small, pocket-sized copy of the New Testament. This volume, measuring roughly 2½ inches by 3¾ inches and bound in what is now very worn leather, contains a significant annotation in my father's handwriting. Inside the front cover, he wrote, in pencil,

27th July, 1922
O Happy Day
That fixed my choice
On thee my Saviour
And my God.

Was this, perhaps, a record of a decision made to become a full member of the Church and an acceptance of the baptismal rite? He was now 19 and his writing lacks the confident, fully-formed script of later years, but this very positive piece of evidence links him with Llewellyn Beechey's Young Men's Bible Class. Beechey was a war veteran whose class, in the post-war years, met at Moriah on Saturdays, and on Friday evenings conducted a 'witness' at Pontymister Crossing. One of a number of battered photographs which have survived from this period shows a group of young men, including my father, all immaculately dressed and photographed indoors. An older figure,which research has shown to have been Llewellyn Beechey' s father, William John Beechey, sits at the front, a bible ostentatiously displayed on his knee. An easy theory is to assume that Beechey, senior, was standing in for his son and that Dad was indeed a member of this much spoken-of group. For my father, during these years, a Saturday meeting might only have been possible during those months of the year when no rugby was being played and this particular snap is remarkable because many of the group have summer flowers in their buttonholes. Another, rather dog-eared snapshot, probably from the early 1930s, and taken in the open air, comprises 10 young men with Dad in a 'commanding' position at the centre of the front row. This group was, in all probability, the Sunday School class which he taught. Another, important photograph, reproduced in *A View From the Hill*, comprises the entire teaching strength of the Sunday School, with the Pastor, the Reverend Iorwerth Hughes, sitting at the centre of the front row. This photograph was taken in 1935 to mark the Sunday School's centenary. My father is in the front row, although well to Mr Hughes' left.

The processes by which Dad advanced through the Sunday School's hierarchy are unclear and I am obliged to rely partially on some of the suppositions that underpin parts of this memoir. Did the date pencilled inside my father's New Testament simply refer to his decision to follow the Lord, or was it the actual date of his baptism? Perhaps the baptism occurred much later. Might his immersion have taken place as part of the stimulating events described in the *South Wales Argus* in its edition of 7th November, 1925? Headed 'Revival at Risca - Sixty Conversions at Moriah Baptist Church - A Remarkable Scene', the article proceeds:

My father is fourth from the left in the back row in this photograph of what was probably Llewellyn Beechey's Bible class at Moriah in the early 1920s. The central figure, however, with a Bible on his knee, is Mr Beechey (Senior), Llewellyn's father.   *Author's Collection*

This Moriah group, surrounding the popular Pastor, The Reverend Owen, includes only three other figures recognised by the author. The man with the boots and the centre parting seated to the left of the minister is Mel Jones. The lady who is partially visible, between Messrs Jones and Owen, was known to me as Mrs Bert Welch, whose first name was Dorothy. The second from the right in the middle row is Frank Wear.   *Author's Collection*

For several weeks, members of Moriah Baptist Church, Risca, have experienced a time of great blessing in which all the other Churches of the district have shared. The work at Moriah commenced with a series of prayer meetings which continued for three weeks. Night after night, decisions were made and conversions registered. Then followed a week's mission conducted by Miss Russell. Several young men were baptised by the Reverend Charles Rees, Abercarn. On Thursday, the Reverend W.H. Williams, Newport, preached and baptised 12 candidates. He then gave the invitation to any who wished to decide for Christ and obey His command to come forward. A movement was seen in the gallery and three men walked into the vestry and throwing off their coats, entered the water. Here each made a confession of faith and were baptised. Afterwards they walked home in their wet clothes. About 60 conversions have taken place and many more are awaiting baptism.

Today, sources at Moriah have been unable to shed much light on this episode, though of the named personalities, my researches show that the Reverend W.H. Williams became the Chairman of the Welsh Baptist Union, and in its edition of 10th April, 1935, the *South Wales Argus* was to report that in this capacity, as a member of a delegation 'representing all the religious denominations of Wales', he lobbied the Prime Minister, Ramsay MacDonald, about conditions in the Principality. My own concern, inevitably, is whether my father was one of the 60 reported conversions in 1925, or whether his solemn inscription in his New Testament, dated 27th July, 1922, is the key.

The year 1922 brought change to Moriah. The Church had been without a Pastor for two years after the departure of the Reverend T. Cynon Jones and in July of that year, services were conducted by Professor T.W. Chance of the Cardiff Baptist College, who might have influenced my father. Chance recommended that the pastor's vacancy should be filled by the Reverend Henry Owen, whom he invited to preach at Moriah. In *A View From the Hill*, Hugh Roberts describes how Chance's letter to the Reverend Owen told of conversions and baptisms that occurred during the period when there had been no pastor and more tellingly, that the Sunday morning congregations totalled approximately 700. Impressively, he added that the evening services attracted 'over 900'. Eventually, Mr Owen accepted 'the call' to Moriah and took up his duties, for what was to be a challenging ministry, on 7th January, 1923.

These events can be set against the background of the colossal difficulties suffered by the mining industry in the 1920s, when unemployment and strikes, particularly the lock-out of 1921, created hardships for which many sought solace through religious observances. Closely linked to this chapel culture was the decline of traditional Welsh Liberalism and the steady ascendancy of the Labour party in the Principality, especially in the mining valleys. Of the 16 Labour members of Parliament returned for Welsh constituencies in the 1924 General Election, 13 were, or had been, prominent trade union officials.[2] Twelve of them were miners and Charles Edwards, the member for the Bedwellty constituency of which Risca formed a part, had been a checkweigher for his Federation colleagues at Nine Mile Point colliery until returned to Parliament for the then newly-formed constituency in 1918. I have quoted elsewhere an allusion by Edwards' eventual successor, Harold Finch, to the links that bound the local Federation leadership to nonconformity, identifying John Woodward, a Wesleyan and Jonah Roberts, a Moriah member, as leaders in whom the Federation membership had absolute faith.

My father's sister, Harriet Mary Jenkins and her husband, Ernest Frederick Jenkins who married in 1911. Their hats and my aunt's gloves indicate a special occasion which may have been their wedding or perhaps the Moriah Anniversary. *Author's Collection*

The Chivers family of Bridge Street was strongly rooted in Moriah Chapel and bound up with its ethos. *A View from the Hill* identifies my grandmother, Mrs Tom Chivers, as the first secretary of the Moriah Sisterhood when this newly-formed group met on 14th January, 1924, and the extant Sisterhood Minute-book, in which the first entries date from January 1925, offers ample evidence that in addition to his mother, my father's sisters were zealous members. Indeed, his younger sister, to whom he was particularly close, Doreen, was the Sisterhood's pianist. When she resigned from this position in 1929, after their mother's death,

> Our Pastor Rev I Hughes presented Miss D Chivers with a salad bowl on behalf of the sisters as a token of the love we held for her. Owing to the death of her dear Mother. She is not able to continue as pianist which post she has held since the commencement of the Sisterhood.[3] [My punctuation mirrors that of the minute-taker.]

In this small, far from affluent community, the presentation custom seemed important. In my grandmother's memory, the family presented Moriah with a handsome set of collection plates, all polished oak and green baize, a gift that in addition to being in memory of Amelia Martha Chivers, might also have reflected their wish to appear generously charitable. Such things would not have been unimportant. The Sisterhood Minute-book also refers to Mrs Tom Chivers (jun.), who would have been my Aunty Gwen, wife of Dad's brother, Tom and Mrs E. Jenkins, Dad's elder sister, Harriet Chivers (1888-1966), my Aunty Hat. This pattern of family involvement with an organisation which stood out in the county at the time as an example to Sisterhoods' other chapels, would clearly have influenced the young Percy Chivers. His membership of the Young Men's Bible Class, and his continued career in the Sunday School, outline a pattern of behaviour in which family and chapel blended significantly.

The Owen ministry appears to have maintained high standards of spiritual intensity which would inevitably have made an impact on my father and on the other youngsters in Llewellyn Beechey's Bible Class. The statistics quoted in *A View from the Hill* are impressive. Mr Owen's first year saw Moriah's total membership rise to 505. The Sunday School had a record attendance of 626; the Band of Hope a weekly attendance of 400, and the Young People's Fellowship about 150. Hugh Roberts has described matters most impressively:

> The second year of Mr Owen's Ministry was equally successful. The Chapel was full every Sunday evening for service and often extra chairs were placed in the aisle. Mr Owen records that on a summer evening, after he had given out the hymn, the light seemed to go out as the congregation stood and partly obscured the windows. The singing, led by the choir, would be given with understanding and feeling, while the choruses would be thundered out in four part harmony, bringing tears to the eyes - particularly with the Welsh hymns.

The hymns may have induced tears, but subsequent events at Moriah were to produce a much greater tristesse. The Owen ministry ended in rancour when most of the deacons and some church officers found themselves ranged against their Pastor on a fundamental issue: could two ladies, one of whom was physically handicapped, be admitted to full membership without the baptismal rite? Hugh Roberts points out that, 'The Church adhered to the Closed Fellowship principle and would only admit baptised believers to full membership', a situation about which, seemingly, there could be no compromise, with the Reverend Owen favouring the ladies' request in the face of the deacons' opposition. Sadly, he felt constrained to leave his post and on 4th January, 1925, in his letter of resignation, the Pastor said,

> Please accept my resignation owing to a decision of a majority of officers to deny rights and privileges of the Church of Christ to those who, because of physical infirmity or organic trouble, are not able to fulfil the letter of the Sacrament of Baptism. The decision appears to me to be in direct opposition to the spirit and practice of our Lord Jesus Christ.

Owen's departure, in less spiritual terms, might be seen as an example of how a good man could be made to bite the dust. Viewed from today's perspective, the deacons' seeming narrowness of outlook will cause concern to those whose interpretations of the usages of Christianity are more liberal. My Aunt Doreen explained the dispute to me. Although she was the Sisterhood's pianist and certainly a staunch admirer of Owen, she sympathised with the ineligible ladies and gave the impression of a regretful sadness about the position adopted by the deacons. I feel confident that in this matter my father would not have sided with the 'majority of officers'. However, allowances must be made for those zealous and dedicated men who sought to conduct the Chapel's business in accordance with what they saw as the correct practice of the Baptist communion. A much less significant episode reveals some of the thinking of those who controlled Moriah's destiny. I can recall an event of the late 1940s, when my father's close friend, Noel Evans, told us that, in his capacity as an

This battered snapshot of Moriah's Reverend Henry Owen with his family was formerly in the possession of my father's sister, Doreen. Its survival is a measure of the high regard which Doreen and her contemporaries had for the minister. His Pastorate lasted from 1923 to 1925 and ended in rancour when Owen disagreed with the chapel elders about the baptism of two physically challenged ladies.   *Author's Collection*

executive of the Rank Religious Films organisation, he had recently offered Moriah Sunday School the use of a cine projector and an accompanying film of spiritual content. He had been told that such things were 'The work of the Devil', and that there was no place for them in the Sunday School.

The light shed on my father's attitudes during these years became a little stronger for me with his accounts of some aspects of the ministry of the Reverend Iorweth Hughes, who was installed as Mr Owen's successor on 28th July, 1926. According to Dad, Iorwerth Hughes began his career at Moriah with 'a dozen good sermons', high praise indeed but added that his later performances were rather disappointing. There was also a minor clash, in a Sunday School setting, or perhaps at a prayer meeting, when in discussion, Mr Hughes may have attempted to illustrate a point by alluding to 'a bank account', though whether this was his own bank account or just any account, is unclear. My father was unhappy with this seemingly elitist reference and long after the event, told me, 'I said that I didn't have a bank account and kept my money in the Post Office!' This crisp exchange may have affected the two men's relationship in later years.

By 1935, my father had progressed through the Sunday School's hierarchy from his position as a teacher for most of the year, to being elected as the Superintendent at a meeting on 14th December. This was certainly the apogee of his career at Moriah and something of which the entire family could feel proud. The Sunday School minute book records his involvement with the details of the school's administration for 1936. Matters such as the appointment of an auditor on 12th January when Brother James was assigned the task; the selection of a new Secretary, Brother Veysey, on 2nd February; the question of the Sunday School's loan to the parent Chapel on 26th April; the invitation to the band that would play on the day of the annual tea-party, (the Abercarn Welfare band), 12th May, 1936; Risca Council's request for guarantees against damage to the Park on the day of the annual tea-party 14th June; my father's suggestion that some Sunday School classes should amalgamate, 23rd August; the accounts of the Sunday School Anniversary, 11th November; the nomination of a delegate for a conference at Cardiff, 22nd November and on 29th November the submission of that delegate's report. Before my father's period of office as Superintendent, he was present when the Committee had expressed its concern at the Ocean Colliery Company's importation of labour from outside the area, an item mentioned in the previous chapter. After he stood down as Superintendent, though maintaining his position as a Sunday School Committee member, he was present when, on 11th April, 1937, another high profile issue received attention. It was 'Pro by Bro G Morgan sec Bro P Chivers', that a report submitted by 'Bros Blackwell and Ivor Roberts', about the 'Spanish Workers' Committee' should be accepted and 'the two brothers continue to represent Moriah S. S. on that committee'. While the Spanish Civil War is not entirely relevant to this memoir and although the minutes contain no other allusions to that conflict at the time, the assault on the democratically elected Spanish government stirred many people's consciences and drew numbers of British citizens, some from South Wales, to fight in Spain, as members of the so-called International Brigade. I have not attempted to scrutinise the Spanish Workers' Committee, as it functioned, at the time, but its position on the agenda at Moriah Sunday School clearly points to a sympathetic

My father is seated in the middle of the front row of this Moriah Sunday School class *circa* 1934. Noel Evans is next to him, wearing a buttonhole. *Author's Collection*

This photograph of Moriah's Sunday School teachers was taken in 1935, probably to mark the school's centenary. *Back row:* H. Ware, A. Griffiths, J. Davies, F. Ivins, W. Stocker, M. Jones, M. Evans, H. Wheel, I. Allsop, G. Morgan. *Third row:* H. Blackwell, G. Gunter, R. Protheroe, J. Ware, R. Thomas, A. Taylor, W. Pritchard, A. Lewis, G. Evans, W. Blunt. *Second row:* Ms L. Veysey, W. Veysey, Ms M. Veysey, Mrs M. Williams, Mrs V. Pritchard, Mrs Hughes (the pastor's wife), Ms D. Richards, Mrs M. Ford, Ms. H. Hopkins, Mrs E. Jones, Mrs Osborne, Noel Evans, Ms A. Gunter. *Front row:* A. Moore, E. Morgan, A. Hodge, Ms E. Bateman, The Reverend Iorwerth Hughes (Pastor), Ms W. Lloyd, F. Johnson, my father, W. Roberts. *Author's Collection*

climate in Risca amongst those members of the Baptist communion whose political agenda leaned to the Left. I know that my father felt strongly about Spain and many years later he told me that had it not been for his family responsibilities, he would have joined the International Brigade.

Moriah Sunday School Committee's work at this time showed how ordinary working men, with perhaps only the rudiments of schooling, proceeded diligently to administer an organisation, which, according to *A View from the Hill*, could list 887 scholars in 1936, the year when my father was Superintendent. It would not have been an easy year for him - I have failed to find his name in Risca colliery's All-Insurances Register for the year - and in all probability he was finding 'a start' in employment wherever he could, perhaps at Southwood Jones's quarry or digging holes in the road for Risca Council. He resumed work at the colliery in April 1937, was advanced to Fireman after due examination for the certificate and as I have described earlier, suffered some kind of breakdown, probably in 1938. It was at about this time that a disillusion with spiritual matters may have set in and his niece, Marian Morris (née Chivers), recalls that one of his remarks at the time was that he could not 'serve God and Mammon'. This remark, almost apocalyptic in its severity, shows that in my father's mind, the pressures of his duties as a colliery fireman, when the working day was all about extracting as much coal as possible, as cheaply as possible, with perhaps a scant regard for bureaucracy and regulations, offered a bleak contrast to the shining ideals of the Christian faith. From this time onwards, he seems to have lost much of his zeal as a member of the Moriah congregation. In later years, when I was taken to the Sunday evening service, there was never any explanation for his absence from the 'second sitting' and the celebration of communion. During my teenage wrangles with him about my own enforced attendance as an escort for my more diligent mother on Sunday evenings (arguments in which I was inevitably bested), his own feelings of unfitness tended to emerge. When I demanded to know why, in spite of requiring me to attend, he was not a regular Sunday evening worshipper, he told me that his Sunday observances had fallen off after he had used bad language 'at work' and that had been an aspect of his remoteness from the Chapel. However, examining this remoteness from today's perspective, I feel that the 'God and Mammon' thesis is more credible. In spite of this, there were many Sunday evenings when, during my childhood, I sat at the end of what was jovially referred to as 'the family pew', a seat which I understood had been ours for a very long time, with other family members, such as a cousin, an aunt and uncle perhaps, and usually one or both of my parents. There were occasions when I was pampered, with a boiled sweet or a piece of chocolate from a sweets-shop proprietor, Theresa Williams, who sat in an adjoining pew.

One occupant of a neighbouring pew during the early 1950s was the manager of Nine Mile Point colliery, Mr Orion Powell, at the time my father's immediate boss. Dad pointed him out to me and instead of being awestruck by the presence of such an important figure, as perhaps a youth in my position would have been in an earlier generation, I wondered why he traipsed all the way down the valley for a Sunday evening service. Having now evaluated some of the pressures involved in managing a Welsh mine in the mid-20th century, I can see how Mr Powell's pilgimages to Moriah may have been his way of seeking God's help in his work. Undoubtedly, Mammon was a hard taskmaster.

Please B Co and return to) Working nights
Police Station Risca) free on Saturdays

3522

FORM OF ENROLMENT IN THE LOCAL DEFENCE VOLUNTEERS.

Name CHIVERS ..... Christian Names. Ernest Percy .....
Block Letters.

XOUM/ 90/1.

Questions to be put on enrolment.

1. What is your name?   1. E. P. Chivers.

2. What is the date and year of your birth?   2. 5/3/03...

3. What is your address?   10 Brookland Road, 3. Risca, Mon

4. (a) Are you a British subject?   4. (a).. Yes.....
   (b) Nationality of parents at birth?   Father (b).. Yes.....
       Mother   Yes
   (c) Name, address and relationship of next of kin wife (c) Ivy Evelyn Chivers 10 Brookland Rd Risca

5. Do you now belong to, or have you ever served in the Armed Forces of the Crown? if so, state particulars of all engagements?   5. ...No......

6. Do you understand that if accepted you will become subject to military law and liable to obey such orders as may be given to you in accordance with instructions for the Local Defence Volunteers issued by the Army Council, but that those instructions will require you to give part-time service only and will not require you to live away from home?   6. ..Yes......

7. Do you understand that your service in the Local Defence Volunteers will be without pay or other emoluments?   7. ...Yes......

8. Do you understand that in the event of your incurring a disability attributable to your service any claim for compensation will be dealt with under the regulations for the time being in force for the purpose which provide in the case of death or permanent disability the same terms as are applicable to private soldiers and their dependants?   8. ...Yes......

9. Do you understand that if you are accepted you will engage to serve in the Local Defence Volunteers for a period not exceeding the duration of the present emergency but that during that period your service may be determined in accordance with instructions issued by the Army Council, by competent authority at any time, or at your own request by fourteen days' notice in writing given by you?   9. ..Yes......

DECLARATION.

I Ernest Percy Chivers do solemnly declare that the answers made by me to the foregoing questions are true and I hereby agree to serve in the Local Defence Volunteers.

Signature of applicant... E. P. Chivers

Date 1/6/40 ...   Signature of enrolling authority. A. H. Drewell

CERTIFICATE OF ACCEPTANCE.

Ernest Percy Chivers ....(name) is accepted for service in the Local Defence Volunteers for the following period:-

GROUP(a) the duration of the emergency G Markham GROUP COMMANDER

20 JUNE 1940 (b) until.................

My father's Home Guard enrolment document (Army Form W3066). This made it clear that he was subject to military law.

Chapter Five

The Defence of the Realm:
The Risca Home Guard and the High Cross Gunners

The Dunkirk tragedy played from 27th May until 4th June, 1940. Anthony Eden, the Secretary for War, by now versed in the scenario of military disaster, had broadcast an appeal for Local Defence Volunteers (LDV) on 14th May.[1] My father joined this new body on 1st June, before the Dunkirk evacuation had been completed. Typically perhaps, he had waited a while after Eden's appeal before taking action. Conservative politicians were not his favourite people and when the Government was headed by a Prime Minister, Churchill, whose tenure of office as Home Secretary, as long ago as 1910, had been marked by a repressive deployment of troops to assist with strike-breaking in the Rhondda, then joining the Colours was not an act to be entered into lightly. However, in a rather sketchy analysis of the period which he offered some years later, he told me that the thought of Hitler landing at Dover, or wherever, had goaded him into action. Of course, the entire South Wales coalfield was populated by workers who shared my father's views about Churchill but who were still prepared to volunteer. Risca's history, and that of all the Monmouthshire valleys, had been affected by industrial strife of some sort, in which workers had confronted management and the owners of pits and foundries. In 1894 there had been ferocious violence between strikers, strike-breakers and police at Pontymister Works, while nearer the time of the LDV's creation, police activity on behalf of law and order during the bitter industrial turbulence of the 1920s and 1930s was fresh in people's memories.[2] A prominent leader of police activity in Monmouthshire had been Risca's own police chief, Superintendent Laurence Spendlove, and it was this individual who was tasked by the government with an important role in the enrolment of Risca's new volunteers. To enter the Risca police station, a handsome, well-appointed edifice, and to submit to a registration process under Spendlove's supervision, would not have been an entirely happy experience for my father. The Ministry of Defence, at my second time of asking, very kindly produced Dad's enrolment document, Army Form 3066, bearing his signature and that of his future Company Commander, A.H. Powell, described as the 'Enrolling Authority'. Five days later, on 6th June, his 'Certificate of Acceptance', on the same document, was signed by C.G. Martyn, described as the 'Group Commander' of the local LDVs. The form makes it clear that he had joined for the war's duration and that he was subject to military law.

All of which may have made my father a touch apprehensive. More youthful recruits had a slightly different perspective. Glyn Hutchings, a seventeen-year-old who lived in Clyde Street, Pontymister, had joined with alacrity soon after Eden's appeal, much to his father's concern. Hutchings senior feared that the new volunteers might quickly become cannon-fodder for the Army proper. However, his son was spotted as a likely lad and speedily became a 'Section Commander', which in the days before the LDV came to terms with a military rank structure, was probably equivalent to Lance Corporal or Corporal. Glyn's elevation was not without its embarrassments. He found himself in command of one of his former teachers at the Pontywaun Intermediate school, Mr Bishop, whose skills were more appropriate to the classroom than to the hurly-burly of the task of keeping the Germans out of Risca. This work began, according to the *South Wales Argus*, in the days immediately preceding 18th June, 1940.[3] On that day, the paper reported, under the heading, 'Risca Volunteers', the first parade of the so-called Risca Company of the Local Defence Volunteers had taken place at the Company Headquarters, a site that may have been the Risca Rugby Club pavilion at the Stores Field, or perhaps the large furniture shop belonging to Messrs Wallace Jones opposite Moriah Chapel. At whichever of these premises the historically important first parade occurred, the assembled Volunteers were addressed by a local notable, the man who had counter-signed my father's application to join-up, Major Claude G. Martyn JP, described by the *Argus* as the commander of the Risca Group and eulogised in a later edition of the paper as 'A man of wide business experience', who was also the Chairman of the Board of Directors of the Royal Gwent Hospital; the Chairman of the Newport branch of the British Legion and one of that body's national vice-Presidents. He was also one of Newport's Harbour Commissioners and a former High Sheriff of Monmouthshire, while at the time of the LDV enlistment he served on the Bench at Newport Magistrate's Court and was clearly one of the locality's great and good personalities.

The *Argus* report of 18th June is very important, given the paucity of official documentation. Not only does it identify the first Commanding Officer of the so-called Risca Group, but it also lists local personalities who had willingly put themselves forward for leadership. The Company Commander was a Mr A.H. Powell and his Assistant Company Commander, Mr C.B.G. Jones, was one of the triumvirate of Jones brothers who ran the Wallace Jones furniture business (and known to his employees as Mr Chris). The *Argus* reported that: 'A strong muster from each platoon were commanded as follows: Risca No. 1 Mr W.D. Matthews; Risca No. 2 Mr G. Thomas; Crosskeys Mr A. G. Moseley; Wattsville Mr J. Hall'. The newspaper also identified the Assistant Group Commander, Captain Walter Phillips, a man who, by the year's end, was the Commanding Officer of what emerged as the 4th Monmouthshire Battalion. Phillips belonged to a well-known Newport business family, while some of the other names would have been instantly recognisable to many Risca folk. Chris Jones of the Wallace Jones furniture emporium has been noted, while there could hardly have been a more readily-identifiable personality than Wilf (Fatty) Matthews, the proprietor of a prosperous grocery store in Commercial Street, Pontymister. A short and exceedingly rotund figure, Matthews was a respected survivor of World War I in which he had served as a member of one of the Bantam battalions. There was no doubt about his spirit, but whether his flesh could have withstood any arduous campaigning as an infantry platoon commander must remain a moot point. While listing Moseley as the commander of the Crosskeys element, the *Argus* omitted to say that he had won the Distinguished Conduct Medal in World War I. In the final list of officers of what became the 4th Monmouthshire Battalion, Home Guard, published in 1944, there is no mention of G. Thomas (Risca No. 2) and J.Hall (Wattsville), two doughty volunteers,

Lieutenant Wilfred Matthews, my father's platoon commander in the 4th Monmouthshire Home Guard Battalion. The photograph was probably taken in June 1940, before uniforms were available when the new organisation was called the Local Defence Volunteers. The brassard probably bore the LDV abbreviation. His rifle was either an extremely scarce Lee-Enfield or a Canadian Ross weapon, with its bayonet still in its scabbard. *Mrs Ruth Burn*

whose careers as LDV/Home Guard leaders may have been brought to an end when the hierarchy changed as the war progressed.[4] As we lived in Brookland Road, Pontymister, it was logical for my father, together with Glyn Hutchings and a group of other Pontymister people, to be allocated to Wilf Matthews' Risca No. 1 Element soon to evolve as No. 5 Platoon, 'B' Company.

However, between its creation in June and its listing in the Army's *Severn Sub-Area War Diary* in December 1940, the 4th Monmouthshire Home Guard Battalion that had evolved from the Risca Group was expected to participate in any actions which might be necessary to repel a German attack on Newport. By the year's end, Captain Walter Phillips was the Battalion's Commanding Officer. He lived at Palmyra House, in Newport and his battalion's headquarters was now in the Emlyn Works in Emlyn Street, Newport, a premises owned by Charles D. Phillips Limited, manufacturers of tents and tarpaulins. The headquarters was at least six and a half miles from Risca and until more documents become available, the 4th Mons Risca-Newport nexus must remain slightly obscure. Phillips' honorific, Captain, must have dated from his World War I service, for it was not until November 1940 that the government agreed to the use of proper military ranks in the Home Guard, though even in December, Phillips is shown as the battalion's CO with only a captain's rank.[5]

By December 1940, the 4th Mons had enrolled 1,790 personnel for whom 992 rifles had been provided, together with 33 Lewis machine guns and six Vickers machine guns. Some time after the war, Colonel Baker, who had been a Home Guard Zone Commander, reminisced at a party in his honour, that at one stage there had only been 10 rifles for each Home Guard battalion, while my father recalled an anecdote about rifle distribution for his platoon. A pitifully small number of weapons, perhaps about six, had arrived for a largish platoon of Volunteers and distribution was overseen by one of the 4th Mons early leaders, soon to become a Second Lieutenant, a man called Percy Bunce, famed throughout the locality and well-known throughout South Wales as a formidable rugby player. Bunce was indeed a star who had narrowly failed to gain a Welsh cap and who handed the newly-arrived rifles to six of his rugby playing cohorts, my father included. There was an inevitable protest from the unarmed majority and articulated by one of the more mutinous members: 'Just because a man plays rugby doesn't mean that he can handle a rifle!' Bunce's reply, delivered in his usual hoarse, gravelly voice, was crushing: 'I've given those rifles to men I can trust!' If eventually some original Home Guard documents about the first six months of the 4th Mons history become available, the reason for locating the battalion headquarters in Emlyn Street, Newport, may become clear. Until then, the War Diary of the Army's Severn Sub-Area for December 1940 must be relied on. This document shows the 4th Mons as part of the overall command of the Officer Commanding Troops, Newport, a title handily abbreviated to OC Troops Newport and identifies the localities liable to attack as Newport Docks and town and 'Chief factories, industrial plants and other installations'. The War Diary goes on to state that two 'stop lines' had been completed on the lines of the Rivers Wye and Usk,

> …that on the Wye to meet an attack from the east and that on the Usk to meet an attack from the south and west. Prepared positions are ready for occupation by reinforcements in case of large-scale enemy landings. Prior to the arrival of reinforcements these localities will be defended by Home Guard units who will reconnoitre the actual posts to be occupied.

The War Diary made interesting provisions for the Home Guard's involvement in local defence:

> The principle of Home Guard defence is a static one and Home Guard Units should operate within a short distance of their homes. With this end in view, islands of defence or localities must be prepared for occupation in emergency and these positions must be held to delay the enemy till the last round or the arrival of reinforcements.[5]

In the light of these decrees, the location of the 4th Mons' battalion headquarters in Emlyn Street, Newport gives the historian something to ponder. When the horrendous threat of a German invasion loomed menacingly during the months following Dunkirk, a concern for the seaport and docks is understandable. Mr Robin Williams of Crickhowell, a kinsman of one of the battalion's officers (Captain, later Lieutenant Colonel W.T. Harris, MC), has very kindly provided me with a contemporary survey of the 4th Mons areas of responsibility during the early days. This document was a kind of press release to coincide with the Home Guard's third anniversary and an edited version appeared in the *Argus* on 22nd May, 1943. It points out that the battalion area then included Newbridge, Abercarn, Crosskeys, Risca, Rogerstone, Bassaleg, Rhiwderin, Rumney, Michaelstone, St Mellons, Castleton, Peterstone, St Brides, Bedwas, Trethomas and Machen. Peterstone and St Brides would have included the muddy Severn estuary and large stretches of flat farmland which the author remembers being planted with tall poles to obstruct aircraft or glider landings. The officer responsible for the shoreline was one of the 4th Mons highly regarded veterans of World War I, Captain W.T. Harris, holder of the Military Cross and a survivor of ferocious fighting whilst serving at Steenbeck, in Flanders with the South Wales Borderers in August 1917.[6]

The tensions of the period immediately following Dunkirk need no emphasis. On midsummer's day, 1940, the *Argus* printed a large silhouette of a German troop-carrying aircraft, the Junkers 52, from which enemy parachutists were likely to descend, an image accompanied by a less than felicitous headline, 'Local Defence Volunteers and all citizens: cut this out and stick it up'. A phrase that has survived from the period describes the LDV's Walking Stick Patrols, earned out by men who were unarmed. Mr Hugh Watkins of Gelli Drive, Risca, recalls these duties, particularly at Pant yr Eos reservoir:

> I remember doing three guards at Pant yr Eos Reservoir. It was summer time and the nights were warm and pleasant. Four members were on duty together. We had no arms but chatted the nights away whilst walking around the dam. Mercifully, no-one ever attacked us.

Glyn Hutchings' account of his duties at the reservoir complements this nicely, although his recollection of the numbers involved does not tally precisely:

> Six of us would form the guard party for the Pant yr Eos Reservoir and the route would be up over the 'Hilly Fields'. One night it was pitch dark and as our guard party were walking up through the fields, one chap walked into the back of a horse which presumably was dozing off. The horse gave a loud neigh, reared up and galloped off, leaving us rooted to the spot! We would have been less frightened if we had seen the anticipated parachute drop. It was thought at the time that attempts would be made to poison our water supplies.

The modern reader will see a farcical element in some of this, but the actual apprehension about invasion was very real. Hugh Watkins recalled his guard duties at the electricity sub-station near the Tyn y Cwm railway bridge, a site where a platoon commander, Wilf Matthews, almost had his career terminated. He was a well-built, portly individual and when challenged by his own sentry in the dense black-out, a certain shortness of breath obliged him to delay his response - a breathing space which, according to my father, almost proved fatal. Luckily, the sentry refrained from pulling the trigger. William Henry Price, a railway worker from Fleur de Lys was not so fortunate whilst driving his car to his place of work on 18th June, 1940. He failed to stop when challenged at a check-point in Maesycymmer. The sentry, not a member of the 4th Mons, fired and Mr Price, though taken to hospital, died on the same day. Similar incidents, all over the country, were to mar the LDV's reputation in those early days.[7]

If road-blocks were an essential feature of the LDV's early deployments, then the surprise which the 4th Mons devised for the German Panzers at Tyn y Cwm deserves a special mention. Glyn Hutchings recalls that,

Anti-tank traps were planned at various points and I remember the railway embankment between the Welsh Oak Inn and the Tyn y Cwm bridge being dug into and barrels of explosive placed there, which were then wired-up to be exploded from Herbert Avenue in the event of enemy tanks using the Risca-Newport road.

Just over 100 years earlier, The Welsh Oak was a rendezvous for the Chartists on their march to Newport, though it must be doubted whether, in 1940, many people bothered to contemplate the pub's early history.

The tension which enveloped the Risca community after Dunkirk and the fall of France shows in some of the meagre local correspondence that has survived. On 25th July, 1940, Chris (Wallace) Jones, describing himself as 'Asst Company Commander of the 4th Batt Mon Regt', wrote to the Clerk of the Risca council:

We have erected a hut near Messrs W.M. Baulch premises for the storage of arms, ammunition etc belonging to our organisation. It will be necessary for us to keep the men there throughout every night to keep guard and we shall be obliged if you would ask your council if they could kindly provide us with light and heat for same. If your council will grant us the above request, we are sure Councillor Baulch, who is the Transport Officer, will see that the privilige [sic] will not be abused.

Trusting you will give a favourable consideration to our request.
Yours faithfully,
C.G.B. Jones

In the distance, the Chartist rendezvous of 1839, 'The Welsh Oak'. In the foreground is the railway embankment where, in 1940, the LDV buried barrels of explosives to be detonated in the event of a German advance along the road from Newport. This 'mine' was to be exploded by means of electric cables connected to a nearby house.   *Author*

Five days later the *Argus* reported that Risca's civil Defence committee had received a letter asking for the installation of heating facilities at three buildings used by the Home Guards. The committee's chairman, Councillor Percy Jerman JP, commented, 'This is not a question of pounds, shillings and pence for we have to win the war and money comes first'. Mr Baulch, referred to in Chris Jones' letter as the Transport Officer, was Pontymister's only funeral director and provider of luxurious Rolls Royce cars for weddings and for general hire. He does not appear again in the admittedly sparse 4th Mons documents of the period, although he attended a celebratory Home Guard dinner towards the end of the war.[8] I was extremely fortunate in being able to converse with his son, Mr Arthur Baulch, who has confirmed the existence of the hut on the forecourt of the family garage.

Yet another prominent Risca citizen who was present at the Civil Defence Committee meeting reported by the *Argus*, was my Headmaster at Pontymister Boys' School, Arthur Vaughan Williams. He proposed to the gathering that the Council's electrical engineer should survey the premises, so in all probability, after the receipt of Chris Jones' letter, other requests were received concerning other buildings. These may have been the Stores Field's rugby pavilion and perhaps a part of the Wallace Jones furniture emporium opposite Moriah Chapel. All was not plain sailing, however, when it came to paying for utilities. Indeed, the sundry premises used by the 4th Mons were usually paid for by the Monmouthshire Territorial Army Association, which, in accordance with a national directive for such bodies, held funds for just this sort of thing. For example, on 6th November, 1940, the TA Association paid Risca Urban District Council 17s. 3d. for supplying heating and lighting to the Drill Hall at Crosskeys and on 3rd April, 1941 handed over £2 15s. 6d. to the Council for expenses incurred by the 4th Mons for the use of a hut at Risca. It is unclear whether this was the hut on the Baulch forecourt or perhaps the Girl Guide hut behind Commercial Street in the vicinity of Wilf Matthews' grocery shop. Lieutenant Matthews, as he was by this time, wrote to the Council about the Guide hut on 13th November, 1941. This particular letter was probably drafted by my father and although it was neatly typed (probably in my father's office at Risca Colliery), the addressee appears in manuscript in the traditional bottom left-hand corner. The hand-writing is my father's.

Matthews was Dad's immediate Home Guard superior whose grocery shop in Commercial Street, Pontymister, was directly opposite Baulch's garage and funeral parlour. Another Home Guard leader, already mentioned, was one of Risca's rugby stars, Percy Bunce. The anonymous process that elevated the town's Home Guard officers - possibly directed by Superintendent Spendlove - would, in Bunce's case, have taken cognisance of his hundred or so games for Cardiff, his selection for three Welsh Trials and the durability of his post-Cardiff days when he led Risca in the highly abrasive Monmouthshire League. As recently as April 1937, Bunce had turned out for Cardiff Past versus Cardiff Present, so his credibility as a tough nut would have been undiminished and there would have been no doubt about his ability to take on the Germans in any battle for Risca. Percy Bunce's rough diamond aspect may have concerned those who sought a more Sandhurst approach to leadership but his rugby football background inspired immense respect. However, would the Germans have known about it? I can remember Bunce calling at our house in Brookland Road on a number of occasions to discuss significant Home Guard matters and, many years later, when I played rugby for Risca, he was the grey eminence with a gravelly voice who virtually ran the club - and never mind the Committee. While Bunce was a personal friend from the good old days of their partnership in the scrum for Risca RFC, my father's links with Matthews were of a different nature. It seems that they worked closely in the 4th Mons B Company where the company stores were my father's personal concern. Glyn Hutchings remembers Matthews with some affection:

> Number 5 Platoon paraded every Sunday morning and mid-week, with guard duties at various points every night. Our commander, Wilf Matthews, was very respectful to his platoon and would address his parade as 'gentlemen and NCOs' while explaining the week activities, etc. Some people may have had a slight dig at his physical stature but he enjoyed the respect of the men as he would engage actively in all the training. On one occasion we were gathered at the derelict farmhouse at the bottom of the Ty Sign Fields. A rope was let down by the Home Guards in the upper storey and the idea was for us to run holding on to the rope towards the house, up the wall and be hauled in through the window by the chaps upstairs! Most of us achieved this ridiculous procedure, including the tubby commander, Wilf.[9]

In July 1940, the LDV, on a Churchillian whim, had its name changed to the Home Guard and on 6th November 1940, Eden's successor at the War Office, Grigg, announced that the volunteers were now to have an army rank structure so that they could feel assured of full and unassailable military status. This was a nice way of saying that in the event of invasion perhaps the Germans would not now shoot the Home Guard out of hand as irregular guerrillas, or *francs tireurs*. The rank structure business inevitably brought some gratification to those who valued their status in the community and who may have been looking ahead to post-war days when, as after World War I, a military career of sorts might redound to one's credit. Obviously, the entire 4th Mons complement of officers and NCOs set to work sewing the appropriate badges on their uniforms, although my mother was not tasked with this until my father's promotion to sergeant in August 1941. His elevation appears to have been the summit of his Home Guard ambition and I can remember him saying at the time, 'They go on to me about taking a commission, but I tell them I've got funny views about class distinction!' These views could have been profitably compared to those held by two other sergeants in B Company, Fred Wilkes, a decorator from Clyde Street, and Jim Weeks, a miner from Wellspring Terrace, both of whom had seen service in the Welsh Guards where class distinction would have been an entire way of life - but of course, far more important things were afoot.

On Saturday 2nd August, 1941, the *Argus* wrote of reports reaching the War Office about Home Guard exercises which had been taking place up and down the country for the past week and which were to continue for another week. Inevitably, a barely-trained volunteer force revealed a number of blemishes and the War Office department which had released this information to the press clearly believed in the importance of putting some of this unsatisfactory detail before the public. The paper pointed out that,

...on the good side it is clear that whatever actual rehearsals of real operations were carried out the turnout of the Home Guards was very good - it often amounted to 80% to 90%. Admirable also [sic] was the keenness of the men. On the other side it was clear that a small proportion of the Home Guard, although keen enough, had not fully learned their job. For this small proportion, it was in some cases the first scheme in which they had participated. They did not know their ground. They did not quite understand the job they were doing and they had not learned to move forward concealed from the enemy...

Reading between the lines of this criticism, emanating from an experienced military source, we can appreciate that the Home Guard's tactical awareness was minimal. The analysis went on to say that, in the next week,

...there will be large exercises including several battalions of Home Guards and all over the country there will be the fundamental weakness of the Home Guard - the little exercises by a company or platoon in the defence of their own particular village or locality.

Although some of the syntax here may be a touch difficult, the overall meaning is clear, and for my purpose, nets in nicely with Glyn Hutchings' account of B Company's mock attack on the Church Road railway station.

This station, in Lower Machen, was just over the hill from Pontymister, in the adjacent Rhymney valley and could easily have served as an inspiration for those cartoonists, like Giles and Emmett, who specialised in situations involving railway architecture in remote locations. All the planning for this attack fell to my father. Our house suddenly acquired a supply of Ordnance Survey maps, some with a scale of six inches to the mile. Browsing over these fascinating blends of geography, history and archaeology left me with a lifelong enthusiasm for maps and atlases, but it was the preparation of the blank ammunition which really intrigued me. Equipped respectively with a wrench and a pair of pliers, my father and Glyn Hutchings sat in our middle room at Brookland Road and carefully pulled apart .303 ammunition, disposing of the lethal bullet and crimping the brass cartridge so that the cordite could not escape. The squeezed cartridge could then be fired harmlessly but noisily, creating the desired martial effect during a mock attack. Piles of this ammunition soon covered our table and presumably, other armourers were also at work in Risca to ensure an adequate supply of blanks. My father was probably chosen to plan the attack because of his local knowledge. After all, anyone brought up in Danygraig would know his way across to Church Road, while his horse-coping on behalf of the Harris farming family must have given him an unrivalled knowledge of the topography. Family lore held that, once upon a time, he had been dispatched from the Chivers home in Bridge Street to collect his sister, Miriam Doreen Chivers (later Mrs Ivor Price), from a party at Llandanglws Farm. Therefore a mock attack over familiar but demanding terrain, down the slope and into the Rhymney Valley must have been a doddle. Glyn Hutchings has kindly produced this account of the planning:

Regarding the Church Road project, your father and I had built up a close working relationship and we were assigned to test the defence of the Church Road Station by the platoon trying to get a small attacking party into the station if possible, without detection - a tall order. I remember meeting Percy on the Saturday afternoon before the exercise. We went over Machen Mountain and planned our route through a wooded area…

Despite research amongst survivors of the 4th Mons Bedwas Company, a formation for whom the attack at Church Road would have served as an opportunity for the rehearsal of a defensive deployment, I have been unable to discover any other details of the operation. Perhaps Dad's promotion to sergeant, dated on his record of enrolment form and Record of Service Aug. 1941, was linked with the scheme's success.

Because he was called-up by the RAF in June 1942, Glyn Hutchings missed the first of a series of Summer Camps arranged by the 4th Mons and described in the *Argus* on 8th July, 1942. My father, as B Company's quartermaster sergeant, would have been deeply committed. The newspaper described the event in glowing terms:

> The first of a series of summer camps organised by the 4th Monmouthshire (Risca) Battalion Home Guard under the command of Lieutenant Colonel Walter C. Phillips was held in ideal surroundings. An attractive training programme was drawn up by Captain A C. Harding MC, and Captain Kenvyn Lewis (Officers Commanding 'C' and 'D' Companies)…A field exercise culminated in a full-scale attack on the camp and during the afternoon the men were fully occupied with such training features as musketry instruction, bayonet fighting, map reading, rifle grenade practice and firing on ranges with .303 and .22 ammunition, together with a 'platoon in attack' introduction ….Home Guard cooks were responsible for cooking arrangements and the food of which there was plenty for every body, was excellently prepared.

Public relations optimism dominates this extract and anyone who has spent more than five minutes in any military organisation can recognise the characteristics of a cheery press release intended to encourage the troops and to boost public morale. From my position as the eight-year-old son of B Company's quartermaster sergeant, I was able to review many of the weapons as they were taken into service. I can remember being allowed to handle, under supervision, a Canadian Ross .303 rifle, a Lewis gun and, frabjous joy, a Thompson sub-machine gun. Later, there was also a Sten gun. Why it was necessary for these weapons to spend any time at 10 Brookland Road was a question to which I certainly did not need an answer. To paraphrase Percy Bunce's remark, the weapons were in the hands of trustworthy personnel. Not all the 4th Mons musketry took place on approved ranges under the vigilant control of hawk-eyed NCOs. Once, Glyn Hutchings and Charlie Tucker failed to get one of B Company's Lewis guns to function during a training session in a field near Pontymister Works. The idea was mooted, there and then, that they should seek advice from Sergeant Murray, an acknowledged expert on the gun and known to be on the afternoon shift in the adjacent steelworks. Murray saw that the problem was all to do with the gas supply to the weapon's return mechanism. Having made the necessary adjustments, he took up a position behind the gun and put a burst of bullets through an oil drum conveniently placed about 50 yards away in the meadow which was the scene of their evening's weapon training. 'It's OK now', he said casually and strolled back to his duties at the steelworks. The discharge of live rounds in a training routine is normally part of an elaborate ritual which the Anglican Church might envy, but on this occasion it seems that the platoon commander, Wilf Matthews, genially gave the gun crew his retrospective blessing and seemed to have approved of their initiative.

The battalion had its share of lighter moments. For example, on Monday 6th October, 1941, the *Argus* reported that the county's Lord Lieutenant, Sir Henry Mather Jackson, accompanied by Lady Mather Jackson, had attended a Field Day which the Risca Home Guard had arranged in the Stores Field. Much later there was the parade which the Home Guard laid on for Her Grace the Duchess of Marlborough and reported in the *Argus* on Monday 25th May, 1942. My father's battalion paraded under the command of Lieutenant Colonel Walter C. Phillips, probably on the preceding Saturday or Sunday, an occasion meant to celebrate the second anniversary of the Home Guard's formation. This may have been the parade which Glyn Hutchings remembers being overseen by our local police chief, Superintendent Spendlove, who uttered the irascible commentary, '...and now, where's that bloody bugle band?' No photographs of this martial display seem to have survived in the local press, although on 27th May, 1942, the *Argus* produced a photograph of the Duchess, surrounded by unctuous local worthies, one of whom was the Pontymister Works manager, Mr Haldane Sullivan. It was quite appropriate for an aristocrat such as the Duchess, Winston Churchill's kinswoman, to visit a mining community during the trying days of war when it was thought that the workers' morale needed a boost. Someone like my father, however, would certainly have wondered what she had been doing when the National Government cut his dole in 1931.

But, for the moment, such things could be set aside and minds focused on winning the war. Where, in 1942, might the Germans have landed? With an apparent nonchalant regard for security, the General Officer Commanding Home Forces confided in the local war correspondent of the *Weekly Argus*, Percy Doble, that enemy airborne forces might have been expected to force a bridgehead from Swansea to Fishguard. Doble wrote in the paper's edition of 11th July, 1942:

> It was the object of those invading troops...to open up the main routes through South Wales, to gain contact with other enemy forces already landed in England. Bridgend, Cardiff and Newport formed the axis of their advance.

Lest it be thought, some 62 years after these fears were published, that Doble had been singled out for special treatment by the General Staff, it is important to point out that in the company of other journalists he had probably been briefed about an extensive signals exercise, an operation involving little or no troop movements. Doble said, 'For a whole day, from one afternoon through the night to the next afternoon, headquarter staffs or regular troops and Home Guards in the South Wales district were on the alert'.

In military parlance, being on the alert could mean anything and I browsed through my father's Home Guard manuals and listened to his anecdotes and wound myself up into my own mildly enthusiastic state of alert. This involved mulling over his instructions that in the event of an invasion, I was to walk, with my mother, along the canal bank to her parental home at Cwmcarn, just a few miles up the valley. His tales of the Molotov Cocktails and of the assiduous practice which the battalion conducted with these devices behind Pontymister School, gave a small boy much to think about. It seemed that these handy projectiles were the Mark Two variety, in that they needed to be thrown with sufficient force against a surface to break the glass bottle so that when its highly combustible contents encountered air, the target was immediately engulfed in flame. An earlier version, which the War Office encouraged the Home Guard to manufacture on a 'Do It Yourself' basis, involved filling a beer bottle with petrol, tar-gas and water. The stoppered bottle was to have two 'Royal Flaming Wax Vestas' (matches), attached by a piece of string.

These matches should be tied in a clove hitch…(and) the bottle must be scratched with a file or a glass cutter circumferentially to ensure easy breakage…These matches will strike on any dry surface but it is as well to keep handy several match boxes, including spares.

This was the language of an instructional pamphlet on how to make 'Molotoff' [sic] Cocktails, issued by the regular army in June 1940.[10] My father's self-igniting versions, according to his enthusiastic descriptions, gave spectacular results when hurled against a wall behind my school. They were a great improvement upon the Mark One, although with a sad smile, he occasionally mulled over the fate of those unbroken Cocktails which had been thrown inaccurately, but with considerable enthusiasm, out of the practice area into the soggy black coal dust or duff at the river's edge. Father and son were able to speculate about what might happen if someone found them and for my part, at least, I was able to wallow in a kind of vicarious anxiety. So far as I know, nothing untoward ever came of the lost Molotov Cocktails.

By 1942, my father's sub-unit, No. 5 Platoon of B Company, had acquired a collection of much more sophisticated weaponry. Glyn Hutchings recalls that long before he left the Home Guard for the Royal Air Force in June 1942, No. 5 Platoon, then 100-strong, 'were all armed with rifles, backed by four Lewis machine guns, two Thompson Sub-Machine guns, two Northover Projectors - kind of primitive mortars, Sten Guns and a supply of hand-grenades'. My good fortune in being able to tap-in to Glyn's memories in this way allows an allusion to yet another weapon, part of which became a permanent item in my collection of military toys. This was the 'Sticky Bomb', or more correctly, the No. 74 Grenade. Glyn Hutchings has,

Vivid recollections of our trip to Mendalgief Field in Newport, where a range had been set up. We were to receive instruction in the use of 'Sticky Bombs' against tanks. The idea was to run from cover to the side of a tank, pulling the pin from the handle of the bomb which looked like a huge lollipop. The casing would spring off and the sticky bomb would adhere to the surface of the tank, exploding inwards against the resistance, with, I assume, devastating effect inside the tank. We had no tanks to practice on, but the holes blasted in the thick iron plates, our targets, raised a few eyebrows.

My souvenir of this practice session, carefully garnered by my father on my behalf, was a specimen of the sticky bomb's spherical casing, garnished with some of the gooey, sticky substance on the inside. It formed a part of my collection of playthings until the day came when it lost its power to intrigue.

A robust military scheme of the type that was essential if the 'General Service' or infantry Home Guard battalion was to begin to cause problems for an invader, gave rise to the case of the subaltern's gold watch. On 9th July, 1942, Lieutenant Colonel Phillips, commanding the 4th Mons, made representations to the Monmouthshire Territorial Army Association, the battalion's financial provider, about a gold watch, belonging to Lieutenant E.J. Thomas. This was, most probably, Emlyn Thomas of Hillside, Risca, the manager of a local chemist's shop. He also played the organ in Moriah Chapel and, when on Home Guard duty, sported breeches and glossy leather gaiters of the type which had made British officers readily identifiable by German snipers during World War I. According to the TA Association's minutes, Emlyn's watch was 'damaged beyond repair during an exercise and recompense of £15, the value of the watch, was claimed'. The meeting's atmosphere that day was not entirely sympathetic to Emlyn. It was resolved that the CO's letter which outlined the sad affair should lie on the table, a delicate way of allowing the matter to receive minimal consideration without being entirely dismissive. A month later, on 13th August 1942, in response to another letter from Phillips, the TA Association resolved that, 'No further action could be taken in the matter'. We never discussed this at No. 10 Brookland Road. Had we done so, I feel confident that a large dollop of Risca *schadenfreude* would have been applied and my father would have commented on the folly of wearing such a valuable watch when engaged in war games.

One of the easier-to-understand endorsements, in someone's neat handwriting, on my father's record of service reads, 'Will attend Street Fighting Course at Birmingham from 30.10.42 to 7.11.42'. This was the first time for my father to be separated from us and his first attendance at any form of instructional, residential course. The syllabus at the General Headquarters Home Guard School in Birmingham dealt with weapon training, battle drill, battle craft, concealment, patrolling, street fighting, defence and attack, night craft, leadership and discipline. His account of how a Vickers machine gun could bring about the demolition of a brick wall, simply by firing in a certain way at this target was, for me, his best anecdote. There were, too, tales of being pulled up the walls of buildings in the way practised by the 4th Mons at Squire Phillips' ruined house, and accounts of the badly-bombed areas of Birmingham which were ideally suited to the tactics which the Directing Staff sought to instil. Wartime censorship tried to hide details of bombed areas from the general public and so traveller's tales of the type that my father brought back to Risca were listened to respectfully.

He left B Company in the Spring of 1943 and his Record of Service shows that on 12th March he was 'Transferred' to Battalion Headquarters, although the purpose of this posting is unclear. Subsequent events show that perhaps he was busy planning some kind of Home Guard career move and that his eyes were on an objective that offered a different option. Although the *Argus* carried the following advertisement long after my father had reached a decision, he would certainly have been made aware of the need for gunners, during his brief sojourn in the 4th Mons Battalion Headquarters. The slightly unusual wartime advertisement in the *Argus* read:

> For AA Battery - Volunteers Still Needed at Newport…Volunteers will be called upon to do duty on the Battery site from 7 pm to 7 am, one night in eight only. While on the site they will be housed and fed by the Army and only called out for actual duty when the occasion demands…

This would not have been the sole recruiting initiative. All Home Guard formations would have been trawled for personnel who were willing and more importantly, able and there would have been a big drive to procure recruits for the seven gunsites with which the Army's Anti-Aircraft Command had surrounded Newport. These sites were at Lodge Farm, Christchurch, Pye Corner, Nash, New House, Pennsylvania and Great Oak, the last-named being my father's eventual destination. These sites, by November 1942, deployed a total of twenty-eight 3.7 inch AA guns. Another unit at Tredegar Park, Lord Tredegar' s seat, deployed 42 rocket launchers. All these sites were manned by Army personnel for whom the Home Guard crews were valuable auxiliaries.[11]

Clearly, my father had reckoned that one night in eight at Great Oak, near High Cross, was infinitely preferable to quartermastering for an infantry battalion with its concomitant exposure to the elements on bleak uplands such as Machen Mountain (Mynydd Machen) and the hilly moorlands with which Risca was surrounded. Transferring from the 4th Mons meant a certain loss of status, for he could not take his sergeant's stripes with him and his Record of Service noted that he 'Reverts to ranks at own request' on 8th July, 1943. On 20th July he bade farewell to the 4th Mons and joined the 71st Heavy Anti-Aircraft Battery of the Monmouthshire Home Guard, a formation which divided up its personnel in accordance with the Army's requirements. His new place of duty was reached by leaving the Risca-Newport Road at a point approximately opposite Bethesda Chapel at High Cross and then by making a steep climb to the bridge over the Crumlin-Newport canal. After the bridge had been crossed, it was then just a mile or so along a lane to the Army's hutted encampment where 612 Battery of 181(M) Heavy Anti-Aircraft Regiment, Royal Artillery, was located. The Battery Commander was Major Saywell, Royal Artillery. Eight Home Guard teams were needed to man one of the four 3.7 inch guns in accordance with the one night in eight roster and Dad's gun team comprised, mostly, personnel from Risca.[12] This team, which was usually on duty on a Tuesday night, was made up as follows:

Jack Beavis, Tyr y Cwm Farm, Danygraig, Risca
Emrys Morgan, Pontymister Foundry
Joe Benning, Manager, Woodley's Butcher's shop, Risca
Ken Miles, Southwood Jones' Brickworks, Risca
Roy Miles, Ken's brother, also from Southwood Jones'
Frank Burston, a Newport coalmerchant
Bert Jones, Station Road, Pontymister
Percy Chivers, Pontymister, Risca Colliery Clerk

It was good to visit Risca and to be able to talk to two survivors of this team, Jack Beavis and Bernard Mitchem, the latter reeling off the names from memory. When I asked Bernard to describe my father's job in that crew, his reply was, 'Well, he was in charge of us!' This confused me because Dad had relinquished his stripes. However, my second request to the Ministry of Defence for information about his Home Guard career produced a photocopy of his Record of Service with a valuable annotation: 'L/Cpl- 28.1.44'. It took him six months to attain the eminence of Lance Corporal and so his position, sitting on a special seat on the side of the 3.7 inch gun and operating two dials, was one of some responsibility. Part of my Risca visit was spent chatting with Jack Beavis' wife, who, interestingly, recalled that her husband's duty at Great Oak was on a Tuesday night because that was the night when another lady stayed to keep her company. Jack Beavis remembered that the Army sent a vehicle to pick him up from the Risca station bus stop, which was, and still is, just a few yards along the road on the Newport side of Moriah Chapel. In all probability this vehicle collected the entire Risca crew for that night's duty.[13]

The transfer of Home Guard personnel from the General Service, or infantry battalions, to the anti-aircraft units where they were badly needed, had a slightly sinister connotation. For so long as the Germans mounted bombing raids on these islands, the Home Guard's hastily trained volunteers were thrust into the harsh reality of a front line that could be attacked at any time. Throughout the war, until the D-Day landings of June 1944 gave the Luftwaffe something else to worry about, South Wales suffered from aerial bombardment, with Monmouthshire receiving 825 high explosive bombs. A further 111 bombs dropped on the county but failed to explode. According to statistics supplied to the *Argus* (20th June, 1945) by the county's police force, there were also 17 incidents caused by parachute mines and 149 by anti-aircraft shells, both exploded and unexploded, not to mention incendiary bombs, ground barrage balloons, crashed aircraft etc.

Many of these statistics can be elaborated by reference to the Home Office's analysis of damage caused to key points, available for all to see at The National Archives at Kew. However, mention of Risca's Superintendent Spendlove in the Army's South Wales War Diary inevitably attracted my attention. On 16th August, 1940 our police chief reported that 10 high explosive bombs had fallen on Goldcliffe, to the south-east of Newport, destroying a shed at Great Newra Farm and killing a number of farm animals. The war came to the Western Valleys on 31st August when the Army reported that two high explosive bombs fell at Nine Mile Point colliery, one of which failed to detonate. On the night of 1st/2nd September, 1940, high explosive bombs fell on Twynbarlym mountain and at a point one mile north of Risca. The War Diary stated that there were no reports of damage or casualties. Two weeks later, on 14th September, incendiary bombs were dropped near Crosskeys and on Twynbarlym, again, when the Army cryptically noted that there were, 'fires on mountainside - quickly under control'.[14] Local gossip would occasionally allude to there having been a land-mine on the Darren, a region on Twynbarlym's shoulder and indeed, one of these incidents might just have been the occasion when, together with my parents, I cowered in our tiny larder, conveniently situated under the stairs at 10 Brookland Road and listened to some horrendous explosions.

As I have said, my father's transfer to the Great Oak gunsite at High Cross took place on 24th July, 1943, a move which, as far as my mother and I were concerned, had no sinister implications. Had the wartime censorship allowed us to learn about the bombing of an AA gunsite at Pye Corner, Nash, near Newport, on the night of 17th/18th May, we might not have viewed the transfer so equably. Two Army personnel at Pye Corner, Gunners Pace and Willis, were killed and four more wounded. The exposed nature of the guncrews' duties is clear from the parent unit's war diary for the night of 17th May:

0237 Raid Alarm. Approximately 30 enemy aircraft in the vicinity of which 50% passed over this GDA (gun defended area). The attack appeared to be directed at the Cardiff GDA, HAA gunsites, Newport 1 (Lodge Farm); 2 (Christchurch); 3 (Pye Corner); 4 (Nash); 5 (New House); 6 (Pennsylvania); 7 (Great Oak); Caerwent 3 & 4 and 'Z' (Rocket) AA site Newport 71 (i.e. Tredegar Park) engaged with a total of 402 rounds…Category 1 success (aircraft destroyed) awarded to Newport 71 and Category 3 success (aircraft damaged) to Newport 7. A bomb dropped on site Newport 3 (Pye Corner) at 0305 hours resulting in casualties to personnel of 432 Battery. Two gunners killed 4 wounded and extensive damage GL transmitter which was replaced within 24 hours. Stand down ordered at 0355 hours.[15]

Newport 7 was of course the Great Oak gunsite and Bernard Mitchem's claim that, 'We got one', or words to that effect in my conversation with him during my Risca visit was perfectly justified in the light of the above diary entry. The South Wales newspapers, without mentioning Pye Corner, also claimed the aircraft for the gunners and identified it as a Junkers 88. However, German historians have helpfully pointed out that, on that raid, a Junkers 88 was shot down by the RAF.[16] I have no idea whether the news of the Pye Corner mayhem reached my father before his transfer to Great Oak. Perhaps the episode was discussed on a Home Guard gossip network but nothing reached us at home. It was probably just as well. My father would give us brief bulletins of his nights at Great Oak. He might report that there had been some excitement and that they had been alerted and perhaps even that the Risca crew had actually fired shots in anger, although I only have vague recollections of these conversations. Seemingly, no helpful duty rosters have survived and one has to make tentative deductions from either the Home Office's notes of bomb damage or, more fruitfully, from the Army's terse War Diaries. What is clear is that my father slogged on at Great Oak, performing his one night of duty in eight, until the Home Guard contingents were stood down on 31st December, 1944.[17] What is clear is that the Germans did not abandon their raids, although after D-Day there was a definite lack of intensity until their launch of the brilliantly innovative Vengeance Weapons, the V-1 and the V-2. The Luftwaffe continued to mount raids throughout 1943, and the Home Office noted that two uneventful sorties were flown over South Wales on the night of 22nd July, a Thursday, and that on the night of Friday 30th July, 1943, 'a single machine crossed the Cornish coast and reconnoitred the Cardiff and Avonmouth areas without incident…'[18] It is probably safe to assume that the Great Oak gunsite stood-to on both occasions, whether Private Chivers, as he still was, would have been involved is problematic. Mrs Jack Beavis was confident that her husband's duty night was on a Tuesday and so perhaps I was on safer historical ground in assuming that my father was certainly sitting on his small seat attached to the side of the 3.7 inch AA gun during the night of Tuesday 17th August, when some 44 hostile aircraft were plotted over north-east and eastern districts of England, dropping bombs on Yorkshire, Lincolnshire, Norfolk, Suffolk, Essex, Kent and Sussex. 'From reports received damage and casualties appear to have been very slight', noted the Home Office. Another Tuesday night's modest excitement for Great Oak occurred on 31st August when three aircraft crossed the east coast of England, while on the night of Tuesday 7th September, two aircraft flew over Essex. Further Tuesday night raids occurred on 21st September (16 aircraft) and on 2nd November, when nine aircraft entered United Kingdom airspace, but stayed away from South Wales.[19]

The following year, 1944, saw the Home Guard's demise when, after the Allies' invasion of Europe, the need for such a force became superfluous. However, in the months preceding D-Day, the Luftwaffe continued to mount raids, mostly on London and eastern England, with approximately 30 aircraft, 'part of a much larger force', as a War Diary put it, attacking South West England and South Wales on the night of Monday 27th March. Meticulous military diarists noted that 1,220 rounds of 3.7 inch and other calibre AA ammunition were expended between 2320 hours on Monday and 0045 on Tuesday by the 'Cardiff, Newport and Swansea GDAs', while the Army's chroniclers whose parent units had a specific interest in the Newport AA batteries, carefully pointed out that as part of the overall effort, these guns discharged 319 rounds of 3.7 inch ammunition, as well as other calibres, in the same time.[20] This would have included the Great Oak gunners, but if the Risca team was exclusively dedicated to the Tuesday roster, then they would have collected a kind of frenetic backwash from the previous night's action and would have been placed at a high state of alert in case the Luftwaffe gave a repeat performance. Another Monday incursion, on 15th May, saw the guns at the Newport 4 site (Nash) in action, with the other weapons, encircling the town, being out of range. In all probability, the Home Guards on the Tuesday roster at the Great Oak site would, once again, have been made aware of what had occurred during the previous night.[21]

It has been noted that on 20th June, 1944, 14 days after the Allies' commenced their invasion of the European mainland, the Army unit at Great Oak, 181 (M) HAA Regiment, lowered its state of readiness, a decision which would certainly have influenced the duties of the unit's Home Guard personnel. Professor Mackenzie, in his work, *The Home Guard*, sheds light on the Government's approach to the citizen army at the time. The Secretary of State for War, Grigg, broadcast to the nation on 6th September, stating that Home Guard operational duties were being suspended and that from then on, all parades were to be voluntary. A decision about a final disbandment was delayed, but my father's Record of Service has a bold franking: '31 Dec 1945 DISBANDMENT of the HOME GUARD'. Clearly, caution had been the watchword at those levels of the country's administrative machine where it was everyone's duty to be prepared, even during the seven months which had elapsed since European hostilities ended on 8th May, 1945. As for the military at the Great Oak gunsite, their formation received instructions to disband on 20th November, 1944, an order which makes it clear that my father's gun team, as well as the other Home Guard teams, were no longer needed.[22]

Possibly the 4th Mons Battalion Headquarters personnel at the Crosskeys Drill Hall after Lt Col W.T. Harris MC assumed command in March 1943. Harris sits in the front row, with the walking stick. Those flanking him may be his four company commanders, all displaying World War I medal ribbons. Next to the man on the motor bike, on his left is a bespectacled Pontymister grocer, Albert Matthews (who must not be confused with another Pontymister grocer, W.D. (Wilf) Matthews, my father's platoon commander). The third figure from the left, in the same row, is Frank Ivins, whose greengrocer's shop was in Cromwell Road. He was made MBE for his services which included much use of his Riley motor car on Home Guard business. His World War I medal ribbons can be easily seen.   *Robin Williams*

The cartoonist, J.C. Walker, has inserted a character representing himself in the bottom right-hand corner of this wonderful sketch of the 4th Mons hierarchy in 1944. *Seated, left to right:* Major Vincent, Major Bird, Lt Col W.T. Harris MC (CO 4th Mons), Captain Walkley. The figures on the table are, *left to right*, Captain Windsor Stark, Captain E.C.L. Harris (CO's brother), Captain Nathan Rocyn-Jones (Battalion Medical Officer), Major Saunders (regular army on secondment).
                                                                      Robin Williams

In the years when our Country

was in mortal danger

ERNEST PERCY CHIVERS

who served 1. June 40 - 31.Decr.44

gave generously of his time and

powers to make himself ready

for her defence by force of arms

and with his life if need be.

George R.I.

THE HOME GUARD

This certificate was presented to all who had served in the Home Guard.

By far the most evocative piece of evidence about my father's Home Guard career is a certificate, signed by the Monarch and issued to all Home Guard personnel. It reads impressively, as follows:

In the years when our country was in mortal danger Ernest Percy Chivers who served 1 June 40-31 Decr. 44 gave generously of his time and powers to make himself ready for Her defence by force of arms and with his life if need be.

George R.I.

On 10th September, 1947, the War Office issued my father with the ribbon to the newly-instituted Defence Medal but despite being entitled to do so, he never took the trouble to apply for the gong itself. He might, perhaps, have pondered the relevance of an official description of the ribbon's colours:

Flame coloured with green edges, symbolical of the enemy attacks on our green land. The black-out is commemorated by two thin black stripes down the centre of the green ones.[23]

My attempt to review my father's Home Guard career, using sketchy documentation, some communication with a few of his fellow volunteers and the perusal of ancient files in the National Archives, has hardly been an epic task but it has nevertheless shed some light on the subject's approach and attitude. His brothers, Tom and Bill, had seen service, on the European mainland, during World War I and their health was damaged. Bill was seriously wounded and Tom suffered from gas inhalation. Combined with the slaughter on the Western Front, this family link had left my father with an acute suspicion of the military establishment. A second European conflict and the threat of a German invasion in 1940 had brought about his enlistment in a volunteer force which, soon after men joined, provided arm bands as their only item of uniform. Perhaps it was this initial lack of uniform, perhaps it was the relatively innocuous term, Local Defence Volunteers, that encouraged a stalwart Labour voter to become a part of the state's armed forces which, in the Army's case, had played an identifiable part in the strikes of 1911, 1921 and 1926. For a former miner, who had experienced the area's industrial turbulence of the 1920s and 1930s, cosying up to the police may have been another issue of conscience, modified, of course, by the acute danger posed in 1940 by the authoritarian and repressive powers, Germany and Italy.

His skill with the English language, his facility for communication, both written and oral, but particularly the former, were a part of the leadership characteristics which brought him two promotions. There was mild pressure from his superiors to take a commission, but this had no effect. Perhaps he attended the final parade of Home Guard units at Newport Athletic Ground, on 3rd December, 1944.[24] The 4th Mons, Risca's Home Guard battalion, were there, as were members of the 71st Heavy Anti-Aircraft Battery, the Monmouthshire Home Guard, the parent unit of the Great Oak volunteers.The apparent finality of those ceremonies might have appealed.

In sum, my father's wartime service was his contribution to the community in a way that was broadly comparable with his duties at Moriah Sunday School in 1936, but without the spiritual overtones implied by chapel attendance. It had been an interesting time.

Chapter Six

Training Officer - A Step Up

Dad's transfer from Risca colliery to Nine Mile Point, where he was to be the 'Training and Welfare Officer', almost coincided with the end of the war in Europe. His final entry in Risca colliery's 'All Insurances Register' was on 28th April, 1945 and the war ended on 8th May. The famous 1945 General Election was to produce a Labour Government and the industry which had provided him with an exceedingly modest, dangerous and uncertain livelihood since he left Pontwaun Intermediate School in 1916, was to be be nationalised. His work in the Risca Office had clearly made a good impression and the Chief Clerk, Walter Lewis, had in all probability, given him a good recommendation when the search for a training officer was initiated. With an extensive knowledge of underground working and a facility for passing on written and oral information, training new entrants to the industry was a task for which he was well-suited.

His welcome at Nine Mile Point was unlikely to have had the same flavour as that accorded to an acquaintance, later to become a friend, Dick Burnett, who, two years earlier, at the age of 20 had also transferred from Risca to The Point. At an initial interview, the manager, Mr Albert Morgan, referred to, behind his back as Albie, asked his new measuring clerk, 'Do you still go to Sunday School?' Dick was able to answer in the affirmative and cited his attendance at the Primitive Methodist Chapel, next to Risca's Public Hall. He knew that his manager had close associations with Risca and that he was a regular worshipper at Moriah. Dick's interrogation was the 1940s equivalent of today's personality tests and certainly sheds light on the mores of those far-off days when chapel attendance was perceived as a strong indication of probity. My father would have had his own views, of course, about the religious observances of mine managers and of how such devotions might have contrasted sharply with the exigencies of the Ocean Coal Company.

Dick Burnett was a junior member of The Point's office hierarchy who frequently cycled with my father from Risca to the colliery. At the end of his day's work, Dad was ready to tell my mother and me about his new colleagues, as indeed he had been, some five years earlier, at Risca. My father's first year at Nine Mile Point was served mostly during Albie Morgan's period as Manager, although there was a brief interlude between his departure, when David Jones managed the colliery, and the arrival of Orion Powell from Treorchy, the last-named being mentioned in the minutes of the colliery's National Union of Mineworkers (NUM) Lodge Committee for the first time on 2nd September 1946.[1] The colliery's under-managers were Messrs Millard and Hopkins, while the colliery's Chief Clerk was Gilbert Jones. The *eminence grise* of the office staff was another Jones, Bill, nicknamed 'Timee' and whose powerful position as the official in charge of measuring the men's underground work stints attracted respect and fear in equal proportions. My father always described him as a 'company man', through and through, who had been at The Point since the shaft was sunk in 1904 and who, when my father arrived, was 63 years old and relieved that Dick Burnett, his subordinate measuring clerk, could perform much of the required leg-work underground. Timee's knowledge of Welsh rugby lore was almost encyclopaedic and he gave quiet amusement with his announcement that whenever he passed through Cardiff Arms Park's Gwyn Nicholls Memorial gate, he would doff his hat 'to a bloody footballer!'

In compiling this memoir, I was very lucky when I was put in touch with two veterans who were Bevin Boys at The Point and whose period of service, in lieu of military service, overlapped my father's time at the colliery.[2] One of these, Eric Gill, lodged with the Harris family at 10 Firbank Terrace, Cwmfelin, and worked with twin brothers, David and John Jones, known locally as Dal and John Twinnie. One of Mr Gill's memories concerns a visit he was required to make to the Colliery Manager's office, where the first words which that august person addressed to him were, 'Don't you take your hat off when you walk into a room?' Gill writes that he never wore a hat but on that occasion he was wearing his miner's helmet! Although Mr Gill is unable to put a date to this socially-charged incident and cannot remember the Manager's name, the event is redolent, surely, of the old days in the industry. My own hunch, necessarily based on limited research, is that the Manager was Albie Morgan, who had some years before, interrogated Dick Burnett about his religious observances.

My other Bevin Boy contact, Pat Regan, known, during his time at The Point as Danny, offered similar anecdotes. He recalls that between 20th December, 1944, when he commenced work and 17th February, 1948, when he was 'demobbed' and returned to a non-mining career, a nightwatchman stood at the top of the pit, 'to see if we had any chopsticks (i.e. firewood) in our socks to take back to lodgings…If caught you are fined five shillings'. His next story sounds as though it involved 'Timee' Jones, but no matter if it was another Jones:

> We had all been home for VE Day and stayed over the holiday so up the dreaded stairs where Mr Jones sat looking at us over his glasses. So first boy up 'Why were you absent?'
> Answered [sic] 'Recuperating from VE Day' which Mr Jones wrote on the chit, the next one, same again. There were 10 of us in line, answer unprintable.

The people holding senior positions in the colliery's hierarchy appropriately directed, channelled and recorded the productive efforts of a workforce which, in 1946, totalled 1,320 personnel. It was a significant year in which the Labour Government, elected in 1945 with a colossal Parliamentary majority, prepared its plans for the long-awaited nationalisation of Britain's coal mines. In 1937, the South Wales coalfield's 135,901 workers had produced 37,773,000 tons of coal. By 1946 the workforce had shrunk to 107,624 personnel who produced, during that year, 20,950,000 tons of coal. The *Colliery Guardian* pointed out, on 3rd January, 1947, that 'South Wales, more than any other coalfield, has been hard hit by chest diseases among miners, caused by dust. This has meant the withdrawal of thousands of men from the mines'. Harold Finch, the compensation secretary to the NUM in South Wales, was more specific when telling a union conference in the same year that, 'more than 7,500 miners in South Wales had been certified suffering from pneumoconiosis in the past two years, 2,400 certified as suffering from other industrial diseases in 1946 and approximately the same number in 1945, a total of 12,000 miners'. Hernia and dermatitis also took a severe toll. Finch, who succeeded Charles Edwards as Bedwellty's Member of Parliament in 1951, said that if 'disablement' could be reduced by 25 per cent, output would improve by 400,000 tons a year. A severe labour shortage afflicted the industry.

My father's assignment as Nine Mile Point's Training Officer was the result of new regulations generated during the war years and which emerged as 'The Coal Mines (Training) General Regulations, 1945', which made specific provision for the appointment of colliery Training Officers. The industry was being dragged into the second-half of the 20th century, a process that could only be enhanced, it was thought, by the nationalisation process implemented on Vesting Day, 1st January, 1947, when the South Western Regional Coal Board, a subsidiary of the brand-new National Coal Board (NCB), took over about 138 undertakings covering 277 pits in the Welsh area alone.

One of nationalisation's most eagerly anticipated benefits for the United Kingdom's miner was to have been a five-day working week. Although not intended for such a group, this was a condition of employment of particular significance to the valleys' rugby football enthusiasts. For rugby-playing miners, getting away on a Saturday had been a serious problem for years and now, it seemed, the difficulty had been removed. Rugby football was of course, not an issue in the summer of 1947 when there was a partial suspension of the five-day week agreement in order to allow voluntary Saturday working to boost production. Thereafter, there were fluctuations in the application of the five-day week agreement and much depended on the overall state of worker-management relations. During the winter and spring of 1949-1950, for example, my father was unable to show up on Saturday mornings to watch our school rugby games, a circumstance for which I held the National Coal Board directly responsible!

It is, I think, very worthwhile to recapitulate the events of Vesting Day at Nine Mile Point. The *South Wales Argus* had carefully chosen a reporter whose skills were certainly appropriate. He wrote in the paper's Vesting Day edition:

Grouped around a newly erected platform at Nine Mile Point Colliery, Ynysddu, eight hundred miners watched one of their own leaders, Mr Arthur Davies, Chairman of the local lodge, hoist the Coal Board flag high over the colliery buildings just as dawn broke above the bleak hills. Then followed the unveiling of the plaque by a 73 year-old miner who has spent sixty years underground - Mr John Chivers, of 41 Clyde Street, Pontymister, the oldest worker in the colliery and 14½ year-old Edward Sidney Cocking, of 39 Pentlwyn Street, Cwmfelinfach, the youngest worker. These ceremonies were greeted by cheers from the assembled workers whose lamps flickered pale light on the black slopes of the valley. They had stood in the bitter cold to listen to speeches of encouragement which recalled the struggles of the past. Tribute was paid to the sacrifices and determination of the older men which had brought about the changeover. Bare-headed men stood in silence as miner Gurnos Rowe blew the 'Last Post' to mark the passing of the old regime and 'Reveille' to herald the new age of nationalisation, dreamed of by the men for years and now an established fact. Mr D.R. Davies, Ebbw Vale, Miners' Agent, said the happenings that morning had been attained by the determination, sacrifice and courage which had been exhibited by the colliers. 'It is

Above: The Mine Rescue Team based at Risca colliery and photographed in 1947. *Left to right:* R. Brewer (Crumlin Training Centre); Haydn Davies (Risca Colliery Manager); F. Lippiard; G. Jenkins; E. Tutton (Captain); E. Sheen (Crumlin Training Centre); L. Lee; W. Whitcombe and P. Chivers.   *South Wales Argus*

Right: My father's medal awarded for 10 years' service with the Crumlin Mine Rescue Team.

B. Withers/Galata Print Ltd

by the major powers at Yalta, in the Crimea, in February 1945, saw Poland finish the war as a country within Russia's sphere of influence, making their homeland particularly unattractive to those Polish soldiers who had spent the war on the side of the western allies, fighting against the Fascist powers. The presence of large numbers of Polish ex-servicemen in the United Kingdom coincided with a serious labour shortage in the newly-nationalised mining industry and, by February and March 1947, an exceptionally harsh winter meant that the country's industries and services were desperately in need of coal and in great need of the necessary labour to mine it.

When, in 1947, the National Coal Board persuaded the National Union of Mineworkers to accept Polish workers in the industry, subject to the agreement of the local lodges, the Board achieved a feat that would have eluded the former owners. When the topic was formally broached at a meeting of the Nine Mile Point Lodge of the National Union of Mineworkers on 14th April, 1947, it was minuted as follows:

> *Polish workers in Pits*
> A circular from divisional Hqrs was read intimating that Poles were being trained and asking the attitude of the Lodge to this matter. The conditions of their employment were set out and safeguards given. After giving this matter careful attention, it was decided to adopt a sympathetic attitude regarding the matter...

Not all the NUM lodges were sympathetic and mine managers tended to quibble about balancing the requirement for mandatory recruit training with the urgent need for workers. Approximately five miles to the north of Nine Mile Point, but also in the Sirhowy Valley, a Mine Training Centre had been set up at Oakdale where, by 16th September, 1947, 1,523 Poles had been trained. Of these, 935 had been absorbed into the pits in South Wales, 514 into pits in other divisions, leaving 56 to be placed. Frustratingly, because many important records have been destroyed or lost, it has been impossible to identify how many of these men ended up at Nine Mile Point in my father's care. Jan Rozek, one of the veterans still to be found in the district, maintains that there were 250 Poles and 'European Voluntary Workers' at The Point at this time, though Dick Burnett offers a much more conservative estimate.[5]

Clearly the impact of these 'immigrants' was something with which the local communities in Ynysddu, Cwmfelinfach and Wattsville came to terms. There were no open manifestations of hostility from a Welsh population which, although inward looking and perhaps narrow-minded, was still capable of displaying warmth and hospitality. If a coal mine was hardly a benign location in which to earn a living, it was a great improvement over, say, fighting your way up the muddy slopes of Monte Cassino, being pursued by the German army which occupied your homeland or being forcibly transported from Poland to Germany to work in a factory.

Jan Rozek, who now lives in Pontllanfraith and who prefers to be called John, was in the latter category. His career, up to the time when he arrived at Nine Mile Point, sometime in 1949, inevitably presented a sharp contrast to that of any of his Welsh contemporaries. It was, however, probably somewhat tame when compared with the careers of his fellow Poles and other European

Jan Rozek, formerly a miner at Nine Mile Point, photographed at his Pontllanfraith home in 2003. *Author*

Voluntary Workers (EVWs). John was born in Brosly, Poland on 22nd October, 1923 and had almost reached his 16th birthday when the Germans invaded the country in September 1939. He had planned to study engineering, but the war put paid to that ambition and he was soon involved with the Polish resistance movement. However, the Germans made him work in an an armaments factory. When eventually the Russians began to roll back the Wehrmacht, the factory was evacuated from Poland to the Brunswick Hanover region of Germany and John continued his career as one of Hitler's slave workers. This phase of his life lasted until 2nd March, 1945, when he was freed by the advancing American army, and a new career beckoned. The Americans recruited him as a member of a Polish contingent that was meant to act as some kind of auxiliary military force to support their occupying army. This Polish force was assigned duties in the Nuremburg area where John caught sight of the Allies' 'star' prisoner, Hermann Goering.

At the time, he would have preferred to settle down in the United States, but despite his period of service as one of their auxiliaries, the Americans told him that he would have to wait for five years before he could obtain naturalization. This was disappointing and so John investigated prospects in the United Kingdom. After being screened by British Intelligence he eventually arrived at Bedwas colliery by way of a Scottish hydro-electric project, a mining school in Lincolnshire and two months at the Oakdale Training Centre in Monmouthshire. He lodged for a while at a hostel at Ystrad Mynach and transferred from Bedwas to Nine Mile Point in 1949, where he became one of my father's charges. However, as he pointed out to me in March 2003, he had little need for the ministrations of any Training Officer, because in addition to his time at the Lincolnshire and Oakdale mining schools, he was experienced as an electrician and as a fitter and had a fair knowledge of sundry electrical functions and equipments. More importantly, at this stage in his career, he started at The Point as a fitter, on a salary of £12 per week.

Although my father had little to do with John Rozek, apart from speeding up the arrival of the papers that naturalized him as a British citizen (a process which John recalls with gratitude), the Training Officer needed to cope with the remainder of the colliery's foreign workers who were by no means as easy to place as Rozek. For someone who had spent most of his life in the mining industry, my father could only have had a limited knowledge of foreigners, at first-hand, as it were. His patronage of the Italian proprietors of the valleys' ice-cream parlours probably comprised the sum total of his experience of aliens and so a letter, dated 24th August, 1949, to my father, from the head of the NCB's Manpower and Welfare Department, Mr G.A. Reicher, who had visited the coalfield, sheds an interesting light on Dad's career at this stage:

Dear Mr Chivers,

Many thanks for your letter of 2nd August and for your very interesting note on foreign labour employed at Nine Mile Point Colliery, which I found on my return from annual leave.

I agree with you that it is much better for the men to settle down slowly and naturally and that this process must take its natural course and cannot be hurried. The temperament of all continental workers differs greatly from that of the British workers with whom they have to mix, and in addition prevailing circumstances, conditions of work, the attitude shown by local communities, personal circumstances, etc. greatly influence the men and have a bearing on the rate of progress made. I think therefore that you are quite right in saying that the men appear to need some preparation in order to meet the circumstances of their new environment. Being emotional and temperamental, and having in many cases passed through the most grievous experiences during and after the war, the continental volunteers are often very susceptible and show a tendency to easy exasperation. It follows that they are easily encouraged, but just as easily disheartened. All this calls for careful treatment when dealing with them. Too rigorous treatment tends to remind them of the camp life through which they passed before coming to this country and often causes a stubborn response. On the other hand, most of them appreciate any kindness and friendliness that is shown towards them. During my various visits to the coalfields, the men have at a number of pits of their own accord called my attention to the friendly atmosphere in which they work and have told me how much it means to them. At first the men find it difficult to understand the natural reserve of the British character and they therefore have the feeling that they are outsiders. When, in addition, they encounter difficulties with upgrading at the pits or with housing problems, they get discouraged. The majority appear to have decided to make mining their career for life and it worries them when they find that the chances for promotion are remote. It is therefore most important that the right angle on this problem should be conveyed to them and that the reasons why they cannot be upgraded as quickly as they had hoped if they worked well, should be explained to them in detail.

The men at your colliery to whom I spoke appear fully to understand the position and you will be pleased to know that they have confidence in the colliery manager and in you.

As to the men's ambition to study and obtain firemen's or other certificates, I am of the opinion that they should be encouraged to do so. I agree that a district cannot be placed under the supervision of a man who only recently came to this country, but I feel that some specialised knowledge would not do any harm to their work in the pits and may, in some cases, even increase their value.

Finally, I should like to say that your approach towards the problems connected with the introduction of foreign workmen, their settling in and final absorption, shows very successful results and I feel sure that the Colliery Manager's and your endeavours and interest are not only greatly appreciated by the men, but also contribute to the best use being made of their capabilities.[6]

I was fortunate to have found this document on a file at the National Archives at Kew. Sadly, there was no trace of the letter to which it is a reply. My father had probably expressed himself in terms that were sympathetic to the colliery's immigrant workers, although one wonders if Reicher's point about 'careful treatment' may have been a response to any hint of a 'no nonsense' approach which he detected in Dad's letter.The NCB document gives us a glimpse of the attitudes of the foreign workers as well as that of top-level management and shows that Reicher's visit to the coalfield had left him with a favourable opinion of The Point's Training Officer as well as of its Manager.

A valuable contribution to this memoir comes from one of my former rugby team-mates at Risca RFC, Fred Whitcombe, who had his own views on the Polish and European Voluntary Workers at The Point:

...I came into contact with the European element who came to us during and after the war. My experience with them was an interesting time and I can say straight away they were excellent handling machinery such as coal cutters, borers, infusion, anything of this nature, great, but put them on anything else (with a pick and shovel) and they would lose all interest, you soon learned that you had to accommodate them to get the best (out) of them. Do this and you had a workman equal to anyone. Reading your letter with your enquiries brings to mind the likes of Chas Rykala, Roman Pukuliki, Stefan Kurkitus all friends and up until I left Ystrad Mynach to return to Risca we used very often to pass the time away discussing our days together at NMP.[7]

I should very much like to have produced valid statistics about the numbers of foreign workers at The Point in the early 1950s but the body which inherited NCB and British Coal records is hamstrung by the Data Protection Act. This organisation based at Iron Mountain, Rumer Hill, Cannock, Staffordshire, can only say that, on an unspecified date, there were 37 personnel with Polish or Slav sounding names on the colliery's roll. Mr Colin Williams, a retired miner who was one of my father's trainees in 1956, recalls that at that time there were approximately 20, or perhaps 30, foreign workers of at The Point. The Iron Mountain figures come close to this, although they could have been valid as late as 1964, when the colliery closed.

Managing a colliery was a job which Dad fancied, despite his lack of any formal qualifications and despite his difficult time as a Fireman. All the NCB's managers needed a degree in mining engineering, the 'ME', and they needed to have passed the examination with a First Class result. It was rather bizarre, perhaps, that at about this time, my father applied for a job, or jobs, managing mines in West Africa. He was interviewed, somewhere in Crumlin, as I recall, but was unsuccessful. I suppose that I was too young and certainly too inexperienced to have interrogated him very closely about these aspirations, although I remember that he said that his long experience of coal-mining might carry him through to an appointment.

'Moonlighting' as a football coupon checker for the Western Pools company in Newport was an easier accomplishment. Every Saturday evening in the winter months my father reported to their premises and was paid 17s. 6d. for approximately four hours' work. Sometimes the checkers would be asked to volunteer for overtime, work carrying an additional 'remuneration', the management's word which Dad found amusing and which he enjoyed repeating. Overtime meant missing the last bus from Newport to Risca and therefore he walked the 6½ miles home. The remuneration was inevitably worth a lot more in the late 1940s than today's equivalent would be and my mother carefully hoarded these pay-packets against a requirement to spend money on the family's summer holiday or perhaps an item of capital expenditure such as the promised wrist-watch for my School Certificate performance in 1948 and a portable radio when I achieved a creditable series of passes in the 1950 'A' Level examination. It is certainly worth mentioning that my parents did not open a bank account until very much later, perhaps in the early 1960s, or thereabouts, and that cash savings were kept in the house.

A memoir of this nature must incorporate some notion of its subject's regular salary. Such important information would not have been entrusted to a talkative teenager and so Kew's National Archives, many years later, must be relied upon for detail. A meeting of the NCB's Deputy Labour Directors was told on 21st July, 1947, '...that by far the greatest number of Training Officers enjoyed salaries in the £400-£500 range...many of these officers had perquisites in addition to salaries'. In the vast majority of cases, such perquisites comprised specially discounted household coal. We certainly enjoyed cheap coal, although as I was frequently tasked with carrying a ton of this precious commodity, by wheelbarrow or with buckets, from the street in which it was dumped to our coal shed at the rear, I viewed the benefit with mixed feelings. Compared therefore to the dire poverty which they had experienced during the early years of their marriage and with his meagre underground pay which was only marginally improved when he became a Fireman, my parents were reasonably well-placed.

Such apparent comfort, however, was not entirely satisfactory for my father who was, it is fair to say, always on the *qui vive* for other opportunities. It was one of these ambitious initiatives which placed him, one Saturday afternoon, in the BBC's radio commentary box at Cardiff Arms Park for an audition. He was under the critical supervision of one of the Corporation's star performers, Alun Williams, and given free rein, by his own account, to deliver a recorded commentary, not on air, on part of the Cardiff versus Llanelli game played on the famous turf below. This initiative, sadly, came to nought, but afterwards he was able to drop several BBC names and reported that a contemporary Welsh media heroine, Mair Jones, composer of the famous ballad, 'We'll Keep a Welcome', was rather plain.

Miss Jones' physiognomy was, however, unimportant to us. Of greater significance was the demise, in Aberdare, of a great aunt, my grandfather's sister, Miriam Davies (née Chivers). In 1953 she bequeathed my father a sum slightly in excess of £500 which almost matched the asking price for a brand-new Austin A30 saloon motor car. The salesman employed by the Newport firm of Jones, 'The Austin People', was another of my rugby football associates, William Boyd Avery. It was Boyd, moving at a speed that exceeded his try-saving runs from full-back, who brought the car to the house for us all to have a trial spin. Soon we were a car-owning family, despite the gloomy advice from sundry relatives about the imminent and considerable expense which such ownership could entail.

Of course, our prosperity hinged on my father's continued employment at Nine Mile Point, where, as we shall see, the portents were not uniformly good.

Chapter Seven

Death of a Colliery: Nine Mile Point to 1964

The eight years during which Orion Powell managed Nine Mile Point saw it make rapid technological progress, thanks to an investment programme and an application of managerial toughness which contained a flavour of the pre-nationalisation days. He and my father seem to have hit it off, with Powell, by my father's reckoning at least, appreciating his experience and ability to get on well with most of the workforce. However, the Training Officer had nothing to do with the acquisition of up-to-date equipment; managerial initiatives in pursuit of modern mining machinery and channelled through the Area General Manager can be traced in the minutes of the NCB's South Western Divisional Board's meetings. Take, as an example, the Samson Stripper, a device which, according to *Coal* magazine (June 1948) was, 'the first major step toward the ideals of fully mechanised continuous mining'. This Mavor and Coulson product travelled along the coal face, cutting off a slice of coal which it then loaded on to a conveyor, thereby dispensing with shot drilling, hand-shovelling and the manual effort of splitting up the conveyor and threading it through roof supports into a new position. At a meeting on 19th September, 1950, the South Western Divisional Board approved the purchase of this machine for Nine Mile Point at a cost of £19,815. The same meeting agreed to spend a further £29,000 for the replacement of obsolete plant and equipment of electricity supply transformers and the conversion to a 3,300 volt supply. A Board meeting on 7th November, 1950 decided to add to The Point's Samson Stripper's versatility by authorizing expenditure of £3,849 for its pneumatic stowing equipment.[1] My retrospective interest in this machine centres on the fact that it was operated by my Uncle, David Jones, who, according to a remark of the Manager's, earned 'good money'. Another operative was John Rozek, the Pole, whose assistance with this chapter has been invaluable.

Further examples of expenditures at Nine Mile Point during the Powell regime include, £4,075 for 100 new coal trams; £7,050 for an electric haulage system; £85,470 for a compressor plant and its ancillary electric motors; £11,000 for an 'overland compressed air main between Nine Mile Point and Risca collieries'; £570 for a shed, on the surface, for 10 cycles and 30 motorcycles; £111,645 for the electrification 'and reorganisation of Nine Mile Point'; £123,519 for four electrically driven air compressors to replace the existing steam compressors (this presumably was a sum additional to the £85,470 for flotation and water clarification plant), and £98,032 for the electrification and reorganisation of the Rock Vein pit.

This brief scrutiny of Mr Powell's managerial years would be incomplete without some glimpses of the man's undoubted toughness and his readiness to take on all comers. Take, for example, the case of the workman whose job it was to oversee the pumps in the surface Pump House. One fine August day, in 1949, he left his workplace to inspect the colliery reservoir, some distance away. He was unfortunate to have been discovered by the Manager who sharply

Orion Powell, the Manager of Nine Mile Point colliery, 1946-1954, sketched by the *Coal* magazine artist in 1950.

Author's Collection

reprimanded him for being absent from his place of duty. In vain did the pumpsman protest that an inspection of the reservoir, during his shift, was a part of this duty. The Manager told him, in no uncertain terms, that he had no right at all to leave the Pump House during the shift and as the Lodge Minutes record, 'any contravention of this matter would be dealt with'. Another surface workman, whose job it had been to clean in and around the West Pit winding machinery, was summarily moved, by the Manager, to another job. Mr Powell, when justifying the switch before the Lodge Committee, said that the cleaner was 'very tottery' on his feet and it was his opinion that he was therefore incapable of doing the job.The matter was one of safety. Indeed, he could have given him two weeks notice, 'in which event there was nothing the Federation [sic] could have done about it'. In the margin of the Lodge Minute book, the Secretary wrote, 'The Manager stated he knew who was behind all this, but that he had better be careful not to leave his work (pump) or he would be for it'. This note is a clear allusion to the pumpsman who had attracted managerial ire by inspecting the reservoir and who had, in all probability, chosen to use the cleaner's abrupt transfer to cause the Manager embarrassment.

A more serious disciplinary matter which attracted the attention of the *South Wales Argus* when it came to court, was the case of the sleeping miners. Under a headline, 'Three Colliers Found Asleep Underground', the *Argus*, in its edition of 9th May, 1952, told how in his evidence before Blackwood magistrates, 'Orion Powell, Manager of Nine Mile Point Colliery, said he saw the three men lying down asleep near the coal face. After an under-manager, Idris Robinson, awakened the men with difficulty, they apologised'. The three miners wrote apologetic letters to the Court and were each fined £2 for contravening mining regulations.

In September 1954 eight workmen were caught riding 'on a journey', this being a technical description for a number of coal tubs or trams and a tempting, but illegal, form of underground transport for miners faced with with a long walk to the pit bottom after their shift. The Lodge Minutes which recorded the incident said, 'The men had agreed to pay ten shillings fines this the manager accepted'.

John Rozek, the Pole who shared working the Samson Stripper with my Uncle Dai, also received the weight of Mr Powell's displeasure. Working afternoons, Rozek took a debilitating blow to his ribs from, as he described it to me, an 'iron bar'. This so concerned the ambulanceman on duty that the workman was told to go home. After showering and changing, he called in at the Ex-Serviceman's Club for a reviving drink and proceeded to the Plaza Dance Hall, where he knew he would find his wife, who, importantly, had their house key. On entering he was mildly surprised to meet Orion Powell, who greeted him civilly with a comment to the effect that he, Powell, thought that John was on afternoons. The workman explained the situation to his Manager, who made no further comment. However, when John reported for his afternoon shift on the following day, he discovered that Powell had 'cropped' his pay for missing part of the previous day's work. For an immigrant Pole, who had endured the harsh vicissitudes of wartime life in his occupied homeland and a period as one of Hitler's slave labourers, this new injustice was insupportable and he protested volubly. The 'cropping' decision was reversed in fairly short order. John was not reluctant to cite further instances of other abrasive encounters which he had experienced with officials.

My father played little or no part in these disciplinary processes; they were not his concern. Yet there are pieces of evidence pointing to the fact that Mr Powell seems to have valued his presence when tricky matters were being handled, whether they were disciplinary or not. When, on 6th June, 1952, the Nine Mile Point Lodge Committee discussed the Manager's reception of its deputation to review how he had disciplined a miner found asleep underground, the Lodge minutes noted that Percy Chivers was in the office when the Manager met the deputation. Although the documents describe matters with a very broad brush, it is clear that the offending miner was told he could resume his old job.

Six months earlier, on 13th December, 1951, 'Mr O. Powell and Percy Chivers attended' a Lodge Committee meeting when the Manager asked for sympathetic consideration for the employment of Italian miners, a project which had little or no hope of success. The Manager 'thanked the Lodge Committee for receiving him, he said he was present to try and get the ban lifted on the employment of Italian labour at Nine Mile Point'. Mr Powell said that for nearly six years he had been faced with a manpower problem and that he needed to remedy the situation. He failed to elicit a positive response. There had been rumblings of discontent at The Point about 'foreign labour' since 1948 and in October of that year, the Lodge Committee had resolved to hold a meeting with the Manager to 'discuss the whole question'. A week later, Mr Powell spoke to the Chairman of the Lodge and admitted to an 'oversight' by 'starting a Pole from Pontypridd' without keeping the Chairman in the picture, an indication of the way in which the wind was blowing. When, in 1951 the NCB sought to invite Italian miners to work in the United Kingdom's collieries, it became clear that this initiative would not succeed in its entirety. Not only were they unwelcome at The Point, but many other collieries also refused to accept them.

On 29th December, 1951, the *South Wales Argus* published a letter from 'Arthur Davies, Miner', of 25 Cobden Street, Crosskeys, who may have been the same Davies who was the NUM Lodge Chairman at the time of the Point's nationalisation ceremonies on 1st January, 1947. The letter dealt succinctly with part of the problem. Headed 'Foreign Labour', it said,

> The introduction of Italian miners is used as an alibi by the NCB for their failure to make the coalmines sufficiently attractive to solve the manpower problem. Conditions in our factories and other sources of employment offer far greater social amenities than the mines. Until the remunerations are sufficient to attract outside labour, the manpower problem cannot be solved. The experience with the Polish miners, the majority of whom left the mines as quickly as they came in should prove that foreign labour is not the solution.

Certainly, employment in the mines' Stygian gloom was hardly an attractive prospect, especially when in December 1951 the minimum wage for underground work (excluding the actual coal-hewing) was £7 0s. 6d. per week.

Surface workers earned £6. 1s. 6d. per week.[2] These were the rates to which the letter-writer referred but he made no allusion to old-fashioned xenophobia. Not everyone was enthralled at the prospect of having to come to terms with a group of Italian fellow-workers, while, of course, Mr Davies was accurate in his description of how the Poles had moved on. John Rozek, who was to marry the daughter of J.O. Davies the Point's Lodge Chairman, told me that certainly, many of the Polish miners found much better rates of pay and more attractive prospects generally, in the Midlands. While it has been impossible for me to produce authenticated statistics about foreign workers at The Point, these figures, gleaned from the minutes of a meeting of the NCB's South Western Divisional Board on 13th October, 1955, offer some clues. On 2nd July, 1947, there were 1,138 Poles and 1,320 EVWs working in the mines in the South Western Division. By 2nd July 1955, there were only 732 Poles and 427 EVWs in the same area, and I have 'guestimated' the numbers of foreign workers at The Point in Chapter Six (*see page 121*).

Clearly then my father's workload in respect of foreigners was diminishing towards the end of the period when Orion Powell was The Point's Manager. I recall the occasional Sunday morning at home when there would be a knock at the door and my father would disappear into our front room with a group of foreign miners, there to discuss the finer points of their working days. He was taking Reicher's advice to heart (*see page 120*), by offering modest hospitality and in all probability, good advice about their careers, all in his own time. One of his blue-covered, National Coal Board ledgers, Code 334, contains a page in his clear, copper-plate handwriting, dated from February through to June 1955. Headed 'Training Face' (a location in that part of the colliery called R 8), it shows that on the day shift during each of the five months there were 15, unnamed colliers, or supervising workmen in charge of a group of trainees, also unnamed, whose numbers varied. There were 12 in February, 8 in March, 11 in April and 9 in each of May and June. There is no way of telling whether any of these were foreign workers or if they were locals. In August 1947, *Coal* magazine, the NCB's house journal, described the system devised by the Deputy Director of Training and Education for the South Western Division, Lieutenant Colonel D.G. Richards, which had 'great success. A three weeks cycle consists of one week at a technical institute, another at a surface training gallery and the third underground'. In all probability, this was the system which my father had been following at Nine Mile Point.

For a man with a penchant for Biblical allusions, my father might have relished their application to a series of meetings (mostly of The Point's NUM Lodge Committee), that began as early as 1950, gatherings where he could easily have envisaged a moving finger which wrote, 'God hath numbered thy kingdom and finished it'.[3] It was hardly the business of the Training Officer to attend Lodge meetings, except when the Manager requested his presence or when the meeting was a joint meeting with the colliery's Consultative Committee, to which my father became the Secretary. The Lodge meeting held on 22nd February, 1950, which he did not attend, was to hear a report about the possible closure of the colliery in 1960-1965. Tait, the NCB's Area General Manager, told the Committee that foreign coal producing countries had now entered the market and were giving very keen competition. However, there was plenty of coal to last until 1960 and while the NCB was prepared 'to help you all we can', the Board wanted to see an output per man-shift (OMS) of 21.8 cwts. This type of statistic was a mantra in the industry. When the Powell era began at the colliery in 1946, the OMS had been between 14 and 15 cwts, achieved of course, before the massive investment in new machinery.

From 1950 to 1964, the colliery's history was to be punctuated by sundry predictions of gloom and doom, some related to the entire mining industry and some focused on The Point itself. For example, there was a joint meeting of the Lodge and Consultative Committees on Wednesday 18th February, 1953. Both my father and Orion Powell are shown in the minutes as members of the Consultative Committee and the gathering was told that, 'in the Sirhowy Valley, only Oakdale and Wyllie were paying'. The Point's finances were not healthy.

Only four days later, on 22nd February, 1953, a Sunday, my father filed into a mass meeting of mining personnel in Cardiff's Capitol Cinema, to hear a joint plea by the NCB and the NUM, for an improvement to 'the very serious position prevailing in the coal industry in this country'. By this they meant the United Kingdom as a whole. Perhaps the delegates were dazzled by the platform talent that was on view: Sir Hubert Houldsworth, the NCB Chairman; Mr Ebby Edwards, the NCB's Labour Director and a respected former secretary of the NUM; Sir William Lawther, NUM President and Arthur Homer the Union's General Secretary, who was a Communist.[4] All pleaded with their audience for more coal to be produced. The country needed an extra eight to ten million tons in 1953 and that year's Coronation holiday would cost the NCB 800,000 tons, while, for the first time, miners were to get two weeks annual holiday, an innovation which, combined with the existing six statutory holidays, meant a national loss in output of four to five million tons. The industry's post-World War I difficulty - a loss of foreign markets - was now being rehearsed in the aftermath of World War II, when foreigners were becoming 'more choosy' and when the beginnings of Europe's Common Market, a project called the Schuman Plan, would have an effect on our own economy. The nationwide state of the coal industry formed the principal burden of the speakers' songs, that day, at Cardiff's Capitol cinema, but South Wales was not let off the hook. The audience was told that the region lost 385,000 tons of coal in 1952 due to 'stoppages and restrictions in outputs', and in the same year showed a deficit of £2,000,000.[5]

When my father returned from this unusual Sunday foray to a Cardiff cinema, he spoke briefly to me about the industry's gloomy outlook. From today's perspective, however, Nine Mile Point's investments in new machinery which characterised Orion Powell's period as Manager, showed his determination to modernise his colliery and to improve output. One month before the gathering in the Capitol, the NCB's South Western Division had authorized an outlay of £123,519 so that The Point could have four electrically-driven air compressors to replace those driven by steam. In May 1953, the same body gave approval for the expenditure of £82,478 for the electrification of the East and West pit winders. This impetus continued throughout the year, and in

October, authorization was granted for the expenditure of £141,751 for the installation of a 'fine coal washer'.

Those were items of machinery. What about the man-management aspect of the quest for coal? How did this search impact on human beings? Dick Burnett, the Measuring Clerk and my father's friend and colleague, has kindly provided me with a glimpse of one aspect of the colliers' lives. Describing their work in the colliery's 'Davages' working place, Burnett says that it was the Measuring Clerk's job to write, 'their names and Coal Numbers on the Office Books every week'. He visited, 'their working places underground with the Manager or Under-Manager, booking the payments for any extra work or conditions. These payments were often strongly argued about'. Dick Burnett's letter merits a fuller quotation:

> I remember some of the numbers each collier had to chalk on every tram of coal they filled. These trams were then hauled by horse and haulage to the surface to be weighed and booked to the collier whose number was on the tram. Any tram that was obviously over-weight would be tipped out and any slag found would be deducted and the slag pile put on display outside the Top Office for all to see as humiliation for the offending collier.

Too much must not be made of the issue of the over-weight trams. Evidence is sparse about payment and output at this time. On one face, the Lodge Minutes for 13th April, 1953 record that 'The wage offered for a 6-day week was £16 10s. 0d.' Later in the year, on 22nd June, the Lodge Committee was informed that certain non-face workers would earn £12 3s. 0d. for 6 days worked. *Coal* magazine eagerly printed some statistics about output in all the NCB's Divisions in 1953: those for the South Western Division, which included The Point, were not too encouraging. In June, six months after the appeal in the Cardiff Capitol, the South Western Division's saleable output of coal was 2,394,100 tons, down from the 2,420,400 tons for the same month in 1952. For the four weeks that ended on 1st August, 1953, the Division's output was 1,471,000 tons. The outputs of individual collieries were not included. *Coal* magazine for August 1953 also told of how the United Kingdom was to buy foreign coal, because stocks of large coal 'particularly for domestic purposes were inadequate'.

Orion Powell's period as Manager was coming to a close. The Lodge Committee grumbled about his methods and one veteran miner, Colin Williams, remembers him as 'a hard man'. Perhaps the pressures of 1953, generated by the state of the industry, as described at the February meeting in Cardiff, were hard to handle. While it is difficult to be precise about dates, this may have been the time when I noticed Mr Powell at services in Moriah Chapel.

Late in 1954, the Manager took my father to what was almost a valedictory Lodge Committee meeting on 20th October. The minutes noted their presence with an interesting rubric, which Dad might have resented: 'In addition to the normal membership, those present were Mr O. Powell, Colliery Manager and P. Chivers, Clerk'. The Manager's intention was to describe some of his plans for the colliery, but he prefaced this with a summary of his period of management, so far:

My father's welfare duties included organizing the Nine Mile Point cricket team which won the NCB's No. 5 Area Cup in 1956. *Back row, left to right:* (?) Gregory; Ivor Richards; Phil Webb; my father; Eddy Eldridge; Ray Parfitt; George Cook (Umpire). *Seated:* Breeze Jones; Edwin Morgan; Ray Beacham (Captain); Mervyn Gilchrist; Tommy Purnell. *At the front:* Adrian Crane; Ambery Dew. Beacham was a combative member of the Lodge Committee who was always ready to challenge the NCB's position on the closure of the colliery and contributed to the discussion of this topic with Lord Robens at NCB headquarters in 1964.   *Author's Collection*

My father is on the extreme right of this group in a photograph perhaps taken in the early 1960s at Nine Mile Point or at Risca colliery.   *Mr John of Cwmcarn*

In 1946, the number of men employed 1320.
In 1954, the number of men employed 1100.
One mile of coal faces opened in 1946 and 47 miles of major roads and returns...With more men employed in 1946 the OMS was 14-15 cwts. In 1954 20 cwts with less men employed.

He followed this with some dense detail about how his ambitions would improve output, about joint development of the Five Feet and Meadow Vein seams, about the closing down of a certain district and about the application of mechanisation, all of which would, 'bring the pits up to date and in his opinion, reduce costs'. The anticipated improvement in output would result in larger pay packets for all concerned. The minutes record that the Committee offered the Manager full support and that 'Mr Powell was thanked'. On 28th December, 1954, the Lodge Committee was informed that Mr Powell was leaving to take up a new appointment in the next few days and so the decks were cleared for his successor, Mr Ron Williams, appointed on 5th January, 1955 on a salary of £1,444 per annum, plus 'free coal'. I have very little information about these moves, and I have been unable to detect whether my father enjoyed the rapport with the new man which he had enjoyed with Orion Powell. My former team-mate with Risca RFC, Fred Whitcombe, successively a shotfirer and deputy at Nine Mile Point, has described the new era, as follows:

Then there was Mr Ron Williams who came to N.M.P with the stated opinion of making a name for himself in order to get the job of Area Manager He told us he was here for just a year and was after production - nothing else. This he achieved by coaling on all three shifts...he certainly did achieve his plan and he broke all records and got his job after one year. On the whole he was a man you could take to.

At its meeting on 23rd January, 1956, the Lodge Committee was informed that,

Mr R.Williams, ME, Colliery Manager had had a new appointment and was leaving at the end of the present month and he was wishful [sic] of attending committee to express his appreciation of help given him during his short time as Manager of Nine Mile Point.

Williams duly attended the next Lodge meeting on 30th January and was given the Committee's best wishes. The South Western Division's Board confirmed the appointment of his successor, K.V. Coleman, at its meeting on 20th March, 1956, at a salary of £1,500, plus free coal. The meeting's minutes said that the appointment was to take effect from 1st April, 1956, but it is unclear who ran the colliery during the managerial *interregnum*.

An incident in the West Pit during the week ending Saturday 23rd August, 1958, reflects the troubled nature of Mr Coleman's period as Manager and also gives a glimpse of a working day underground. The Lodge Committee was told that,

...the belts would not go and the Manager came into the face and instructed the men to unload the belt which they did for 80 yards but it still would not go and he asked them to take more off. The men asked what they were going to be paid for this job and were told he would discuss this at the end of the shift and instructed the men to further unload the the the belt which they refused as it was additional work and the men were told the belt had started to move. The Manager then told the men to go out for refusing to carry out his instructions. The Chairman (of the Lodge, Mr J. Woodward) was contacted and they were advised to carry out this instruction.

This brief extract encapsulates some of the colliery's difficulties and illustrates the problems affecting Coleman, some of which may have contributed to bouts of illness that he is reported to have endured. Underlying problems of a more serious nature emerged by the following spring and my father, had he been present at a joint meeting of Lodge members and NCB officials on 20th April, 1959, might have had further recourse to the Book of Daniel. As it was, the moving finger allegory was assuming greater significance. Gittens, the Miners' Agent, told the meeting that the 'overall production factor here is very low, compared to other areas and it must be improved otherwise the losses would increase and will eventually lead to the colliery being closed...' Although Mr Gittens was entrusted to pass on such sinister information, there were others present who had greater clout: Rhys Davies, the Labour Relations Officer for the South Western Division; Mr Tomkins, the General Manager for No. 5 Area; Mr Maddox, the Area Production Manager; Mr E. Jones, the NCB Agent; Mr R. Jones, the Group Accountant and Mr Miller, the Area Wages Officer. Also present were Coleman, the Manager, Idris Robinson, one of his Under-Managers and of course the Lodge Committee.

The Minutes reflect the serious position, not only of Nine Mile Point colliery but also of the industry throughout the United Kingdom. There was a decline in coal sales and although production was increasing, orders were not forthcoming from householders. Oil was in great demand for domestic purposes and the equivalent of 4 million tons of coal was being used every year. Furthermore, oil had only increased in price by $7\frac{1}{2}$ per cent. The country's gas and electricity boards were turning to oil ,while open cast coal was being produced at a cost of 15 shillings per ton. Perhaps the Lodge Committee could detect a bitter note when they were informed that wages costs at the colliery were 15 shillings more, for every ton of coal mined, than the average costs for the area, i.e. No. 5 Area, as a whole. Indeed, the colliery had the Area's highest production costs. The minute taker produced the following crucial summary from the speech of Mr Tomkins, the Area General Manager: 'We need an extra output per manshift ... and the colliery is on the list for closure unless the situation can be resolved'.

What followed was clearly a free and frank exchange of views between managers and the managed. One of the Lodge members, Ray Beacham, engaged in an acerbic exchange with Rhys Davies, the Divisional Board's Labour Relations Officer, which the minutes probably express a little more economically than was actually the case: 'Mr Ray Beacham objected to the statement made by Mr Rhys Davies of the Lodge being organised to do as little as possible and he said so to the Area General Manager'. Clearly, this was an abrasive meeting at which the analysis placed before the Lodge by higher management was difficult for the former to accept.

During the remainder of 1959, Lodge meetings were told that things were pretty serious; that there was a manpower shortage and that an output per manshift of 24 cwts was needed or closure was a distinct possibility. By 4th January, 1960, the Lodge noted that Nine Mile Point's Training Face had been closed down, proof, if any was needed, that recruits for the industry were in short supply.

My father's position must have been perceptibly changed by the closure of the Training Face, although certainly there were duties throughout the colliery which the training regulations still required him to perform. There is a contrast, too, between the managers' attitudes to his role. Orion Powell valued his presence whenever tricky situations and issues were under discussion, but the young and ambitious Ron Williams, aged 29 at the time of his appointment, may have been happier to plough his own furrow. The welfare aspects of my father's work were also significant and the successes of the colliery's cricket XI under his management present an interesting contrast to the miners' apparent failure to perform adequately underground. Before the depressing events of the 1960s, the Nine Mile Point cricket team reached the Area Shield final in 1952, losing to Beynon colliery. *Coal* magazine for November 1952 reported that The Point 'went in first ...and scored 63 for 9 wickets, B. Jones making 35', but their opponents scored 64 in the 17th over of a limited-over contest. Four years later, in 1956, my father was delighted when his team, captained by Ray Beacham, won the Area Shield in a final played at Ystrad Fawr.

The Training Officer's duties required a fair amount of walking along the colliery's underground roadways and by 1960, despite the closure of The Point's Rockvein Pit in that year, there were still fair distances for a 57-year-old to cover during his working day, a period that was mostly, a gentlemanly nine to five arrangement. My father suffered with an arthritic hip, a condition which, by 1963, the doctors had decided to alleviate with surgery and the operation and his lengthy recuperation took him completely 'out of the loop' at Nine Mile Point. This period coincided with the NCB's plans for the colliery's closure when the Board's Chairman, Lord Robens, took a firm grip of the industry, a process that could provide a separate narrative, but which can only be alluded to briefly in this memoir.[6]

Robens, who had served in a Labour Government, was appointed in 1961, by the Conservative Prime Minister, Harold Macmillan and swiftly implemented a series of corrective procedures that he deemed necessary for a healthy coal industry. The mines were overmanned, both underground and on the surface and retained a management structure from the days when coal held a virtual monopoly in the fuel market. Cheap oil, North Sea gas and nuclear power competed with coal and so brought forth a number of combative initiatives from the new Chairman: there was a massive sales campaign to limit the damage inflicted by the new competition and an intensive mechanisation programme which meant job losses. He also initiated an administrative reorganization. During his 10 years as Chairman, productivity increased by more than 50 per cent and as production was concentrated in profitable coalfields, the number of pits dropped from nearly 700 to fewer than 300.[7] As we have seen, profitability was a problem at Nine Mile Point, and the Lodge

Committee had been reminded of the possibility of closure on a number of occasions. The early years of the Robens chairmanship nevertheless saw The Point obtain permission for some capital expenditure, with £33,680 authorized in March 1962 for a new 'panel' in the Lower Blackvein seam and £18,676 granted in February 1963 for washery improvements. The available Divisional Board documents are imprecise about the Area General Manager's request, in September 1962, for the astonishing sum of £1,792,752 for the 'reconstruction' of Nine Mile Point, but there is no evidence that this sum was made available. Nor is there any supportive material showing that a request for the expenditure of £25,000 on a new 'slum' at the foot of a shaft was ever approved. Meanwhile, the moving finger continued its work.

The movement for closure was well under way by 4th January, 1964, when the NCB compiled a brief for the Minister of Power:

> Collieries such as Nine Mile Point, Cambrian, Harry Stoke (and) Rhigos have been the subjects of major capital schemes which have failed…The losses sustained by the South Western Division over recent years have been a considerable burden on the industry…

The coalfield's geological problems were cited, difficulties recently discovered to have become acute at The Point and now used as a part of an argument in which the general sense was to achieve closure. Ten days later, the South Western Divisional Board agreed, 'in principle, that the Nine Mile Point Colliery, in the Number 5 (Rhymney) Area, should be closed in or about April 1964'.

The Board eventually decided that the colliery would close on 25th July and between January and June a seemingly measured dialogue between the NCB and the NUM presented, so far as some of the documents show, a reasonable management and a concerned union. A sharper tone however, can be detected in Harold Finch's *Memoirs of a Bedwellty MP*, where the author tells of how, 'Strenuous endeavours were made by the Nine Mile Point Lodge to prevent the closure. These included a public meeting at Cwmfelinfach at which I was one of the speakers; but the NCB adhered to its decision to close down the pit for economic reasons'. Initially, the Board sought a two-stage closure in 1964 but this was changed to a one-off event for 25th July with another 12 months to be devoted to the salvaging of economically viable material.

On 15th April, the South Western Board and the NUM seem to have engaged in a careful negotiating process, by which the latter put forward a suggestion and the Board courteously rejected it. The NUM's suggestion had been for The Point's Davages 'area' to be reopened, but,

> THE BOARD REAFFIRMED
> the views they had expressed…that as development of this area would be costly, very speculative and could not be justified on any technical grounds, they have no alternative to the closure of the colliery…

Events accelerated during the next few months and the Area General Manager was ordered to press on with negotiations with the union for the redeployment of Nine Mile Point's personnel to neighbouring pits such as Penallta, Bedwas and Risca.

By 27th May, 1964,

The Board decided that the Colliery must close because of the exhaustion of the economically viable coal. The take is limited and heavily faulted and the remaining reserves are in isolated pockets. Due to the mining difficulties, a profit of £32,300 in 1962 was turned into a loss of £305,000 in 1963.

In the month of April 1964, Nine Mile Point suffered a financial loss of £10,400 which equated to a loss of 18.4 shillings per ton of coal. It is unclear whether these facts, in their entirety, were relayed to the union, particularly as the Divisional Board's letter in which they were set out and directed to the NCB's headquarters in London, was endorsed, 'Secret'.[8]

Labour and Management came face to face across a conference table at Hobart House in London, on 3rd June 1964 .This was virtually a final court of appeal when Lord Robens, surrounded by the NCB's experts, listened courteously to a strong team fielded by the Nine Mile Point NUM Lodge Committee, led by its Chairman, Stan Holvey. The die was well and truly cast by this time and, 40 years on, the impression remains that although the NCB was prepared to listen to arguments, the corporate mind was already made up. NUM representatives, there to support the colliery's Lodge Committee, pointed out that at the union's South Wales Area Conference the majority of members were opposed to the colliery's closure; furthermore, the Lodge had agreed to longer stints and productivity had correspondingly boomed from an output per man shift (OMS) of 9 cwts to 23 cwts. However, this had worsened 'due to difficulties on the M.11 and L.18 faces'. When Ray Beacham's turn came to speak, he stressed how many of the valuable social activities of the surrounding villages depended on the Workmen's Hall and the Miners' Welfare Institute. If The Point's labour force was redeployed to other pits, as was planned, Beacham stressed that, 'Some men at the colliery lived in Cwmcarn, Crosskeys, Pontymister and Risca and that these were further from the receiving collieries than was Wattsville'.

As a former member of the Distributive and Allied Workers' union, Robens could probably see where the NUM 'was coming from', although such an idiom would have seemed strange to him. Having listened to other speakers, he said that 'the Board would give full and careful consideration to what had been said and would reach a decision as soon as possible'.[9] However, nothing stood in the way of closure and the available documents, particularly the minutes of the meetings of the South Western Divisional Board, show that despite the Lodge Committee's brave showing at Hobart House, the colliery closed on 25th July.[10]

Despite the long approach to the closure, it still came as a jolt to The Point's 630 workmen, approximately 270 of whom were to go to Penallta colliery, where their former workplace's reputation for abrasiveness preceded them. Fred Whitcombe, by now an Overman, recalls that the Penallta colliery manager, Mr Llewellyn, whom he describes in unflattering language, was determined 'to bring this rabble to heel very quickly - confrontation was in the air…' However, this narrative would stray from its principal purpose if I were to explore the working lives of those who left The Point, not only for Penallta but for Risca, Britannia, and Bargoed collieries in July 1964. Holvey, The Point's

Lodge Chairman, told the NUM Conference that he was more than satisfied with the way the case for keeping the pit open had been presented to the NCB. This slightly ambiguous endorsement, appeared in *Coal News* (July 1964), the revamped successor to the NCB's former house journal, *Coal*.

Amongst those assigned to Risca colliery was The Point's Training and Welfare Officer. My father endured his hip operation in August 1963 and by the time of the Nine Mile Point closure and after a long period of sick-leave he had recovered sufficiently to return to work. Risca was, of course, rich in memories and perhaps it was a suitable place where he could begin to contemplate retirement. Long ago, with his brother Bill, he had walked from Cross Keys station, along Pandy Lane for their colliery shifts. Bill had left mining for a safer and more rewarding Civil Service career. My father had stuck to it, riding out the 1921 and 1926 strikes as a young bachelor with few responsibilities and placing his wage packets on his parents' Bridge Street table. His marriage in 1929 and my birth in 1933 brought weighty commitments at a time when South Wales endured the Depression and work was hard to come by. From 1937 onwards the mining industry seemed to pick up at the prospect of a European war. My father's appointment as a Fireman at Risca colliery coincided with the coalowners' voracious demands for output and in common with many other Deputies in the industry, he had succumbed to intolerable pressures. Staff appointments as a clerk and as a Training Officer restored his confidence and utilised his administrative and man-management skills. At last he had prospered.

The gloomier reminiscences were perhaps a faint memory as in 1964 and 1965 he worked at Risca. County Councillor Keith Griffiths was the Secretary of Risca's NUM Lodge at this time and has kindly assisted with this portion of the memoir. He remembers that my father possessed 'the driest, quickest wit' and that his work encompassed training and welfare, both at Risca and with the final activities at The Point, where salvage work was in progress.

Perhaps my father's duties were not too onerous at this time. He was intrigued to discover amongst the colliery's files some grim details about the Risca explosion of 15th July, 1880, which he copied into a notebook. I have included as an Appendix this small but important historical fragment - a sad catalogue of the fatal injuries sustained by 120 men and boys, with occasional allusions to the identifying garments which they wore. The incorporation of such a document in a work of this nature is meant to underline my father's interest in history and perhaps his need to demonstrate mining's horrifying capacity to destroy communities. Perhaps too, it was a similar instinct that led him to take me, as a child, to the canal side graveyard of the victims of the Blackvein explosion of 1860.[11]

However, in 1965 at Risca colliery, he had clearly resolved to retire. Risca's NUM Lodge, faced with the need to make a farewell presentation, not only to my father, but to 33 other retirees, invited a distinguished ex-miner to perform this duty. They chose Wales's first-ever Secretary of State, James Griffiths MP, who was not only a former miner but an individual with an exemplary trade union and Labour party background. Griffiths had been deeply involved in the General Strike of 1926 and by 1934 was President of the South Wales Miners' Federation. Two years later he was elected as a Labour MP for Llanelli which he represented until 1970. His CV was replete with significant posts in a series of Labour Governments but the evening of Saturday 27th November, 1965 found him in the Crosskeys Miners' Institute on Pandy Lane, a step from the so-called 'Penniless Corner'.[12] Each retiree was presented with a clock. Each clock bore a small brass plaque commemorating the event and the recipient's NUM credentials. In a piquant twist to this final episode of my father's mining days, the Risca Lodge had bought his clock, and those presented to the other retirees, from the local firm of Percy & Wilfred Phillips. These brothers were themselves former miners who by dint of hard work had acquired appropriate qualifications and had been in practice for a number of years as opticians, as jewellers and as watch repairers. My father knew them well and had worked alongside them during their mining days. Perhaps he saw a certain quaintness in receiving a clock supplied by a former mining colleague?

In his speech, the distinguished guest said: 'Risca is one of the communities for which I have a deep regard and I would like to pay tribute to all those men and women who have built this community'.

My father of course, was deeply concerned about another, more rewarding kind of tribute. Before The Point's closure and before the hip operation, the NCB issued him with a statement showing his salary and superannuation contributions. This shows that on 5th April, 1963 his salary was £998 13s. 0d. and in the 12 months up to 30th March of that year, he had paid 4 per cent of this amount in superannuation contributions. I have no further evidence about his pay, but perhaps, by the time of his retirement, it had reached the magical four figures and he became 'a thousand a year man'. A tax return for 1969, the last year of his life, shows that his annual pension from his 'former employer' was £353 and that his Old Age Pension, described by his sister Hattie as, 'The Lloyd George', after its originator, was £234. In his will, published in the *South Wales Argus*, for all to see, he left my mother '£3,079 16s. gross, £3,005 11s. net', a sum that comprised mostly National Savings certificates and Premium Bonds. There was also a modest amount of cash in a recently-opened bank account, my parents' first and one and only bank account, at Barclays Bank, Tredegar Street, Risca.

Perhaps the financial records of the other retirees at the Crosskeys Institute on 27th November, 1965 may have yielded broadly similar statistics bearing evidence of hard work and thrift. Perhaps some owned their own houses. Just after the war, the Oddfellows offered my parents 10 Brookland Road for about £350. However, they were prudently reluctant to take on such a commitment, being apprehensive of the maintenance costs involved. As the house was rather large for their needs and because my father's hip problem had not entirely disappeared after his operation, my parents moved in 1968, to a modern, ground-floor flat at Britannia Close, Pontymister. It was owned by the local council and its occupancy was the result of diligent canvassing of those who held key positions in the organisations controlling such premises. I think that my father was quite proud that his circle of acquaintance included folk who could be approached in this way.

When he retired, the Austin A30 was traded in for a brand-new Austin 1100, a purchase funded by a maturing insurance policy.

At £630, it was my father's most expensive acquisition.

My father, *left*, with Tom Wilcox. Date uncertain.   *Author's Collection*

Chapter Eight

My Father's Friends

A man's circle of friends says much about him. My father's friends all belonged to the same working-class group, although one or two, by diligent work on their shoe-laces, managed to pull themselves up into a higher social stratum. Those who came to the house were specially favoured and could be relied upon not to commit any social gaffes in my mother's presence. There were rare occasions when someone was asked to stay for supper - although this honour was usually conferred upon family members and would mostly occur on Sundays after the evening service at Moriah Chapel. The remains of the Sunday joint would have been available and the vegetables speedily converted to 'bubble and squeak'. As an only child, I found the advent of a visitor slightly awe-inspiring but there were periods when dramatic events from the colliery might have been discussed - a relatively trivial roof-fall perhaps, a damaged conveyor or, more likely, an irascible manager. On these occasions I would offer spasmodic attention, but when people who had been away from Risca during the war, or because of their jobs, offered anecdotes, then naturally my ears flapped. One friend owned a motor-car and therefore had a lot to offer. There was always the chance that he would take us all for a drive.

Really close friends, like Tom Wilcox of Penrhiw, always came to the rear entrance. This was a covered passageway between our house and the Dyers' premises at Number 8 and known to us as 'The Gully'. Its door was noisy and distinctive and not unlike Tom's arrival. He always hummed a tune, a bit like Pooh Bear perhaps, but it was usually an unrecognisable melody which my father believed was used to conceal shyness. Tom's musical enthusiasm mostly found an outlet in the chapel choir, where, together with my father (in his chapel attending days), he sang bass, and his substantial figure, always in the front row, upstairs, to the congregation's right, was as familiar to me as that of the Conductor, Jimmy Westlake. My father and Tom enjoyed long walks together, mostly in the lanes behind Penrhiw and I have no doubt that serious issues, like work or perhaps Tom's income tax return, formed the principal topic of conversation. I was occasionally allowed to be present on these occasions and sometimes I was invited in to the Wilcox's tiny house where I might be given some refreshment by his wife, Gladys. There was a great solidity about Tom, not just because of his physical bulk - although of above-average height for a miner he tended to run to fat - but because of an unwavering straightforwardness and unworldliness, the latter ascribed by family members to his having been over-mothered as a child. This zealous parent could hardly have been faulted when Tom joined a 'stay-down' strike at Risca colliery in 1935. Mrs Wilcox (senior) prepared a daily meal for her son and saw that it was sent down the pit for him. He was a team captain when colliery conveyors came into use and was inordinately proud of this distinction, but his enthusiasm for working at dangerous places 'on the coal', that is, at the actual coal face, resulted in a number of bad accidents, the lot of many workers in that position. His love of gardening and of outdoor pursuits blended nicely with my father's interests, when in 1941 they planted and harvested six rows of potatoes on a local farm, the property of Tom's uncle, old Bill Charles. I remember this episode quite well because I was pressed into service as a potato gatherer. Bill Charles was something of an institution locally and his livestock were seriously superannuated, a position that changed when, soon after, he sold up to a Mr Grisewood, held to be related to a famous BBC broadcaster of the day, Freddie Grisewood. The Grisewood family may have been intrigued by Tom's conversational style, in which the word 'Thunning', which I always assumed was a corruption of the more explosive 'Thundering', was the nearest he ever came to swearing. However, he did use this word quite frequently and when addressing colleagues, friends and family he tended to use 'thee' or 'theece', marking himself out, quite clearly, as someone on whom the rapidly spreading 'BBC English' had no great impact. Tom's niece, Sidonie Herbert, has described him as 'an innocent' who had probably never grown up properly and who gave his spare money to his sister, Mercy, who was more able to take care of it by putting it safely in the Post Office. No-one else in his life, except perhaps my father, who was entrusted with the completion of his income tax return, was able to perform such a function. Tom's initial reaction to the horrendous Aberfan disaster in October 1966 was to throw some shovels into a car and to drive, with his son, Eddy, to the stricken school in order to be a part of the rescue attempts. His death, when he was in his sixties, was a blow to my father.

If Tom Wilcox was a friend who was allowed to visit us via our back gully, then Ivor Beacham was on a more formal footing and always came to the front door. Beacham, one of my father's colleagues at the Risca colliery office, had been born with a severe handicap that had stunted his growth and he was a tiny, fragile figure for whom special blocks were attached to the pedals of his Ford Eight car. During the last years of the war, this vehicle was a relatively recent acquisition and he liked my father to accompany him on special familiarisation trips so that he could gain driving proficiency. My mother and I were always hopeful that Ivor would invite us along for the ride and indeed there were a few journeys to places like the Wye Valley, in a vehicle powered by an engine that was much younger than the car's chassis. A member of Ivor's family was serving at a military base where there were rotating guns powered by Ford Eight engines. An exchange was arranged and a spanking new 'power pack' was installed in Ivor's Ford. The War Office's opinion about this procedure never seemed to have been a problem. The Beachams were a well-known Crosskeys family and Ivor's brother, Arthur, achieved eminence as a scrum half for the town team, though his father felt that this frivolous activity should be subordinated to the more serious business of academic study and advised his son to curtail his rugby career. Mr Beacham's approach proved to have been entirely justified when Arthur became a University professor of Industrial Relations, firstly at Aberystwyth and latterly in the Antipodes. Perhaps a stronger link between Ivor and my father was their shared appreciation of the *New Statesman and Nation*, to which Ivor subscribed and which my father inherited after it had been finished with. As it turned out, I became number three in the line of readership.

I have difficulty in remembering whether I was ever allowed to read letters which my father received from his friend Ray Tucker who, during the war, found himself serving as an army officer in East Africa. Tucker's unpropitious upbringing in that part of Risca that was sometimes called Sponford's, after its Victorian builder, had probably played a small part in his military advancement, but it is more likely that his managerial status in peacetime with Woolworths and Marks & Spencer was much more significant. According to my father, Tucker's childhood had been marred by a an involuntary twitching of the head which encouraged other children, unkindly, as is the way with these things, to call him 'Nodder'. When my father briefed me about Tucker, prior to an elaborate visit (they stayed for a few days) which he and his wife made to our house in Brookland Road, sometime during the late 1940s, he told me about Tucker's encounter with authority at Pontywaun Intermediate School during World War I. A master, 'Tank' Hughes, fumbled in his pocket, produced a coin, and ordered Tucker to go to the newsagent's and buy a copy of *The Times*. Unfortunately, Mr Hughes, who had been brought up in a Welsh-speaking part of the Principality, spoke heavily accented English which was not always easy to grasp. Tucker received the impression that he was required to go to a shop window where a clock was displayed, to check the time. He returned briskly and told 'Tank' that it was ten past three. He was cuffed and the coin was repossessed. Such a tale does little justice to Ray Tucker, who began his commercial career with Woolworths and then transferred to Marks & Spencer, becoming a dynamic store manager with both organisations before World War II intervened. The Army was clearly pleased to commission a man of such wide experience in the business of supplying things and at home we were intrigued to receive his letters and the occasional photograph from his base in East Africa. My father used Tucker's career to discourage me from showing any interest in the world of business. According to one of Tucker's anecdotes, he had once managed a store in Dorchester which was close to the residence of the firm's founder, who, naturally, liked keeping an eye on things in the shop. This led to him dropping in, picking up an item of merchandise and finding some fault with it. Tucker said that it seemed inevitable that the great man's thumb would go straight into an over-ripe piece of fruit, but such embarrassments were insignificant when compared with the 'sales hysteria' that could pervade the entire M&S organisation. My father always trotted out this discouraging phrase, coupled with Tucker's name, whenever I showed any interest in selling as a career.

Careers of any sort had not always been easy to find in the valleys during the bleak inter-war years and the statistics about migrating workers were quite depressing. Amongst those who had sought a job in Canada for example, was one of my father's early boon companions, Bill Everson. Sometime in the 1920s, perhaps during a colliery strike, my father and a group of friends had pitched a tent in the vicinity of Pant yr Eos reservoir and enjoyed life in the open air. A key man in these arrangements was the cook, Bill Everson, who hailed from a point somewhere between Grove Road and Crosskeys, probably the Risca Road. My first awareness of Everson had been wartime letters with a Canadian postmark. Then came the writer himself, on one occasion wearing the uniform of a sergeant in the Royal Winnipeg Rifles, in which formation, we were given to understand, he was a regimental cook. With a neatly trimmed moustache and his sergeant's stripes, not to mention a transatlantic nasal inflection to his voice that matched my embryonic impressions of Hollywood, there is no doubt that he cut a dashing figure. The uniformed visit must have been immediately before, or perhaps just after, D-Day. At the end of the war and fairly soon after Germany's collapse, Bill Everson returned, this time with the spoils of war, a pocketful of watches, all of which were for sale. My mother was not best pleased when my father agreed to part with £6 for a splendid Swiss specimen that was, and still is, waterproof and shockproof, with a luminous face that bore the trademark, 'KM Zentra'. My mother's point was that friendship ought to have produced a more generous deal. After all, £6 was not a trifling sum to us in the post-war period. She was unimpressed by the watch's provenance and its alleged origins as a piece of German military equipment. I retain an impression of Everson's tale of how, during an advance, he had helped himself to the contents of a German watchmaker's shop, simply by sweeping a counter-top's worth of timepieces into his unbuttoned battledress blouse. Somehow, I had always thought that this was the origin of my father's watch, but years later, Bill Everson told me that he had acquired it from one of Germany's many displaced persons. Looking back, I am not entirely clear about the nature of my father's relationship with Everson in those post-war years. Once he came to the house and tried - but failed - to get my father to go out with him, possibly on a pub-crawl, although this was unclear. Then there was the occasion when Everson accosted Dad after the Sunday evening service outside Moriah chapel and asked for a hand-out. There was a swift transfer of funds, possibly a half-crown and the recipient disappeared. Somehow, I think that my mother disapproved of Bill Everson and my subsequent contacts with him were very brief. Once, I recall chatting to him while he was up a ladder, painting a house in Commercial Street and much later (and after my father's death) while he was sitting on the bench which the Council had placed in a shaded position on the main road, just outside Pontywaun School. The watch was resurrected as a topic of conversation and on this occasion its origin was definitely ascribed to one of Germany's many displaced persons, or 'DPs'. That was my last conversation with Bill Everson.

If Everson was a military figure with transatlantic associations, then Reginald Noel Fisher Evans was a powerful personality whose associations with Hollywood and the British film industry brought a distinct whiff of glamour into our part of the Western Valleys. Tucker's life, as I have briefly portrayed it, illustrated a process by which a Risca boy might haul himself up by his bootlaces, but the impressive saga of Noel Evans dazzled us all. Not only had he tugged on his bootlaces with mighty strength, but to mix the metaphor, he had gone into orbit. This is perhaps one way to describe his ascent to a barrister's qualification, his appointment to the Secretaryship of a J. Arthur Rank company, Religious Films, his promotion to the wartime rank of Major in the army and a post-war career which saw his return to the film industry and a career incorporating work as a film producer. Noel's visits to our house in Brookland Road were amongst the most interesting events of my childhood.

Obviously, smooth executive types were thin on the ground in Risca and not even the most thrusting of the area's insurance agents, the most eloquent of our chapels' preachers, nor the most learned of our medical practitioners could approach Noel in the matter of charm and charisma. I was also dazzled by his car, an impressive Ford Pilot, a vehicle that was twice the size of Ivor Beacham's re-engined Ford. He also played the organ at services in Moriah, on the occasions when he could be spared from his civil or military duties in London or in occupied Germany.

Noel was approximately nine years younger than my father and they had shared an upbringing encompassing Bridge Street, Pontywaun School and Moriah Chapel, where Noel held office at roughly the same time as my father. His father Matthew Evans, was an ordinary working man, not unlike my grandfather, Thomas Herbert Chivers. Indeed they both sported a Kitchener-type moustache, Matt Evans's being much the more impressive. Noel's career at Pontywaun was more profitable than my father's and in September 1927 the *South Wales Argus* listed that year's School Certificate results in which Reginald Noel Fisher Evans passed in 'English and Literature; Mathematics including Trigonometry; Book-keeping and Shorthand'. Noel was on the verge of a career which few Risca folk of his background in the 1930s could aspire to. Theresa Thorn, the Gray's Inn librarian, wrote to me as follows:

> Noel Fisher Evans was admitted to Gray's Inn on 22nd January, 1935. His entry in the Register of Admissions describes him as an undergraduate of the University of London and Clerk to the Director of Education for Monmouth and states that he was the second son of Matthew Evans of Risca, Newport. Noel was Called to the Bar in 1939...

The dry, concise language of the archivist seemingly makes no concession to the vast efforts which Noel gave to a rigorous study programme, much of which was carried out in his own time. My father always acknowledged this work and told of his own attendance at the Risca evening classes where Noel taught Economics during his preparation for the Bar.

Noel secured a post where, it seems, a legal qualification was a *sine qua non* and he became an executive or perhaps the company secretary in a relatively new film company that the flour miller, Arthur Rank,[1] had set up in 1933 when it was called the Religious Film Society and which became Religious Films Limited on 8th December, 1938. It was about this time that Noel Evans was recruited by Rank, whose inherited family flour-milling business seemingly gave him ample funds and time to indulge an enthusiasm for spreading the Gospel by the most modern means, the movie camera. Noel's diligent self-improvement, chapel background and urbane personality would have shone forth at interview and impressed the teetotaller Rank, whose Methodist Sunday school teaching in Reigate would not have seemed a million miles away, doctrinally speaking, from Noel's experiences at Moriah.

The war intervened and Rank lost Noel's services to the Army for the duration. During his leaves in Risca we learned how he had been promoted lance corporal after playing a mouth organ to boost morale during a route march. I think that this is something which we would have expected. However, it was my father's positive intervention, from his position of influence in the 4th

Mons (Home Guard) 'B' Company stores, that was to play a significant part in Noel's new career. The time arrived for him to be interviewed as potential officer material. An appropriate wheeze was for his recruit's original battledress to be swapped for a new one from the Home Guard stores. The new uniform, free from the ever-so-slightly used appearance of its predecessor, completed the picture of a potential officer cadet and Noel got through his interviews and training, to be commissioned as a Second Lieutenant in the Royal Army Ordnance Corps on 24th April, 1943.

Just over two years later, Noel was a Major on the legal staff of the Control Commission in the defeated and devastated Germany, where his career was to receive a nasty jolt. It requires a major adjustment to our thinking, in the prosperous Europe of the 21st century, to recall the awfulness that was Germany in 1945. The position of conquerors of a country that was very much down and out was bedevilled by military, economic and geo-political issues which affected soldiers at every level. In essence, the occupying armies were well cared for and, for the most part, well housed and immeasurably better off than a German populace living in extremely difficult conditions and swollen by displaced persons and a demobilising Wehrmacht. The German currency of Hitler's day, the Reichsmark, was virtually worthless and an elaborate, unofficial barter system was in place in which coffee, cigarettes and luxury goods such as cameras and nylon stockings played an important part in a flourishing black market. The British Commander-in-Chief, Field Marshal Montgomery,[2] decreed that his troops were not to exploit this situation and that in particular, there was to be no looting of German goods and property.

It could not have been easy, for a chapel-raised Risca boy, who held senior commissioned rank, to find himself living as a conqueror in the rugged, almost frontier-like conditions of an occupied enemy country. Indeed, it could not have been easy for all those troops, fed-up and far from home, who found themselves, four months after the war had ended, being obliged to administer a defeated enemy country. On the morning of Friday 9th November, 1945, when Elstow's delivery boy pushed our *Daily Express* through the letter-box of 10 Brookland Road, it became clear how difficult life had become for my father's friend, Noel Evans. I was an eager 12-year-old, keen to scan the paper as soon as it had arrived. One headline, that day, took my eye: 'Padre with pistol liquor store raid. 3,900 bottles taken in lorries'.

This turbulent priest, Captain John Birnie Allan, of the Royal Army Chaplains' Department, was accused, at a Court Martial in Munster, Germany, of stealing a quantity of alcohol from a German civilian. An alternative charge to that of theft was one of seizing the drink contrary to good order and military discipline. This Army padre was not alone; there were five other officers arraigned before the court on the same charges, one of whom, sadly and surprisingly, was Noel. On the evening of 18th September, 1945, in an officers' mess at Bunde, the six officers, according to the prosecutor, were discussing an illicit store of liquor which one of them, a Lieutenant Tyrrell, of the Army Catering Corps, had discovered that afternoon. *The Times* (9th November edition) report of the court proceedings said that, 'Between them it was agreed to go and get some'. Indeed *The Times* gave a succinct account:

At 9 o'clock, a three-tonner, another lorry and at least two other cars took the officers to the place which Tyrrell had visited...On the way they told the driver 'Don't be afraid. This is an official raid'. The apparent ring-leader, chiefly because he could speak German, was Captain Allen...At his command, the store was opened and the cases loaded into the lorries. The prosecution said that a witness would say that he thought Captain Allen had a pistol. Captain Allen would say, the prosecution continued, that all he had in his hand was a tyre gauge enclosed in a black leather case, for what purpose it was unknown.

Another of the accused, Captain Catchpole of the Royal West Kents and the holder of the Distinguished Conduct Medal, agreed that he had taken a Sten gun on the raid, but stated that this was to comply with the Army regulation that arms should be carried when one or two vehicles were out. *The Times* of 10th November provided a valuable summary of the proceedings:

> Lieutenant Tyrrell said he told Captain Allen, who acted as interpreter, to inform the German at the wine store that the stuff taken away would be paid for in the normal way. Captain Allen...said there had been a lot of chaff in the Mess about the scarcity of drinks and that he received information purporting to disclose where supplies were available. He agreed to go with Tyrrell expecting perhaps that they would get a couple of dozen bottles. He was angry when he discovered that a lorry and other officers had come along. Tyrrell had assured him they were going to buy supplies and he thought they were entitled to purchase stocks not frozen by the Military Government. He told the German at the wine store: 'There is to be no robbery. British officers do not rob'.

Naturally, this Court Martial was big news in Risca. My 25-year-old cousin, Marian Chivers, later Mrs Stanley Morris, was going about her duties as a teacher in Danygraig Primary School when a colleague, Mrs Lewis Lewis, née Veysey, brought the previously-unnoticed trial to her attention. It was a scenario that Dylan Thomas could have made much of. Moriah Chapel, where Noel Evans' father was a deacon, was agog. In a chapel culture that reviled drink, the business of relieving the Germans of 3,900 bottles of booze was not viewed favourably. I naturally mentioned it to my father, who reacted in a tight-lipped manner. Far away in Germany, however, Field Marshal Montgomery showed no reticence in confirming the Court's findings that Captain Allen should be dismissed the service for conduct prejudicial to good order and discipline; that Lieutenant Tyrrell should be cashiered for stealing, while the three others, including my father's friend, Noel Evans, were given severe reprimands on the charge of seizing and taking the 3,900 bottles. The most junior officer amongst the six accused, Lieutenant William Brown, was found not guilty.[3]

It was everyone's bad luck that in the chaotic military occupation zone, a mere four months after the war against a reviled enemy had ended, stringent orders had made it an offence to behave as these officers had behaved. There seems to have been confusion about whether the authorities had officially 'frozen' the liquor store as the prosecution sought to point out, or whether it was truly 'illicit', as Noel had told the investigators was his belief, prior to the Court Martial. As a 12-year-old, I received very little 'inside' information. I may have heard my father say, much later, that Noel thought that the stuff had been properly paid for or perhaps it was that he had thought that it was 'OK', but no other information came my way.

Despite the blot of the court's 'severe reprimand' and despite the nature of the commodity that had been involved, Rank the teetotaller Methodist seems to have allowed Noel to put all this behind him. So far as we were concerned, he returned to civil life with the Religious Films organisation in London and regularly, each Christmas time, seasonal greetings came our way on specially printed, personalised cards from an up-market address in Belgravia, No. 6 Eaton Gate. Noel called too, whenever he was able, and I cravenly hung around, listening to his tales of sundry film actors, of his trips to the States on ocean liners, of his nodding acquaintance with the rich and powerful and above all, about his boss Mr Rank. I remember once that Sonja Henie, the Scandinavian ice-skating film star, was one of the names 'dropped' at No. 10 Brookland Road. All of this was glorious stuff for a youngster. I wasn't bothered about any old Court Martial. Noel was a heroic figure for me.

His administrative role with Rank seems to have been interchangeable with a job as a film producer, and the journal *Kinematograph Weekly*, in its edition of 2nd August, 1956, carried the following headline: 'Mr Rank is Co-author of this Film'. A review followed:

Mr J. Arthur Rank is the co-author with Mr R.N.F. Evans of the story of *Shield of Faith*, a fifty minute film that was trade shown last week by Religious Films Limited. It is based on the actual air disaster of some years ago when about 80 Welsh Rugby Football enthusiasts were victims of a crash when returning from a rugby international. On to this the screen writer, Mr Lawrence Barrett has grafted a sincere and moving sermon on the power of faith represented by the courage of the village parson, who, although his only son was killed in the crash, thinks only of bringing comfort to his fellow sufferers. Stars of the commercial stage and cinema, Mervyn Johns, Adrienne Corrie and Emrys J Jones carry the main parts with telling conviction...[4]

It was not until I researched this material that Noel's dynamism and eclectic talents were clarified. The film was obviously based on the dreadful episode that had affected Risca so badly in the Spring of 1950. Prominent local people, young and old, died when their Tudor aircraft crashed when attempting to land at Llandow airfield after returning from a rugby international match in Belfast, where Wales won the Triple Crown. Risca was traumatised by a disaster in which 80 people had died, many from the locality and many of them well-known. Our General Practitioner, Doctor Paterson, died in the crash, a severe personal loss, quite obviously, for his patients and for his practice. Noel's film, if the review is to be believed, seems to have struck the appropriate notes, even if the fictional parson was meant to represent the script writer's wish to blend the themes appropriate for a Religious Films product. Unfortunately, there are no copies available for a leisurely contemporary assessment.

Some records show that in 1965 Noel produced at least two more 'religious films', one entitled *Recalled to Life*, which sought to derive spiritual guidance from Sidney Carton's speech in *A Tale of Two Cities* and another entitled *African Stonehenge*. The latter followed winners of the Duke of Edinburgh's Award on a trip to Africa.

Noel went on to become a magistrate and was Chairman of the Westminster Bench. He also became Chairman of the Inner London Branch of the Magistrates Association; Chairman of the Westminster Licensing Committee; Chairman of the Westminster Gaming and Betting Committee; a member of the Committee of Magistrates and a member of the Court of Quarter Sessions of Inner London. Despite these grand appointments, he maintained his links with Risca and would call occasionally on my parents who would diligently pass on appropriate bulletins to me. Sadly, he died on 22nd July, 1983, aged 72. The Gray's Inn journal, *Graya*, published the following obituary:

Reginald Noel Fisher Evans was called to the Bar by Gray's Inn in 1939 and died on 22nd July, 1983, aged 72. He was long a prominent and popular figure in the Inn, although he did not practise. Slender, elegant, well-groomed, soft-spoken, extremely sociable, he played a considerable part in the life of Hall. For many years after his war service in the army he was a regular diner and contributed much by his quiet humour to the conviviality of the table and of the spontaneous entertainments which so often enlivened Hall after dinner. He did not perform himself, but he was a great encourager of the performances of others. He helped much in organising the annual smoking concerts, uproarious set pieces of music, song and party tricks; one of the best services he rendered to these was to bring young Peter Ustinov, master of unforgettable monologues, whose wit shone brightest in such intimate surroundings. One of the foremost assistants of the late Lord Rank and principal director of his Religious Films Limited, he was much in touch with the world of entertainment. Incidentally, his Welsh origins had given him a minute and accurate knowledge of Scriptural citations, which he could place with astonishing precision. In the revival of the Gray's Inn Debating Society after the war, he played a prominent part, particularly in organising the exchange visits of teams of members of Gray's Inn and the King's Inns, Dublin. For many years he was a very active Justice of the Peace for the County of London. He was a most loyal Welshman and loved the border country of Abergavenny, Monmouthshire, the Black Mountains and Brecon and the little inns which gave hospitality there. Hall should remember such men as he and hope that their like will not fail.

That piece of prose must surely be one of the finest testaments about any Risca man and is certainly the only one of its type to have been penned about any of my father's friends.

I never met Ivor Davies, the Best Man at my parents' wedding in 1929 and his name as a witness on their marriage certificate is barely a reinforcement of the brief character sketch which my father gave me. He was a close friend it seems, but was referred to as 'Davies', and described as a good rugby player whose life ended tragically. Like many others, Davies was driven by economic circumstance to migrate to Coventry where chronic asthma induced him to consult a medical 'expert' of dubious qualification. By my father's account, the pain produced by this expert's recommended injections drove Ivor Davies to suicide.

Juggling my assessments of those friends whom I was lucky enough to meet, and in an effort, perhaps, to produce some kind of pecking order, I wonder if mentioning Ivor Roberts at this stage in my essay, is entirely fair. Ivor was Jonah's son and had enjoyed a rugby career not unlike my father's. Together they ran a mile in five minutes, no mean achievement in the 1920s. Ivor's son, Hugh, recalls how, during the lean years of the Depression, our fathers had discussed the possibilities of easing their lot by means of a well-executed bank raid, a fantasy totally alien to their careful chapel upbringing and childhood in Bridge Street. I remember Ivor as a jolly giant who must have been a formidable forward in his days with the Risca and Cross Keys clubs and who, when shewn the silver cup that I had won as a member of the Risca Athletic team in 1952, counselled me against 'pot hunting'.

Other names worthy of mention in this essay belong to some of those who sat alongside my father at Pontywaun School. He was one of the 'School Scholarship Holders', pupils who paid no fees because of their success in an entry examination and some of his contemporaries in that category were well-known to me during my days in Risca: Gwyn Edmunds and Austin Davies were to be my teachers, years later; Raymond Tucker has already featured in this portion of the memoir and Oliver Graham Sutton achieved distinction when he became the Director of the Meteorological Office. One of my father's contemporaries became a Member of Parliament in the Labour interest, for East Dumbartonshire, in 1951.This was Cyril Raymond Bence who was not a scholarship holder, but according to the Pontywaun School records in the Monmouthshire archives at Cwmbran, he was a 'fee paying scholar. Such implied affluence could have had something to do with his attitude to authority and in particular, could have influenced his relations with the Headmaster, The Reverend 'Boss' Williams. My father's yarn about Bence concerned the half-orange which the future MP hurled against the ceiling of a newly-decorated classroom, where it stuck. 'Boss' Williams demanded of the class that the perpetrator should own up. There was no response. Suddenly, Bence said, 'Sir, doesn't it look like a butterfly?' He was given six of the best.

During my schooldays, it seemed that Risca was a place where my father knew almost everyone - or perhaps he knew everyone who mattered - and when my eyesight needed professional attention, I was set before Mr Wilf Phillips, optician, watch repairer and jeweller, at his premises in Tredegar Street. It was mildly surprising to hear my father address the proprietor by his first name and impressive to be told later that he was an ex-miner who, after rigorous home study, was a qualified optician. Together with his brother, Percy Phillips, Wifred had perfected a system by which they could manufacture artificial eyes from plastic and thereby provide what may have been a profitable alternative to the long-established glass eye.

My father's friends provided an interesting kaleidoscope of character and personality, a thesis perhaps which children can substantiate at any time or place. However, like my father, many of these friends bore the marks of the hard times through which they had lived. The life of a working man in Risca during in the first half of the 20th century was no bed of roses.

Postscript

The valley communities' histories in the 20th century have an extra edge when studied against the background of one man's career and lifestyle. Undoubtedly, the wonder of the coal industry's development in the 19th century invites the historian to take a sharper view of its vicissitudes during the 1920s and 1930s. Protracted and gargantuan struggles between the coalowners and the 'Fed' in these years saw the former in the ascendant. My father, together with thousands of his fellow workers in the Welsh coalfield , became a casualty, although of the walking-wounded variety. His bitterness about long periods of unemployment and about the cut in his dole payments was only slightly modified after he was assigned to the colliery office and then to the position of Training and Welfare Officer.

The coal industry's nationalisation in the wake of the Labour party's 1945 electoral triumph brought the coalfields much satisfaction and optimism. However, my father was to be disappointed at the enduring militancy of many NUM lodges. He would shake his head sadly and say something about how they were 'spoiling it'.

His involvement in community activities such as rugby football and more significantly perhaps, with the affairs of Moriah Chapel, were much more than rites of passage. The latter was probably a by-product of Amelia Martha's rigorous yet caring family skills. My father's enthusiasm for rugby football owed much to his father's near-fanatical support for the national team and to his brothers' successes with the Risca club. Many young men enjoyed the sport but fewer enjoyed admission to the townships' prominent teams and even fewer were equipped and motivated to devote time to chapel work. My father's decision to serve with the Local Defence Volunteers, soon to be called the Home Guard, was another type of community service performed under wholly exceptional circumstances - the imminent threat of invasion which, for the 4th Mons alone, was to produce over 1,700 fellow volunteers by December 1940.

His younger sister, Doreen, recalled that as a schoolboy, my father always had his head in a book. He certainly read a lot when I was at home and our middle room at Brookland Road was furnished with a capacious glass-fronted book-case holding the family's collection of books, some of which he would press upon friends who shared his interests. I still have many of these works, of which Orwell's *Road to Wigan Pier* is certainly the most dog-eared and annotated with Dad's neatly pencilled comments endorsing or challenging the writer's opinions.

Nothing could make him forget the serious mistake he made when he left Pontywaun School after a brief, one year sojourn. His only son would not be allowed to make such an error, especially after receiving intensive and protracted paternal coaching for the 1944 'scholarship' examination. Determined and vigorous supervision of my subsequent academic career was to follow, a vigilance which my father relaxed only after that part of my life concluded.

I have cause to be grateful.

Appendix One

Football Miscellany

A list of some of the teams in some of the games that have been mentioned.

Risca Harlequins versus St Julians at the Stores Filed, Risca, 29th January, 1921

Risca: Nicholls, Clarke, Hurford (Capt.), Mitcham, Lewis, Milton, Jones, Chivers, C. Evans, H. Evans, Nelson, Allsop, Brooks, Brimble, Gibbons.

St Julians: Thomas, Osmond, Adams, Woods, Barry, Hill, Taylor, Slade (Capt.), Ward, Harris, Morgan, Davies, Williams, Knight, Powell.

Result: Risca 28, St Julians 6

Risca RFC's Trial Game, 3rd September, 1921

Whites: James, Challenger, Lewis, Hurford,Morgan, Davies, Griffin, Dowling, Ralph, Cooper, Brimble, Allsop, Noble, Chivers, Evans.

Stripes: Harris, Smith, Miles, Gill, Phillips, Lowry, Jenkins, Bunce, Hall, Woods,Brimblee, Nicholls, Jerman, Roberts, Guy, Jones.

Result: Whites 18, Stripes 0.

Bath versus Crosskeys at The Recreation Ground, Bath, 20th October, 1923

Bath: H.J. Commin, W.J. Gibbs, A.E. Anderson, G. Woodward, Dr F.A. Meine and Morley, H. Vowles and T. Lloyd, C. Mannings, W. Sheppard, R.S. Chaddock, L. Bisgrove, Lt T. Rose, L.J. Richardson, C.E. Carruthers.

Cross Keys: Lyons, Benson, Hicks, Burnett, D. Williams, C. Howell, Reeves, Rowe, Steve Morris, W. Hicks, Evans, P. Blakemore, P. Chivers, Millard, Parfitt.

Note: Both teams fielded seven forwards and eight backs, in accordance with Bath's current practice of 'the five-eighth game'. The game ended in a 3-all draw.

The Centenary Game, played at Rugby School, 1st November, 1923, England and Wales versus Scotland and Ireland

England and Wales: Fred Baker (Newport), Rowe Harding (Swansea), H.M. Locke (Birkenhead Park), R.A. Cornish (Cardiff), T. Johnson (Cardiff), W.J.A. Davies (Portsmouth Services, Capt.), C.A. Kershaw (Portsmouth Services), W.W. Wakefield (Leicester and Cambridge University), T. Voyce (Gloucester), G.S. Conway (Rugby), Luddington (Devonport Services), Tom Roberts (Newport), Ambrose Baker (Neath), S. Morris (Cross Keys) and G. Michael (Swansea).

Scotland and Ireland: W.E. Crawford (Lansdowne), G.V. Stephenson (Queen's University, Belfast), D.J. Cussen (Dublin University), A.L. Gracie (Harlequins), H.W. Stevenson (United Services Portsmouth), W.E. Bryce (Selkirk), J.C. Dykes (West of Scotland), J.H. Bannerman (Glasgow High School), J.C.E. Buchanan (Stewartonians), L.M. Stuart (Glasgow High School), D.S. Davies (Hawick), T.R. Lawrie (Melrose, W.P. Cullopy (Bective Rangers), T.A. McClelland (Queen's University, Belfast) and R.Y. Crichton (Dublin University).

Result: England and Wales 21 points, Scotland and Ireland 16 points.

It was this game which inspired my father to write his short story, *The Dress Suit*, which 'starred', suitably disguised with different names, his friends and heroes, Steve Morris and Tom Roberts.

Llanelli versus Cross Keys, at Stradey Park, 4th February, 1924

Llanelli: D.B. Evans, Garfield Phillipps, Albert Jenkins, Mortimer Evans, Cecil Williams, A. John and D.E. John, Bobbie Evans, W. Lewis, Evan Phillips, Cliff Williams, B. Ferris, Wyndham Hopkins, Fred Harries and Arnold Rogers.

Cross Keys: Reg Lyons, T.R. Benson, Ossie Hicks, B. Burnett and D. Williams, H. Rowe, and Fred Reeves, A.H. Evans, W. James, P. Chivers, C. Phillips, A. Blakemore, R. Herrera, W. Millard and W. Hicks.

Result: Llanelli won, 8-nil.

Risca versus Cross Keys, at The Stores Field, Risca, 21st November, 1925

Risca: Attwell, T. Smith, E.J. Pettiford, Ivor Jones, S. Davies, Blackler, Milton, F. Oram, P. Bunce, I. Pask, W. Beavis, P. Chivers, Geo. Lewis, Richards, H. Dallimore.

Cross Keys: H. James, L. Perkins, B. Tovey, G.J. Lewis, A. Martin, H. Bates, T. Pugh, T.A. Green, R. Herrera, W. Williams, J. Hayes, C. Phillips, W. James, E. Davies, W. Hicks.

Result: Risca 13, Cross Keys 3.

Appendix Two

Moriah Chapel Miscellany

The bookplate on the inside cover of my father's Sunday School prize for 1912 listed Moriah's Pastor and the Sunday School officials:

Pastor:	Revd T. Cynon Jones
Superintendent:	Mr William Pritchard
Assistant:	Mr William Jones
Treasurer:	Mr William Budding
Secretary:	Mr Walter Veysey
Regis. Secretary:	Mr Robert Banfield

Extract from the Minute Book of the Moriah Chapel Sisterhood for 16th May, 1927:

Meeting held on May 16th
Mrs Hughes* presiding
Mrs Tom Chivers† took the reading today, Paul's Letter to Philemon...

Extract from the Minute Book of Moriah Sunday School for 2nd February, 1936:

Special Meeting of The Sunday School held February 2nd 1936.
Pastor# in the Chair.
Business: To select a new secretary in the place of Bro E.C. Morgan, who resigned through removing from district.
Bro Walter C. Veysey was elected to that position.
List of officers for 1936, is now as follows

Supt.	Mr Percy Chivers
Assist.	Mr Albert Lewis
Sec	Mr W.C. Veysey
Reg. Sec	Miss Winnie Lloyd§
Treas	Mr Arthur Hodge

* Wife of the Pastor, The Reverend Iorwerth Hughes
† My father's mother, Amelia Martha Chivers (née Tucker).
# The Reverend Iorwerth Hughes
§ My father's first cousin

Appendix Three

The 4th Mons: June 1940 to July 1943

Documentary evidence dealing specifically with what became known as The Risca Battalion is hard to come by. On 18th June, 1940, the *South Wales Argus* reported that the 'Risca Company' of the Local Defence Volunteers had held its first parade and had been addressed by a local notable, Major Claude G. Martyn, whom the paper described as 'the commander of the Risca Group'. If this piece of reportage can be relied on, it seems that some time had elapsed since Eden's broadcast of 14th May, and so the newspaper report may have resulted from the easing of the wartime censorship to permit readers to be informed. Perhaps, too, there had been wrangles behind the scenes about publishing. The Army's Severn Sub-Area War Diary for December 1940, states that the 4th Monmouthshire Battalion of the Home Guard, under the overall command of Lieutenant Colonel D.G.C. Murphy, the Commanding Officer of the Newport-based 5th Battalion of the South Wales Borderers and described as 'OC Troops Newport', had their headquarters in Newport at the Emlyn Works, adjoining Kingsway. This factory, the property of Charles D. Phillips Limited, manufactured tents and tarpaulins. The December 1940 War Diary listed the 4th Mons Commanding Officer as Captain W.C. Phillips, of Palmyra House, Newport. It is highly probable that during these early days, the battalion's job, in conjunction with other formations, was to defend Newport and to keep the local roads clear of the enemy. When the Emergency Committee of the Monmouthshire Territorial Army Association met on 8th January, 1942, its minutes recorded that the 4th Mons Headquarters had been transferred on 5th January from Emlyn Street, Newport, to the Crosskeys Drill Hall, clearly reflecting the reality of the battalion's role in and around Risca, Bedwas, Newbridge, Abercarn and St Mellons. Captain W.C. Phillips was soon to appear in the documents as Lieutenant Colonel Walter C. Phillips, until succeeded in March 1943 by Lieutenant Colonel W.T. Harris, MC. By this time the battalion's hierarchy comprised:

Commanding Officer: Lieutenant Colonel W.T. Harris, MC
OC A Company (Abercarn): Major G. Probert
OC B Company (Risca): Captain A.H. Powell
OC C Company (St Mellons): Major T.R. Hughes
OC D Company (Bedwas): Major Emrys Walters
Quartermaster: Captain H.V. Goldthorp
Medical Officer: Major Nathan Rocyn-Jones.

Appendix Four

The Great Oak (High Cross) AA Gunsite

This gunsite was part of the Army's Anti-Aircraft Command. It housed Number 612 Battery of Number 181 (M) Heavy Anti-Aircraft Regiment. In May 1943, the Battery Commander was Major W.L. Saywell of the Regular Army.

Home Guard personnel on this site performed one night's duty in eight and belonged to Number 71 (Monmouthshire) Home Guard Heavy Anti-Aircraft Battery, commanded by Colonel Thomson, whose responsibilities included Home Guard personnel serving at other Army gunsites.

Appendix Five

Extract from Nine Mile Point's NUM Lodge Notes 26th August, 1957 to 5th May, 1958

The following list is taken from The Point's NUM Lodge Minutes, numbered in the Swansea University Archives as NUM/L157 Vol. 26. The Minute Book is dated 'from 26th August, 1957 - 5th May, 1958'. No precise date is attached to the list, which was meant to be a rota of Lodge Committee members who would attend conferences in this order. I have included it as a valuable nominal roll and historical record.

1. Colwyn Thomas
2. Jim Haynes
3. Ivor Huggins
4. Hadyn [sic] John
5. Bert Williams
6. Cliffe Brooks
7. Chas Wakefield
8. Trevor Williams
9. Arthur Davies
10. Bryn Pritchard
11. Ray Beacham, Vice Chairman
12. Jack Farmer
13. Chris Johnstone
14. Joe Woodward, Chairman
15. George Gregory
16. Ned Hatton
17. Will Paul
18. Cliffe Clarke
19. Gordon Rawlings
20. Ron Donaghue
21. Jonathan Davies

Appendix Six

Risca Colliery Explosion, 15th July, 1880

My father copied these details from a document in the Risca Colliery Office. I have tried to follow his style of copying which I feel sure is a replica of what he read.

Risca Colliery Explosion 15th July 1880 120 men and boys killed

The following are details of bodies brought out after the explosion:

Alf Shore. Body mutilated, legs off and one arm; back of head blown off.
W. Edmunds; two arms blown off.
William Palmer, identified by son-in-law, W. Avery.
Mark Emery, nr Tredegar Arms, Pontymister. Shirt patched with large plaid on sleeves. Under shirt also worn. Both shirts lengthened with another colour. Vest with sleeves patched with brown winsey. Finger hood in packet. Stockings knitted blue worsted grafted with drab colour. Fustian trousers. Wide leather strap, large buckle. Boots, no patches with long laces in one, short in the other. Cravat Black and white plaid. Identified by cravat and shirts. Aug 17 1880.
Daniel Moore, nr Glyn Chapel, Pontymister. Soft cap commonly worn. Red cravat. Fustian trousers. Black cloth vest. Blue stockings, new boots, sock of leather in one. Piece of cloth in the other. Identified by boots and wife (?). Black pieces and strap. Aged 19. Aug 1st 1880.
George Evans, nr Long Bridge Risca. New cord trousers with a key in the pocket. Brown woollen knitted stockings white tops and black stripe gray vest. Boots nearly new. Strap joined near buckle with a wax end. Identified by strap, trousers, boots, key. Aged 55. Brought to bank Aug 7th 1880.
Stephen Bush, nr Long Bridge, Pontymister. Shirt (ordinary), Fustian trousers verge watch no. unknown. Blue worsted stockings white tops. Boots much worn and patched on sides. No strap. Braces cotton, lengthened by string and walking stick no watch 1542 (capped). Identified by watch stockings trousers, beard. Age 64. Brought to bank Aug 7th 1880.
William Bush, nr Long Bridge Risca. Shirt fancy flannel white and black plaid. Trousers striped cloth. Stockings blue worsted white tops. Boots cossacks with buttons up front. Strap with iron buckle. Identified by boots trousers shirt.
Edward Wilcox, commonly Chap from the fair, nr Church, Risca. Shirt (ordinary). Trousers cord patched. Broad buff belt worn by soldiers. Knitted stockings. Boots much worn at toes (cut). Stockings orange colour. Identified by trousers strap stockings and boots. Age 30. July 31st 1880.
Thomas Summerhill. Lodge at Wm Morgan, Moriah, Ponty. Clogs no stockings. Shirt old black and white striped sleeves cut out. Small worsted cord trousers much patched. Oct 9th 1880. Badly decomposed. WH.
George Poole. Lodge Wm Morgan Moriah Pontymister. Cloth trousers, check flannel shirt cotton collar. Feet cut out of stockings. Legs only worn sewn at one end act as socks. Clogs worn.
William Stafford nr Moses Slaughter house, Risca. Shirt with short sleeves. Boots nearly new. Identified by Wm Hayes. Brought to bank Aug 7th 1880. Age 13.
Frederick Ball nr Goods station, Risca. Boots newly tapped, narrow patch around front of one boot. Fustian trousers with duck patches on each knee & bottom. Stockings much

darned feet & legs with blue and white worsted. No strap. Duck braces double buttoned. Ruptured on right side and wears a truss. Identified by truss & boots & features. Also by brother in law J. Davies. Age 36. Aug 7th 1880.

Thomas Wooley nr Miners' Arms Risca. Shirt Welsh flannel with large patch in front of same material. Stockings knitted much darned. Vest blue cloth with patches under arms. Boots new. Trousers fustian patched fustian & Duck piece let in at the Bottom. Tooth out in front upper jaw. Tobacco loose in vest pocket. Identified by boots trousers & strap. Tooth. Aug 20th.

Samuel Tucker nr Riflemans Arms Risca. Welsh flannel shirt plaid much patched short sleeves original colour washed out. Fustian trousers duck patches. Stockings rather light darned a little in feet. Strap no buckle tied with string. Boots old much patched. Bunions very large on each foot.

Edward Edwards nr Riflemans Arms Risca. Shirt plaid, much patched Fustian trousers old and patched Stockings knitted brown, quite new white tops. Boots much worn, one patched on toe the other cracked by heel. Tobacco box of tin. Small strap nearly new. Identified by son Ed Edwards also boots strap & tobacco box 31st Aug 1880 Age 51.

No 109. Clothes blown off except top of trousers & piece of shirt.

William Ashman nr Batemans Shop Risca Shirt fancy check flannel short sleeves. Trousers fustian much patched with fustian on knees. Cloth patch on seat with narrow stripes also calico patch on seat Stockings worsted light blue old & darned. Boots good condition. Strap buckle sewn on with twine.

Henry Baker nr Batemans shop Risca. Shirt ordinary, good condition. Trousers fustian old and patched with fustian. Stockings old and darned in feet. Red Cravat. Boots tip loose. Strap fastening end smaller than Buckle end. Back leather in one piece. Knife in trousers pocket - white handle. Vest, cloth. Identified by knife & trousers. Age 24 Aug 7th 1880.

Jesse Sage nr Batemans shop Risca. Shirts two worn. Under shirt thick spotted flannel. Outer shirt then mixture of cotton and flannel. Cord trousers good condition. Stockings black and white speckled quite new. Boots light, bottoms bad. Strap wide with buckle. Tobacco box iron. Identified by trousers boots strap & tobacco box. Aug 7th.

William Harris, Copper works Risca. Shirt old & patched with linsey. Fustian trousers patched with duck on seat. A plaster on one ankle covered with calico & sown on. Boots light and nailed with a piece cut out of ankle of one to suit the above sore. Strap wide with traps buckle. Identified by boots strap & trousers. Aug 23 1880.

William Lester, Copper works Risca. Shirt grey tuck in one sleeve. Fustian trousers patched in two places on leg with jean…Stockings blue worsted darned in feet. Boots one new tip on toe causing it to appear longer than other. Back leather strap passing through for fastening. Another strap around trousers, one of them wider than the other. Vest, fustian front jean sleeves & back. Vest under of cloth. Knife in trousers pocket likely to be identified by Sergt Williams. Red Cravat. Identified Thurs July 22 by cravat strap, boots & stockings. Shirt vest and knife.

Lewis Price, Darran Lane Risca. Trousers corded. Patched & lengthened with Duck. Shirt striped with collar of Red Merino, sleeves cut off. Boots, light - fronts worn short no toe tips. Strap narrow strap fastenings man & bat on front. Stockings cotton light brown Stripe on top. Broken heels.

George Smith, Darren Lane, Risca. Shirt ordinary, patched on shoulders & elbow. Trousers duck. Covered cloth leather knees & seat. Stockings knitted, magenta with white tops. Boots light, nailed: no tips on toes, tips on heels. Strap about 2 ins in width. Age 24. July 30 1880.

William Mills, Darran Lane Risca. Shirt striped flannel. Old undershirt, new piece of as pad [sic]. Drawers two pair of calico long reaved on bottom. Fustian trousers not patched. Braces, one broken. Lengthened with string. Strap thin narrow has a double-headed snake hook fastening. Stockings worsted, drab, ribbed & darned feet and ankles. Boots not watertight. Good condition. Identified by pieces of shirt, pieces of calico drawers, pieces of trousers & features. Lower part of body blown off.

John Breeze, Canal Row, Abercarn. Shirt fancy plaid flannel with patches of white flannel on shoulders. Stockings dark ribbed darned in feet. Vest blue plaid large pattern. Drawers black & white plaid quite new. Trousers duck patched with same. Boots watertight, tongues cut, being too tight. Cloth cap, patch on top, piece of duck in front used for carrying lamp in naked light mines. Identified by shirt, drawers, trousers & by brother in law. Age 23. Aug 3.

Thomas Waters, Chapel of Ease Abercarn. Shirt front made separate & let in. Shirt red & grey, sleeves grafted with another colour. Trousers light blue cloth, patched with duck on both legs, the bottom of which are not sewn down. Also a piece cut out of the flaps from inside in a circular form from the cloth. Stockings light grey knitted. Darned feet & ankle. Boots, heavy patch on heel not certain for both. Strap joined in middle made of two pieces. Cap ordinary. Aug 24.

Lewis Harris, Spiteful Row Abercarn. Aug 19th age 35.

Thomas Jones, Cross Roads, Abercarn. Had bad knee through injuries received in Abercarn explosion. Wears the top of stocking over the same. Marked heavily with small pox. Aug 21st.

Daniel Lewis, Pontywain. Little finger off right hand. Brought to bank, Thursday July 22 1880.

Llewellyn Lewis, Boy, Pontywain. July 22nd.

John Hicks nr Bridge, Pontywain. One arm. False arm strapped to elbow. Crossplate with hook attached - screwed in. Age 55. July 28th 1880.

Charles Carey, Pontywain, age 23. Aug 1st 1880.

Thomas Lewis, Pontywain, Fireman. Aug 17 1880.

Henry Adams, Pontywain, age 44. Aug 1.

John Daley, nr Bridge, Pontywain. Aug 20th 1880.

Wm Davies, Rees Row, Pontywain. July 24th 1880.

Rees Leyshon, Rees Row, Pontywain, July 22. Age 44.

Charles Mead, Rees Row, Pontywain. Identified by Jas Williams, Aug 30th 1880.

Robert Lugg, Rees Row, Cwmcarn Age 40. Identified by son Aug 31 1880.

David James, nr Eagle, Pontywain. Age 40, July 30 1880.

Thomas Dale, Foresters Row, Pontywain. Silver plate in roof with false teeth (owing to cancer). Makers name on plate. Age 46. Sep 11 1880.

David Brake, Pontywain. Aug 20th 1880.

Simon Gulliver, Crosskeys. Watch value £7-10-0 in brass case. Identified by son. Aug 12th 1880.

Joseph Horler, Crosskeys. Age 32, July 27th 1880.

John Millsom, Buck Farm, Risca. Shirt ordinary, new, tucked sleeves. Trousers black cloth mended in fork. Stockings grey worsted. Boots new, flat nails in bend of foot. Knife likely half pruner. Broad strap and back leather. Age 20. Identified by brother Alfred. Aug 11th 1880 7.30 pm.

Jeremiah Hurley, nr Station, Pontymister. Age 22. Aug 11th 1880.

Henry Harvey, Buck Farm, age 41. Identified by brother James, Aug 13th 1880.

Samuel Williams, Colliers Row, Risca. Identified by brother Aug 27th 1880.

Mark Crook, Colliery Row. Watch with name engraved inside. Identified by brother. A. Crook. Sept 11th 1880.

Lewis Harvey, Buck Farm, Aug 26 1880. Identified by boots & trousers.

Rosser George, Cubola Houses, nr Ventilator. Aug 18 1880.

William Henry Marsh, Old Blackvein Houses. Identified by belt bearing inscription, Gibraltar. Age 19. Aug 8th 1880.

Uriah Edwards, Newtown. Overman. Identified by scribe knife, pocket knife. Age 33. Aug 12th 1880.

A postcard view of Risca colliery.

James Jones, lodger with Taliesin Jenkins, Newtown, age 17. Identified by Taliesin Jenkins, Aug 11th 1880 at 7.45 pm.

William Benny, Newtown. Identified by hairy back. Aug 9th 1880.

Tom Wallace, boy, Newtown.

Thomas Lent, Newtown. Identified by truss, age 36, July 26th 1880.

Isaac Theophilus, no. 63 Newtown. Age 47. Identified by features. Aug 1880.

George Vaughan, Newtown Hotel. Identified by clothes, Sept 28th 1880.

Thomas Griffiths, no. 4 Newtown. Identified by clothes. Aug 12th 1880.

Stephen Powell, 61 Newtown. Oct 11th 1880. Much decomposed. WH.

James Powell, 61 Newtown, age 19, Aug 25th 1880. Identified by boots.

Edward Jay, 52 Newtown. Identified by double truss. Sept 8th 1880.

Thomas Thomas, 15 Newtown. Identified by mother, Aug 7th 1880.

Lewis Leyshon, 17 Newtown, Aug 21st 1880. Identified by clothes.

George Yemm, 21 Newtown. Age 40. Identified by truss July 30th 1880.

Meshac Yemm, 21 Newtown. Identified by clothes.

Alfred Baker, 21 Newtown. Identified by brother Charles Baker Aug 7th 1880.

William West, 43 Newtown. Identified by name on tobacco box & by John Simonds, Aug 11th 1880. Much decomposed.

Philip Jones, 6 Newtown, Aug 10th 1880. Identified by watch No. 90913.

William Sheen, Ynysddu. Found in Sage's Heading Aug 11th 1880. Identified by his brother. Age 45. Much decomposed.

Thomas Edwards, Full Moon. Identified by missing tip of finger & wenn on neck. Aug 17th 1880.

William Palmer, Crosskeys. Identified by shirt, boots, strap & by J.W. Avery.

Samuel Dix, Crosskeys, age 51. Identified by clothes. Aug 11th 1880.

Thomas Dix, Crosskeys. Age 26. Identified by 4 false teeth in front. Aug 7th 1880.

David Lewis, age 31, lodging Thos Kenvin, nr pit. Identified by missing finger. Aug 12th 1880.

Lewis Williams, Full Moon. Aug 8th 1880. Identified by 'tea kettle' on cover of tobacco tin.

Simon Harris. Identified by clothes & boots. July 23rd 1880.

William Francis alias Davies commonly called Mockyn. Identified by clothes. (Telegram Mr John Francis, 11 Glandwr Terrace, Llwynypia, Tonypandy.)

William Hayes. Identified by son, Wm Hayes July 31st 1880. Brought to bank July 30th age 54.

Evan Hayes. Identified by brother Wm Hayes. Age 27 Aug 7th 1880.

Wm Charles age 45. Legs off. To be taken direct to Risca Church for interment. Father dependant. Wm Morgan, Moriah, to act in this case.

John Jones, age 34. Identified by clothes.

Joseph Everett. Identified by Jonah Tovey, Aug 21st.

Winding gear at Cwmcarn colliery. *David Williams*

Acknowledgements

I owe a considerable debt of gratitude to those who have assisted me with this project. I must firstly acknowledge support from my wife Ann, who has always been ready to read preliminary drafts, to offer constructive comments and to proof-read final versions. My son, Paul Chivers, who drew my map and his brother, David Chivers QC, have been similarly involved. The staffs of libraries and archives have always been helpful, particularly Elisabeth Bennett, the Archivist at the University of Wales, Swansea, her deputy, Susan Thomas and the staff of the Miners' Library at Hendrefoelan House. The Gwent County Archivist, David Rimmer and his colleagues Anthony Hopkins and Colin Gibson have frequently taken considerable trouble to find the information which I requested, while the Glamorgan Archivist, Susan Edwards, together with her diligent colleagues, have always provided strong support and co-operation. My visits to the Glamorgan Archives in Cardiff necessitated overnight accommodation and I am deeply grateful to my cousin, Dorothy Kendal who, together with her husband John, always provided generous hospitality. Much praise accrues for the staffs at the British Library, at the Colindale Newspaper Library and at the National Archives at Kew. Publicising my requirements was important and I am grateful to Walter Jones, the Risca correspondent of the *South Wales Argus* for including my appeals in his regular column.

The following is a list of family members and friends who have contributed, and I am very grateful for their unstinting collaboration:

Donald Adams, Arthur Baulch, Mrs Beechey, Ruth Burn, Len Bowden, Mr and Mrs John Beavis, Professor Arthur Beacham, Dick Burnett, George Bridgeman, Christine Brewer, Raymond Chivers, Tom Cowlin, F.W.J. Davies, Coco Edwards, Richard Evans, Mrs Alan Evans, Professor David Egan, Eric Gill, Carol Graves, County Councillor Keith Griffiths, Mrs Green, Isabel Harris, The Reverend John Hayward, Sidonie Herbert, Islwyn Howe, Glyn Hutchings, Mary Leblanc, Bill Macey, Bernard Mitchem, Marian Morris (née Chivers), W. Hugh Phillips, Bronwen Price, Doreen Price (née Chivers), Mary Prosser, Pat Regan, Hugh Roberts, Jan Rozek, John Sims, Dr John Sweetman, Theresa Thom, Ceri Thompson, Glyn Tucker, John Wadge, Ken Wallace-Jones, Hugh Watkins, Fred Whitcombe, Colin Williams, Robin Williams, Ross Williams, Paul and Bente Withers.

Primary Sources

War Office files, labelled 'WO'; National Coal Board Files, labelled 'COAL'; Home Office Files, labelled 'HO' (National Archives, Kew).

South Western Division of the Coal Board Files also labelled 'COAL' (National Archives, Kew).

Minutes of the Monmouthshire Territorial Army Association, labelled D.766 (Gwent Record Office, Cwmbran).

Correspondence of the Oxford House Educational Settlement, Risca, labelled D 2357 (Gwent Record Office, Cwrnbran).

Risca Urban District Council file dealing with the Risca Home Guard, serial 896/C (Gwent Record Office, Cwmbran).

Minutes of Risca Council Meetings (Gwent Record Office, Cwmbran).

Minutes of the Nine Mile Point NUM Lodge Committee, labelled NUM/L/57 (Library, University of Wales, Swansea).

NUM, South Wales Area: Report on Conference of Representatives of Divisional Area and Consultative Committees, February 1953 Serial SWCC, (Library University of Wales, Swansea).

Paybooks and National Insurance Registers for Risca colliery, labelled DNCB (Glamorgan Record Office, Cardiff).

The Minutes of the Sunday School Committee and the Minutes of the Sisterhood: Moriah Baptist Chapel, Risca. (These documents are in the possession of the Pastor, The Reverend John Hayward.)

Register of Electors for the Bedwellty Division of Monmouthshire 1930 and 1932 (Gwent Record Office Cwmbran).

Monmouthshire Marchers' Council Document August 1933 (South Wales Miners' Library, Hendrefoelan House, Swansea.)

The Report of the Royal Commission on Safety in the Coal Mines 1938. Command 5890 (British Library).

4th Monmouthshire Battalion Home Guard: Press Releases. (Documents in the possession of Mr Robin Williams, Crickhowell.)

Bibliography

Books

Harry W. Barstow, *Gladiators of a Roman City, A History of Bath Football Club* (Bath FC and Corsham Publishing Company, 1986).
Brian Collins and Terry Powell, *Old Crumlin to Pontymister* (2 Vols, Stewart Wiiiiams, Barry, 1981 and 1982).
The Concise Dictionary of National Biography (OUP, 1994).
D.E. Davies, *Cardiff Rugby Club 1876-1975* (2nd Ed., Starling Press, Risca, 1976).
David Egan, Coal Society, *A History of the South Wales Mining Valley, 1840-1980* (Gomer Press, 1987).
H.J. Finch, *Thirty Years a Bedwellty MP* (Starling Press, Risca, 1972).
Hywel Francis and Dai Smith, *The Fed: A History of the South Wales Miners in the Twentieth Century* (University of Wales Press, Cardiff, 1998).
L.L. Gordon, *British Battles and Medals* (4th Edition, Spink, 1971).
The Gwent Schools Resource Book, Monmouthshire Record Office, Cwmbran.
Gareth Hughes, *One Hundred Years of Scarlet* (Llanelli RFC, 1983).
A.V. Jones, *Risca: Its Industrial and Economic Development* (New Horizon Books, 1980).
B.P. Jones, *Sowing Beside All Waters* (Gwent Baptist Association, 1985).
Joseph Jones, *The Coal Scuttle* (Faber and Faber, 1936).
Ray Lawrence, *The South Wales Coalfield Directory* (Ray Lawrence, Oakdale, 1998).
S.P. Mackenzie, *The Home Guard* (OUP, 1995).
K.O. Morgan, *Rebirth of a Nation: Wales 1880-1980* (OUP, 1982)
W.H. Morris, *Kidwelly Tinplate Works: A History* (Kidwelly Heritage Trust).
R. Page-Arnot, *The South Wales Miners, 1914-1926* (London 1976).
Alfred Robens (Lord Robens of Woldingham), *Ten Year Stint* (London 1972).
H.J.A. Roberts, *A View From the Hill, A History of Risca and Moriah Baptist Church* (Moriah Baptist Church Risca 1986).
Rothmans Rugby Yearbook, 1982-3.
David Smith and Gareth Williams, *Fields of Praise* (University of Wales Press on behalf the Welsh Rugby Union, 1980).
Jack Strickland, *Risca Rugby, Days of Glory* (Starling Press Risca, 1983).
Who's Who in Wales 1920 (Western Mail, Cardiff, 1921).
Ivor Wilks, *South Wales and the Rising of 1839* (Croom Helm, 1984).

Newspapers and Periodicals

The Times
The South Wales Argus
The South Wales Weekly Argus
The Football Argus
The South Wales News
The Western Mail
The Western Daily Press
The South Wales Echo and Express
The Daily Express
The Daily Worker
The South Wales Miner
Coal
Coal News
The Colliery Guardian
Llafur
The Cinema
Educational Screen
Kinematograph Weekly

References

List of Abbreviations used in References

'A' Branch   Part of a military headquarters dealing with personnel, manpower etc.
CO   Commanding Officer
CG   *Colliery Guardian*
DNCB   National Coal Board Records in the Glamorgan Record Office
FA   *Football Argus*
'Fed'   The South Wales Miners Federation
HQ 4AA   Headquarters, No. 4 Anti-Aircraft Group
HO   Home Office Files at the National Archives
(M) HAA   Medium Heavy Anti-Aircraft Regiment
NUM   National Union of Mineworkers
'Q' Branch   Part of a military headquarters dealing with equipments, clothing, etc.
SWA   *South Wales Argus*
SWN   South Wales News
SWWA   *South Wales Weekly Argus*
WO   War Office files in the National Archives

Chapter One: The Search for Black Gold

1. See Ray Lawrence, *The South Wales Coalfield Directory* (pub. R. Lawrence Oakdale, Blackwood, Gwent, 1998), p.162.
2. Glamorgan Record Office, Cardiff. DNCB 23/227, October 1917-April 1918.
3. See Lawrence, *op. cit.* p.440.
4. See K.O. Morgan, *Wales Rebirth of a Nation* (OUP, University of Wales Press, 1982), pp.181-183.
5. See Hywel Francis and Dai Smith, *The Fed A History of the South Wales Miners in the Twentieth Century*, (University of Wales Press, Cardiff, 1998), Appendix IV.
6. J.M. Roberts (1873-1931).
7. See H.J. Finch, *Memoirs of a Bedwellty MP* (Risca 1972),p.60 *et seq.*
8. See R. Page Arnot, *South Wales Miners 1914-1926*, (London, 1976), Chapter Seven.
9. Correspondence between trade associations and the Newport Board of Guardians at The Gwent Record Office, Cwmbran.
10. Letter to the author from Mrs Mary Prosser (née Harris), 5th June, 2002.
11. See David Egan, Coal Society. *A History of the South Wales Mining Valleys 1840-1980* (Gomer Press, 1987), p.119.
12. SWA 29th May, 1926.
13. The *South Wales Argus* covered proceedings in the Magistrates' Court in its editions of 30th August; 20th September; 21st September; 22nd September and 1st October, on which date the defendants were committed to the Monmouthshire Assizes. The paper reported the Assize case in its editions from 23rd to 29th November. Hywel Francis and Dai Smith (*op. cit.*) offer a more considered evaluation on p.64.
14. SWN 1st February, 1927.
15. The Labour Party had achieved a historic success at the 1923 General Election when it formed a minority government headed by Ramsay MacDonald. The party took 20 seats in Wales, with Edwards re-elected in Bedwellty. This Government endured endemic industrial troubles and fell after an unsuccessful prosecution of the editor of the *Daily Worker*. The Zinoviev letter featured in Labour's defeat in the 1924 election, when the party won 16 Welsh seats. Edwards retained Bedwellty. A second Labour administration formed in 1929 and, overwhelmed by catastrophic economic conditions, was transformed into a National Government headed by MacDonald in 1931. For this, MacDonald was excoriated by the Labour Party.
16. Risca Urban District Council Minutes, 1927, at the Gwent Record Office Cwmbran.
17. SWA 8th March, 1927.
18. SWA 22nd May, 1928. The *South Wales Argus* carried a number of reports about unemployment and short-time working, both at Nine Mile Point and at Risca colliery. On 31st January, 1928, the paper reported a meeting of the 'Fed's' Tredegar Valley District at which the Miners' Agent, George Davies, reported that 'Nine Mile Point, where 2,000 men are employed had been idle

for two weeks during the month. Risca Colliery, where 1,500 men are employed, had also been idle for one week'. Interestingly, Charles Edwards MP and Harold Finch, his eventual successor in the constituency, were both present. Approximately one month later, on 25th February, Davies told a similar meeting that the two collieries 'were working irregularly and had been idle at times for two or three weeks at a stretch on account of depression of trade'. Edwards and Finch also attended the meeting.

19.   Glamorgan Record Office, Cardiff. DNCB 23/297. These papers indicate that at the end of the quarter, i.e. 1st April, 1928, 621 men were employed at the colliery.
20.   SWA 2nd June, 1928: article by Finlay Gibson, Secretary of the Monmouthshire & South Wales Coalowners' Association. Also SWA 21st June, 1928.
21.   SWA 11th September, 1928.

Chapter Two: *That Old Football...*

1.   To call a tiny handbook, published by a medical company, a 'diary' is a slight exaggeration. Amelia Martha used it for sundry jottings, especially recipes. The entry dealing with Partridge may have been made by one of her sons.
2.   See Jack Strickland, *Risca Rugby Days of Glory* (Risca 1983), p.41 and *Who's Who in Wales* 1920. This reference work lists Partridge as a son of the late Jason Partridge of Risca and mentions his service during World War I in the Welch Regiment and in The South Wales Borderers.
3.   See Hughes, *One Hundred Years of Scarlet* (Llanelli, 1983), p.249.
4.   See Strickland, *op. cit.* p.40. The nickname derives from an ancient anecdote of how, once upon a time, Risca folk sought to imprison a cuckoo in a fenced enclosure. The bird simply flew over the fence and was not seen again. Similar stories can be detected in rural communities in other counties and countries.
5.   See David Smith and Gareth Williams, *Fields of Praise* (University of Wales Press, on behalf of the Welsh Rugby Union, 1980), p.259.
6.   See Harry W. Barstow, *Gladiators of a Roman City - A History of Bath Football Club* (Bath 1986), p.55.
7.   See Strickland, *op. cit.* pp.62-64 and D.E. Davies, *Cardiff Rugby Club 1876-1975* (second ed. Starling Press, Risca 1976), p.214. Davies delivers important statistics about Percy Bunce's career with Cardiff, for whom he played 107 games between 1926 and 1929.
8.   See Finch, *op. cit.* pp.21-23. The book also contains a group photograph showing my Uncle Harold with Finch in the early 1920s and relates that '...Mr Chivers later attended the Labour College in London'. This came as a surprise, there having been no reference to this in any of the many family history discussions in which I participated.
9.   FA 13th March, 1926 and 20th March, 1926. The latter edition earned a retrospective commentary on the game by a Talywain 'scribe' who said, 'Football was at a discount at Risca on Saturday...So bad did the situation become that two of the visiting players and one Risca man were given their marching orders'.
10. FA 17th April, 1926. A sense of perspective is important here. The dispute in the coal industry and the imminence of the General Strike (which began at midnight on 3rd May), could have degraded news about rugby football.
11. Works of reference all agree that Thompson received one 'cap' before 'going north'. A fairly reliable source listing rugby union international players is *Rothman's Rugby Yearbook*. In this instance, the author used the 1982-83 edition.

Chapter Three: *Gardener, Father, Fireman, Clerk*

1.   This rather hasty comment, overheard during my childhood, was probably accurate as far as it went. However, on Wednesday 15th May 1935, the *South Wales Argus* carried the following report: 'Pontymister Tinworks (Partridge Jones and John Paton), is to re-open on Thursday and work will be found for 140 unemployed. With the exception of ten weeks from June 1932, the works have been idle since November 1931'. How the situation may have affected Ernest Jenkins (my Uncle Ern), and his modest affluence, is unclear.
2.   Gwent Record Office, Cwmbran. D 2357: 'Correspondence Regarding Classes at Oxford House'. Letter from the Warden of Oxford House to Mr Cameron 1st November, 1932.

3. This account of the march is in a document entitled, 'The Monmouthshire Hunger March of August 1933', published by the Monmouthshire Marchers' Council at the National Unemployed Workers' Movement office, Queen Street, Abertillery. The author discovered this document at the South Wales Miners' Library (a part of the University of Wales, Swansea) at Hendrefoelan House, Gower Road, Swansea. See too, SWA, 30th August, 1933. Walter Jones was a prominent local trade unionist, and Communist Party member who became a Risca Councillor. The author remembers him making a brief presentation to primary school children, during World War II, when he spoke about the need to collect salvage for the war effort.

4. Aneurin Bevan (1897-1960). MP for Ebbw Vale 1929-1960. As Minister of Health he set up the National Health Service in 1948.

5. See, *The Gwent School Resource Book: the Depression in Monmouthshire 1934.* (Information supplied to the author by the Gwent Record Office.)

6. CG 12th June, 1936: extract from evidence laid before the Royal Commission on Safety in Coal Mines.

7. See Francis and Smith, *op. cit.* Chapter Four.

8. See Francis and Smith, *op. cit.*, p.286.

9. See Francis and Smith, *op. cit.*, p.131.

10. SWWA 5th October, 1935.

11. SWA 25th July, 1933 and 7th April, 1936.

12. Moriah Chapel Sunday School Minute Book,1935.This document was very kindly loaned to the author by the Reverend John Hayward. My father's commitment to the Chapel and to the Sunday School is set out in the chapter entitled, 'God and Mammon'.

13. James Griffiths (1890-1975). Labour MP for Llanelli 1936-1970; Minister of National Insurance in the Labour Government, 1945; Secretary of State for the Colonies 1950-51.

14. Arthur Lewis Horner 1894-1968. Member of the British Communist Party from 1920. President South Wales Miners Federation 1936. Published autobiography, *Incorrigible Rebel* (1960).

15. CG 3rd October, 1947, quoting *The Lancet* article, of 6th September, 'Coal Miners' by J.N. Morris.

16. James Henry Thomas (1874-1949), a native of Newport, Gwent, who in addition to holding high office in the National Union of Railwaymen was Labour, later National Labour, MP for Derby from 1910-1936; Colonial Secretary 1924; Lord Privy Seal 1929-1930; Dominions Secretary 1930-1935; Colonial Secretary 1935-1936. Ostracized by the Labour Party for joining the 1931 National Government.

Chapter Four: God and Mammon

1. See J.H.A. Roberts, *A View From the Hill - a History of Risca and Moriah Baptist Church* (pub. by Moriah Baptist Church, Risca, 1986), p.292.

2. See Morgan, *op. cit.* p.273.

3. The Minute Book of the Monah Sisterhood was kindly loaned to the author by the Reverend John Hayward.

Chapter Five: The Defence of the realm:
   The Risca Home Guard and the High Cross Gunners

1. See S.P. Mackenzie, *The Home Guard* (Oxford University Press 1995), p.31.

2. See A.V. Jones, *Risca - Its Industrial and Social Development* (New Horizon Books, 1980), pp. 68-72. Also, Francis and Smith, *op. cit.* p.131 and *supra*.

3. SWA 18th June, 1940 and 26th June, 1940. Confusingly, on the second date, the *Argus* published another nominal roll of 'Volunteer Officers'. This said: 'Group and Company Officers of Risca Group of Local Defence Volunteers are: Group Commander, Lieutenant Colonel W. Downes Powell; Assistant Group Commanders, Major Claude G. Martyn, DL JP, Captain Walter C Phillips'. This could have reflected sundry local political influences or it may simply have been a question of availability. In any event, Phillips became the CO of the group of Volunteers soon to be described as the 4th Monmouthshire Battalion.

4. National Archives (Public Record Office) Kew. WO 199/3217. The archives also hold a number of national lists of Home Guard officers.

5. National Archives WO 166/1314. (*Severn Sub-Area War Diary December 1940.*)

6. Information supplied by Harris's kinswoman, Mrs Isobel Harris. Harris was promoted to command the 4th Monmouthshire Battalion of the Home Guard in 1943.

7. *Daily Worker* 29th June, 1940. Mr Price's Death Certificate shows the cause of death as 'the result of injuries sustained by being accidentally shot at the Viaduct, Maesycwmmer Mon.'

8. This copy of an undated menu was kindly given to the author by Mrs Green of Risca, whose father, Lieutenant A.E. (Albert) Ford, served in the 4th Mons.

9. Letter to the author from Mr Glyn Hutchings. The derelict farmhouse, according to my father, was the 17th century building that had probably been the home of a famous Risca figure, Squire Phillips. Phillips may have been an antecedent of the 4th Mons CO. Walter Phillips.

10. National Archives: WO 199/1887. Southern Command letter 24th June, 1940.

11. National Archives: WO 166/11219: the War Diary of 45 AA Brigade January 1943.

12. Interview with Bernard Mitchem, 2nd February, 2001.

13. Interview with Mr and Mrs Jack Beavis 2nd February, 2001.

14. National Archives: WO 166/1247. 'G' Branch War Diary (South Wales Area) August-September 1940.

15. National Archives: WO 166/11661. 181(M) HAA Regiment's War Diary 18th May, 1943. Fatal casualties kindly identified, for the author, by the Commonwealth War Graves Commission.

16. Letter to author from German Archives, Potsdam.

17. Each member of the Home Guard was presented with a certificate of service, signed by the Monarch. On this document the stand-down is dated 31st December, 1944. However, on 20th June, 1944 the state of readiness of my father's parent formation was decreased to 'A': National Archives WO 166/14833: 181(M) HAA Regiment's War Diary 20th June, 1944.

18. National Archives: HO 201: Damage Appreciation of Key Points and Industrial Damage (KPID); also WO 166/10988: Severn Sub-Area War Diary 31st July, 1943.

19. National Archives: HO 201, KPID.

20. National Archives; WO 166/14201 : Western Command 'G' Branch War Diary, 27th-28th March, 1944. Also WO 166/14629; HQ 4AA Group War Diary 27th March, 1944. Also WO 14833 181 (M) FIAA Regiment War Diary 27th-28th March, 1944.

21. *ibid*, 15th May, 1944.

22. National Archives: WO 166/14630: HQ 4AA Group War Diary 'A' and 'Q' Branches, November 1944: 20th November Disbandment instruction received for 181 (M) Regiment, also 612 Battery - my father's formation at Great Oak.

23. See Major L.L. Gordon, *British Battles and Medals* (4th Ed., London, 1971), p.350.

24. National Archives: WO 166/14456: War Diary, HQ South Wales District, 3rd December, 1944. Also SWA 4th December, 1944.

Chapter Six: Training Officer - A Step Up

1. Nine Mile Point NUM Lodge Minutes, 2nd September, 1946. (These minutes are available in the Library Archives at the University of Wales, Singleton Park, Swansea.)

2. The 'Bevin Boys', as they were known colloquially, were an important part of a wartime programme of directed labour devised by the Minister of Labour and National Service, Ernest Bevin (1881-1951). Men could be compulsorily drafted into the mines instead of undergoing military service. The *South Wales Argus* published an outline description of the scheme on 2nd December, 1943.

3. *Coal* Magazine, June 1947, pp.18-19. May be seen at the National Archives Kew: COAL 71/1.

4. Dr Noel Nathaniel Wade was a highly regarded doctor whose surgery, during the author's early days, was at a house called Gardd y Graig in Pontymister. Wade qualified at the University of Edinburgh in 1901 and moved to Risca in 1908, where he practised until approximately 1958. During this period, he also served as the district's Medical Officer of Health and it was perhaps in this capacity that he conducted the First Aid classes attended by my father. His son, Dr Michael Treharne Wade, also practised in Pontymister and another son, Dr Roger Noel Wade, who played rugby for Newport, emigrated to Australia.

5. Interview with Mr John (Jan) Rozek, 5th March, 2003 and correspondence with Mr R. Burnett. The NCB's recruitment scheme was not limited to Poles but eventually included men of other nationalities such as Yugoslavs. Documents of the day lumped all together as European Voluntary Workers (EVWs).

6. Letter dated 24th August, 1949, addressed to 'E.P. Chivers, Esq, Welfare and Training Officer, Nine Mile Point Colliery, Abercarn, Mon. National Archives, Kew, COAL 26/651. (Abercarn was a local NCB administrative centre.)

7.   Letter to the author from Mr F. Whitcombe, one of several in which he kindly provided information for this project. Mr Whitcombe served at Nine Mile Point as a Fireman and Overman.

Chapter Seven: *Death of a Colliery: Nine Mile Point to 1964*

1.   The minutes of the NCB's South Western Divisional Board are available in the National Archives. See COAL 6/153, 19th September, 1950 and 7th November, 1950. (The Divisional Board met in Cardiff.)
2.   Wages varied as between the type of work performed and whether or not a man worked at the actual coal face. The Nine Mile Point NUM Lodge Minutes for 8th January, 1950, 13th April, 1953 and 22nd June, 1953 shed light on this all-important topic. For a comprehensive survey, see Francis and Smith, *op. cit.* p.438, *passim.*
3.   The Bible: The Book of Daniel, Chapter Five, verse 26.
4.   Sir Hubert Stanley Houldsworth, first baronet (1889-1956). Chairman National Coal Board 1951-56. Ebenezer Edwards 1884-1961, NUM Secretary 1944-1946; chief Labour Relations Officer, NCB 1946-1953; President Trades Union Congress 1944-1945. Sir William Lawther 1889-1976, distinguished miners' leader; Labour MP for Barnard Castle 1929-1931 and first President of the NUM.
5.   NUM, South Wales Area: Report on Conference of Representatives of Divisional Area and Colliery Consultative Committees, held at The Capitol Cinema, Cardiff, 22nd February, 1953. Library of University of Wales Swansea. Reference: SWCC, Nine Mile Point Lodge (NWA) 42.
6.   Alfred Robens (1910-1999), Lord Robens of Woldingham. Life Peer, 1961. Member of Labour Governments, 1947-1951. Chairman, National Coal Board 1961-1971.
7.   See Robens, *Ten Year Stint* (1972), *passim.* Also, Lord Robens' obituary, *The Times,* 20th June, 1999.
8.   Letter from Mr E.A. Lewis, secretary to the NCB South Western Division Board to Mr Cowe, NCB secretary, Hobart House, London, 27th May, 1964. National Archives, COAL 74/1085.
9.   Note of a meeting between representatives of the NCB and the NUM at Hobart House, London SW1 on 3rd June, 1964. National Archives COAL 74/1085.
10. Undated (but probably July 1964) document filed at the National Archives in the series COAL 74/1085 with a file number 21387.
11. See, Roberts, *op. cit.* p.91.
12. See *supra,* 'Gardener, Father, Fireman, Clerk', footnote 13. The *South Wales Argus,* in its edition of 29th November ,1965, reported that 17 miners had received presentations. However, County Councillor Keith Griffiths clearly recalls that there were 34 and that the 'Press' had made a mistake.

Chapter Eight: *My Father's Friends*

1.   Joseph Arthur Rank, first Baron Rank (1888-1972). Flour Miller, film magnate and devout Methodist.
2.   Bernard Law Montgomery, First Viscount Montgomery of Alamein (1887-1976) Field Marshal 1944; Commander-in-Chief of British Army of the Rhine (BAOR) 1945-1946.
3.   *The Times,* 15th December, 1945. Also National Archives WO/9.
4.   See, *Kinematograph Weekly,* 2nd August 1956, and *Educational Screen,* October 1955. The British Film Institute (BFI) in London's Tottenham Court Road holds these and other film journals.